# The Lay of
# Havelok the Dane.

---

Early English Text Society.
Extra Series. No. IV.

DUBLIN:         WILLIAM McGEE, 18, NASSAU STREET.
EDINBURGH:      T. G. STEVENSON, 22, SOUTH FREDERICK STREET.
GLASGOW:        OGLE & CO., 1, ROYAL EXCHANGE SQUARE.
BERLIN:         ASHER & CO., UNTER DEN LINDEN, 20.
NEW YORK:       C. SCRIBNER & CO.; LEYPOLDT & HOLT.
PHILADELPHIA:   J. B. LIPPINCOTT & CO.
BOSTON, U.S.:   DUTTON & CO.

# The Lay of
# Havelok the Dane:

COMPOSED IN THE REIGN OF EDWARD I, ABOUT A.D. 1280.

FORMERLY EDITED BY SIR F. MADDEN FOR THE ROXBURGHE CLUB,

AND NOW RE-EDITED FROM THE UNIQUE MS. LAUD MISC. 108,
IN THE BODLEIAN LIBRARY, OXFORD;

BY THE

REV. WALTER W. SKEAT, M.A.,

AUTHOR OF "A MŒSO-GOTHIC GLOSSARY," EDITOR OF "PIERS PLOWMAN"
"WILLIAM OF PALERNE," &c.

LONDON:
PUBLISHED FOR THE EARLY ENGLISH TEXT SOCIETY,
BY N. TRÜBNER & CO., 60, PATERNOSTER ROW.

MDCCCLXVIII.

## OXFORD
UNIVERSITY PRESS

Great Clarendon Street, Oxford OX2 6DP
United Kingdom

Oxford University Press is a department of the University of Oxford.
It furthers the University's objective of excellence in research, scholarship,
and education by publishing worldwide. Oxford is a registered trade mark of
Oxford University Press in the UK and in certain other countries

© The Early English Text Society 1868

The moral rights of the authors have been asserted

Database right Oxford University Press (maker)

First Edition published in 1868

All rights reserved. No part of this publication may be reproduced,
stored in a retrieval system, or transmitted, in any form or by any means,
without the prior permission in writing of Oxford University Press,
or as expressly permitted by law, or under terms agreed with the appropriate
reprographics rights organization. Enquiries concerning reproduction
outside the scope of the above should be sent to the Rights Department,
Oxford University Press, at the address above

You must not circulate this book in any other form
and you must impose this same condition on any acquirer

Published in the United States of America by Oxford University Press
198 Madison Avenue, New York, NY 10016, United States of America

British Library Cataloguing in Publication Data
Data available

Library of Congress Cataloging in Publication Data
Data available

Extra Series, 4

ISBN 978-0-85-991951-7

# CONTENTS.

TITLEPAGE. The engraving represents the seal of Great Grimsby, described in § 19 of the Preface, p. xxi.

PREFACE. § 1. The former edition of 1828. § 2. The present edition. § 3. Plan of this edition. § 4. Notices of the story by Early Writers: the longer French Version. § 5. The shorter French Version. § 6. Peter de Langtoft (1307). § 7. Rauf de Boun (1310). § 8. A Brief Genealogy, Herald's Coll. MS. (ab. 1310). § 9. Metrical Chronicle (ab. 1313). § 10. Robert of Brunne (1338); ed. Hearne. § 11. Robert of Brunne; Lambeth MS. § 12. French Prose "Brute" (1332). § 13. English Prose "Brute," MS. Harl. 2279. § 14. Gray's Scala Cronica (ab. 1360). § 15. Eulogium Historiarum (1366). § 16. Henry de Knyghton (1395); Warner (1586); Webster (1617). § 17. Danish traditions. § 18. Lincolnshire traditions. § 19. Seal of Great Grimsby. § 20. Sketch of the French "Lai." § 21. Gaimar's abridgment. § 22. Sketch of the English Lay. § 23. Possible date of Havelok's reign. § 24. Story of "Edwin of Deira." § 25. On the names "Curan" and "Havelok." § 26. Description of the MS. § 27. Grammatical forms in the Poem. § 28. On the metre. § 29. On the final -e, &c. ... ... ... ... ... ... i

EMENDATIONS, &c. ... ... ... ... ... ... liv

THE LAY OF HAVELOK ... ... ... ... ... 1

NOTES TO "HAVELOK" ... ... ... ... ... 87

GLOSSARIAL INDEX ... ... ... ... ... ... 105

INDEX OF NAMES ... ... ... ... ... ... 157

# PREFACE.

§ 1. THE English version of the Lay of Havelok, now here reprinted, is one of the few poems that have happily been recovered, after having long been given up as lost. Tyrwhitt, in his Essay on the Language and Versification of Chaucer, has a footnote (No. 51) deploring the loss of the Rime concerning Gryme the Fisher, the founder of Grymesby, Hanelok [*read* Havelok] the Dane, and his wife Goldborough; and Ritson, in his Dissertation on Romance and Minstrelsy—(vol. i. p. lxxxviii. of his Metrical Romanceës)—makes remarks to the same effect. It was at length, however, discovered by accident in a manuscript belonging to the Bodleian library, which had been described in the old Catalogue merely as *Vitæ Sanctorum*, a large portion of it being occupied by metrical legends of the Saints. In 1828, it was edited for the Roxburghe Club by Sir F. Madden, the title-page of the edition being as follows:—" The Ancient English Romance of Havelok the Dane, accompanied by the French Text: with an introduction, notes, and a glossary, by Frederick Madden, Esq., F.A.S. F.R.S.L., Sub-Keeper of the MSS. in the British Museum. Printed for the Roxburghe Club, London. W. Nicol, Shakspeare Press, MDCCCXXVIII." This volume contains a very complete Introduction, pp. i—lvi; the English version of Havelok, pp. 1—104; the French text of the Romance of Havelok, from a MS. in the Heralds' College, pp. 105—146; the French Romance of Havelok, as abridged and altered by Geffrei Gaimar, pp. 147—180; notes to the English text, pp. 181—207; notes to the French text, pp. 208—210; and a glossary, &c., pp. 211—263. But there are sometimes bound up with it two pamphlets, viz. "Remarks on the Glossary to Havelok," by S. W. Singer, and an "Examination of the Remarks, &c.," by the Editor of Havelok. In explanation of this, it may suffice to say, that the former contains some criticisms by Mr Singer (executed in a manner suggestive of an officious wish to display superior critical acumen), of which a few are correct, but others are ludicrously false; whilst the latter is a vindication of the general correctness of the explanations given, and contains, incidentally, some valuable contributions to our general etymological knowledge, and various remarks which have proved of service in rendering the glossary in the present edition more exactly accurate.[1]

§ 2. Owing to the scarcity of copies of this former edition, the committee of the Early English Text Society, having first obtained the approval of Sir Frederic Madden, resolved upon issuing a reprint of it; and Sir Frederic having expressed a wish that the duty of seeing it through the press should be entrusted to myself, I gladly undertook that responsibility. He has kindly looked over the revises of the whole work,[2] but as it has undergone several modifications, it will be the best plan to state in detail what these are.

§ 3. With respect to the text, the greatest care has been taken to render it, as nearly as can be represented in print, an exact copy of the MS. The text of the former edition is exceedingly correct, and the alterations here made are few and of slight importance. Sir F. Madden furnished me with some, the results of a re-comparison, made by himself, of his printed copy with the original; besides this, I have myself carefully read the proof sheets with the MS. *twice*, and it may therefore be assumed that the complete correctness of the text is established. It seems to me that this is altogether the most important part of the work

---

[1] In particular, we find there a complete proof, supported by some fifty examples, that, *as* can be traced, through the forms *ase, als, alse, also*, to the A.S. *eall-swa*; a proof, that in the difficult phrase *lond and lithe*, the word *lithe* [also spelt *lede, lude*] is equivalent to the French *tenement, rente*, or *fe*; and, thirdly, a complete refutation of Mr Singer's extraordinary notion that the adverb *swithe* means *a sword!*

[2] In the same way, *William of Palerne* was prepared by me for the press, subject to his advice; see *William of Palerne*, Introduction, p. ii.

of a *Text* Society, in order that the student may never be perplexed by the appearance of words having no real existence. For a like reason the letters þ and p (the latter of which I have represented by an italic *w*) have now been inserted wherever they occur, and the expansions of abbreviations are now denoted by italics. For further remarks upon the text, see the description of the MS. below, § 26. Sidenotes and headlines have been added, but the numbering of the lines has not been altered. The French text of the romance, the title of which is *Le Lai de Aveloc*, and the abridgment of the story by Geffrei Gaimar, have not been here reprinted; the fact being, that the French and English versions differ very widely, and that the passages of the French which really correspond to the English are few and short. *All* of these will be found in the Notes, in their proper places, and it was also deemed the less necessary to print the French text, because it is tolerably accessible; for it may be found either in vol. i. of Monumenta Historica Britannica, ed. Petrie, 1848, in the reprint by M. Michel (1833) entitled "Le Lai d'Havelok," or in the edition by Mr T. Wright for the Caxton Society, 1850. An abstract of it is given at p. xxiii. The Notes are abridged from Sir F. Madden's, with but a very few additions by myself, which are distinguished by being placed within square brackets. The Glossarial Index is, for the most part, reprinted from Sir F. Madden's Glossary, but contains a large number of *slight* alterations, re-arrangements, and additions. The references have nearly all been verified,[1] and the few words formerly left unexplained are now either wholly or partially solved. I have now only to add that a large portion of the remainder of this preface, especially that which concerns the historical and traditional evidences of the story (§ 4 to § 18), is abridged or copied from Sir F. Madden's long Introduction, which fairly exhausts the subject.[2] All extracts included between marks of quotation are taken from it without alteration. But I must be considered responsible for the re-

---

[1] I say *nearly*, because I have not been able to verify *every* reference to *every* poem quoted. I have verified and critically examined all the citations from the *poem itself*, from Ritson's Romances, Weber's Romances, Laȝamon, Beowulf, Chaucer, Langland, and Sir Walter Scott's edition of Sir Tristrem (3rd edition, 1811).

[2] To this, the reader is referred for fuller information.

arrangement of the materials, and I have added a few remarks from other sources.

§ 4. NOTICES OF THE STORY OF HAVELOK BY EARLY WRITERS. There can be little doubt that the tradition must have existed from Anglo-Saxon times, but the earliest mention of it is presented to us in the full account furnished by the French version of the Romance. Of this there are two copies, one of which belongs to Sir T. Phillipps; the other is known as the Arundel or Norfolk MS., and is preserved in the Heralds' College, where it is marked E. D. N. No. 14; the various editions of the latter have been already enumerated in § 3. This version was certainly composed within the first half of the twelfth century. From the fact that it is entitled a *Lai,* and from the assertion of the poet—" Qe vn *lai* en firent li Breton "—" whereof the Britons made a lay "—we easily conclude that it was drawn from a British source. From the evident connection of the story with the Chronicle called the *Brut,* we may further conclude that by *Breton* is not meant Armorican, but belonging to *Britain.* The story is in no way connected with France; the tradition is British or Welsh, and the French version was doubtless written in England by a subject of an English king. That the language is French is due merely to the accident that the Norman conquerors of England had acquired that language during their temporary sojourn in France. From every point of view, whether we regard the British tradition, the Anglo-Norman version, or the version printed in the present volume, the story is wholly English. It is not to be connected too closely with the Armorican lays of Marie *de France.*[1]

§ 5. We next come to the abridgment of the same as made by Geffrei Gaimar, who wrote between the years 1141 and 1151. In one place, Geffrei quotes Gildas as his authority, but no conclusion can easily be drawn from this indefinite reference. In another place, he mentions a feast given by Havelok after his defeat of Hodulf—*si cum nus dit la verai estoire*—" as the true

---

[1] "The word Breton, which some critics refer to Armorica, is here applied to a story of mere English birth." Hallam; Lit. of Europe, 6th ed. 1860; vol. i. p. 36. See the whole passage

history tells us." As this feast is not mentioned in the fuller French version, and yet reappears in the English text, we perceive that he had some additional source of information; and this is confirmed by the fact that he mentions several additional details, also not found in the completer version. That the lay of Havelok, as found in Gaimar, is really his, and not an interpolation by a later hand, may fairly be inferred from his repeated allusions to the story in the body of his work. There are three MS. copies containing Gaimar's abridgment, of which the best is the Royal MS. (Bibl. Reg. 13 A xxi.) in the British Museum; the two others belong respectively to the Dean and Chapter of Durham (its mark being C. iv. 27) and to the Dean and Chapter of Lincoln (its mark being H. 18). It is curious that the Norfolk MS. contains not only the fuller French version of the story, but also the Brut of Wace, and the continuation of it by Gaimar. Gaimar's abridgment, as printed in Sir F. Madden's edition, is taken from the Royal MS., supplemented by the Durham and Lincoln MSS. See also Monumenta Historica Britannica, vol. i. p. 764. It is important to mention that Gaimar speaks of the Danes as having been in Norfolk since the time that Havelok was King, after he has been relating the combats between the Britons and the Saxons under the command of Cerdic and Cynric. Another allusion makes Havelok to have lived long before the year 800, according to every system of chronology.

§ 6. The next mention of Havelok is in the French Chronicle of Peter de Langtoft, of Langtoft in Yorkshire, who died early in the reign of Edward II., and whose Chronicle closes with the death of Edward I. Here the only trace of the story is in the mention of " Gountere le pere Hauelok, de Danays Ray clamez "—Gunter, father of Havelok, called King of the Danes. The allusion is almost valueless from its evident absurdity; for he confounds Gunter with the Danish invader defeated by Alfred, and who is variously called Godrum, Gudrum, Guthrum, or Gurmound. He must have been thinking, at the moment, of a very different Gurmund, viz. the King of the Africans, as he is curiously called, whose terrible devastations are described very fully in Laȝamon, vol. iii. pp. 156—177, and who may fairly be supposed to have lived much nearer to the time of Havelok; and he must further have confounded this Gurmund with Gunter. For the account of Robert of Brunne's translation of Langtoft's Chronicle, see below, § 10.

§ 7. But soon after this, we come to a most curious account. In MS. Harl. 902 is a late copy, on paper, of a Chronicle called *Le Bruit Dengleterre*, or otherwise *Le Petit Bruit*, compiled A. D. 1310, by Meistre Rauf de Boun, at the request of Henry de Lacy, earl of Lincoln. It is a most worthless compilation, put together in defiance of all chronology, but with respect to our present inquiry it is full of interest, as it soon becomes obvious that one of his sources of information is the very English version here printed, which he cites by the name of *l'estorie de Grimesby*, and which is thus proved to have been written before the year 1310. "The Chronicler," says Sir F. Madden, "commences, as usual, with Brute, B. C. 2000, and after taking us through the succeeding reigns to the time of Cassibelin, who fought with Julius Cæsar, informs us, that after Cassibelin's death came Gurmound out of Denmark, who claimed the throne as the son of the eldest daughter of Belin, married to Thorand, King of Denmark. He occupies the kingdom 57 years, and is at length slain at *Hunteton*, called afterwards from him *Gurmoundcestre*. He is succeeded by his son Frederick, who hated the English, and filled his court with Danish nobles, but who is at last driven out of the country, after having held it for the short space of 71 years. And then, adds this miserable History-monger: 'Et si entendrez vous, que par cel primer venue de auaunt dit Roy Gormound, et puis par cele hountoux exil de son fitz Frederik, si fu le rancour de Daneis vers nous enpendaunt, et le regne par cel primere accion vers nous enchalangount plus de sept C auns apre, *iekis a la venue Haneloke, fitz le Roy Birkenebayne de Dannemarche, q̄ le regne par mariage entra de sa femme.*'—f. 2 b.

" After a variety of equally credible stories, we come to Adelstan II.[1] son of Edward [the Elder], who corresponds with

---

[1] "The Chronicler writes of him, f. 6. 'Il feu le plus beau bacheleir qe vnqes reigna en Engleterre, *ceo dit le Bruit*, par quoy ly lays ly apellerunt *King Adelstane with gilden kroket*, pour ce q'il feu si beaus.' We have here notice of another of those curious historical poems, the loss of which can never

the real king of that name, A. D. 925—941. He is succeeded by his son [brother] Edmund, who reigned four years [A. D. 941—946], and is said to have been *poisoned* at Canterbury; after whom we have ADELWOLD, whose identity with the Athelwold of the English Romance, will leave no doubt as to the source whence the writer drew great part of his materials in the following passage :

Apres ceo vient Adelwold son fitz q̄ reigna xvj et demie, si engendroit ij feiz et iij filis, dount trestoutz murrirent frechement fors q̄ sa pune file, le out a nom *Goldburgh*, del age de vj aunz kaunt son pere Adelwold morust. Cely Roy Adelwold quant il doit morir, comaunda sa file a garder a vn Count de Cornewayle, al houre kaunt il quidou͞ie (sic) hountousment auoir deparagé, quaunt fit *Haueloke*, fitz le Roy Byrkenbayne de Denmarche, esposer le, encountre sa volunté, q̄ primis fuit Roy Dengleterre et de Denmarch tout a vn foitz, par quele aliaunce leis Daneis queillerunt g$^e$ndr̄ (sic) mestrie en Engleterre, et long temps puise le tindrunt, *si cum vous nouncie l'estorie de Grimesby*, come *Grime* primez nurist Haueloke en Engleterre, depuis cel houre q'il feut chasé de Denmarche &c. deqis al houre q'il vint au chastelle de Nichole, q̄ cely auauntdit traitre *Goudriche* out en garde, en quel chastel il auauntdit Haueloke espousa l'auauntdit Goldeburgh, q̄ fuit heir Dengleterre. Et par cel reson tynt cely Haueloke la terre de Denmarche auxi comme son heritage, et Engleterre auxi par mariage de sa femme; et si entendrez vous, q̄ par la reson q̄ ly auauntdit Gryme ariua primez, kaunt il amena l'enfaunt Haueloke hors de Denmarche, par meyme la reson reseut cele vile son nom, de Grime, quel noun ly tint vnquore Grimisby.

'Apres ceo regna meyme cely Haueloke, q̄ mult fuit prodhomme, et droiturelle, et bien demenoit son people en reson et ley. Cel Roy Haueloke reigna xlj. aunz, si engendroit ix fitz et vij filis, dount trestoutz murrerount ainz q̄ furunt d'age, fors soulement iiij de ses feitz, dont l'un out a noum Gurmound, cely q̄ entendy auoir son heire en Engleterre; le secound out a noun Knout, quen fitz feffoit son pere en le regne de Denmarche, quant il estoit del age de xviij aunz, et ly mesme se tynt a la coroune Dengleterre, quel terre il entendy al oeps son ainez fitz Gurmound

be sufficiently deplored. The term *crocket* (derived by Skinner from the Fr. *crochet*, uncinulus) points out the period of the poem's composition, since the fashion alluded to of wearing those large rolls of hair so called, only arose at the latter end of Hen. III. reign, and continued through the reign of Edw. I. and part of his successor's."

auoir gardé. Mes il debusa son col auxi comme il feu mounté vn cheval testous q̃ poindre volleyt, en l'an de son regne xxiij entrant. Le tiers fitz ont a noun Godard, q̃ son pere feffoit de la Seneschacie Dengleterre, q̃ n'auo͡ut (sic) taunt come ore fait ly quart. Et le puisnez fitz de toutz out a noum Thorand, q̃ espousa la Countesse de Hertouwe en Norwey. Et par la reson q̃ cely Thorand feut enherité en la terre de Norwey, ly et ses successours sont enheritez iekis en sa p͡ce (sic) toutdis, puis y auoit affinité de alliaunce entre ceulx de Denmarche et ceulx de Norwey, a checun venue q̃ vnkes firent en ceste terre pur chalenge ou clayme mettre, iekis a taunt q̃ lour accion feut enseyne destrut par vn noble chevallere *Guy de Warwike*, &c. Et tout en sy feffoit Haueloke sez quatre fitz : si gist a priorie de *Grescherche* en Loundrez.'— f. 6 b.

" The *Estorie de Grimesby* therefore, referred to above, is the identical English Romance before us, and it is no less worthy of remark, that the whole of the passage just quoted, with one single variation of import, has been literally translated by Henry de Knyghton, and inserted in his Chronicle.[1] Of the sources whence the information respecting Havelok's sons is derived, we are unable to offer any account, as no trace of it occurs either in the French or English texts of the story."

§ 8. " About the same time at which Rauf de Boun composed his Chronicle, was written a brief Genealogy of the British and Saxon Kings, from Brutus to Edward II., preserved in the same MS. in the Heralds' College which contains the French text of the Romance. The following curious rubric is prefixed :—*La lignée des Bretons et des Engleis, queus il furent, et de queus nons, et coment Brut vint premerement en Engleterre, et combien de tens puis, et dont il vint. Brut et Cornelius furent chevalers chacez de la bataille de Troie,* M. CCCC. XVII. *anz deuant qe dieus nasquit, et vindrent en Engleterre, en Cornewaille, et riens ne fut trouee en la terre fors qe geanz, Geomagog, Hastripoldius, Ruscalbundy, et plusurs autres Geanz.* In this Genealogy no mention of Havelok occurs under the reign of Constantine, but after the names of the Saxon Kings Edbright and Edelwin, we read : ' ATHELWOLD auoit vne fille *Goldeburgh*, et il regna vi. anz. HAUELOC esposa meisme

[1] See below, § 16.

cele Goldeburgh, et regna iij. anz. ALFRED le frere le Roi Athelwold enchaca Haueloc par Hunehere, et il fut le primer Roi corone de l'apostoille, et il regna xxx. anz.'—fol. 148 b. By this account Athelwold is clearly identified with Ethelbald, King of Wessex, who reigned from 855 to 860, whilst Havelok is substituted in the place of Ethelbert and Ethered."

§ 9. "Not long after the same period was written a Metrical *Chronicle of England*, printed by Ritson, Metr. Rom. V. ii. p. 270. Two copies are known to exist,[1] the first concluding with the death of Piers Gavestone, in 1313 (MS. Reg. 12. C. xii.), and the other continued to the time of Edw. III. (Auchinleck MS.). The period of Havelok's descent into England is there ascribed to the reign of King Ethelred (978—1016), which will very nearly coincide with the period assigned by Rauf de Boun, viz. A.D. 963—1004."

> '*Haueloc* com tho to this lond,
> With gret host & eke strong,
> Ant sloh the Kyng Achelred,
> At Westmustre he was ded,
> Ah he heuede reigned her
> Seuene an tuenti fulle ʒer.'
> MS. Reg. 12. C. xii.'

"This date differs from most of the others, and appears founded on the general notion of the Danish invasions during that period."

§ 10. Before proceeding to consider the *prose* Chronicle of the Brute, it is better to speak first of the translation of Peter de Langtoft's Chronicle by Robert of Brunne, a translation which was completed A.D. 1338. At p. 25 of Hearne's edition is the following passage:

> 'ʒit a nother Danes Kyng in the North gan aryue.
> Alfrid it herd, thidere gan he dryue.
> *Hauelok*[2] fader he was, *Gunter* was his name.
> He brent citees & tounes, ouer alle did he schame.
> Saynt Cutbertes clerkes tho Danes thei dred.
> The toke the holy bones, about thei tham led.

[1] The poems in MSS. Camb. Univ. Lib. Ff. 5. 48 and Dd. 14. 2 resemble this Chronicle, but do not mention Havelok's name.
[2] *Hanelok* in Hearne, throughout, but undoubtedly *contra fidem* MSS.

Seuen ȝere thorgh the land wer thei born aboute,
It comforted the kyng mykelle, whan he was in doute
¶ Whan Alfrid & Gunter had werred long in ille,
Thorgh the grace of God, Gunter turned his wille.
Cristend wild he be, the kyng of fonte him lift,
& thritty of his knyghtes turnes, thorgh Godes gift.
Tho that first were foos, and com of paien lay,
Of Cristen men haf los, & so thei wend away.'

"This is the whole that appears in the original, but after the above lines immediately follows, in the language of Robert of Brunne himself (as noted also by Hearne, Pref. p. lxvii.), the following curious, and to our inquiry, very important passage:"

'Bot I haf grete ferly, that I fynd no man,
That has writen in story, how Hauelok this lond wan.
Noither *Gildas*, no Bede, no Henry of Huntynton,
No William of Malmesbiri, ne Pers of Bridlynton,
Writes not in ther bokes of no kyng Athelwold,
Ne Goldeburgh his douhtere, ne Hauelok not of told,
Whilk tyme the were kynges, long or now late,
Thei mak no menyng whan, no in what date.
Bot that thise *lowed men vpon Inglish tellis*,
Right story can me not ken, the certeynte what spellis.
Men sais in Lyncoln castelle ligges ȝit a stone,
That Hauelok kast wele forbi euer ilkone
& ȝit the chapelle standes, ther he weddid his wife,
Goldeburgh the kynges douhter, *that saw is ȝit rife.*
& of Gryme a fisshere, *men redes ȝit in ryme,*
That he bigged Grymesby Gryme that ilk tyme.
Of alle stories of honoure, that I haf thorgh souht,
I fynd that no compiloure of him tellis ouht.
Sen I fynd non redy, that tellis of Hauelok kynde
Turne we to that story, that we writen fynde.'

"There cannot exist the smallest doubt, that by the 'Ryme' here mentioned 'that lowed men vpon Inglish tellis,' the identical English Romance, now before the reader, is referred to. It must therefore certainly have been composed prior to the period at which Robert of Brunne wrote,[1] in whose time the traditions respecting Havelok at Lincoln were so strongly preserved, as to

---

[1] This proof is rendered unnecessary by the citations from it by Rauf de Boun in 1310, and by the age of our MS. itself.

point out various localities to which the story had affixed a name, and similar traditions connected with the legend, as we shall find hereafter, existed also at Grimsby. The doubts expressed by the Chronicler, as to their authenticity, or the authority of the 'Ryme,' are curious, but only of value so far as they prove he was ignorant of the existence of a French Romance on the subject, or of its reception in Gaimar's historical poem."

§ 11. "But on consulting the Lambeth copy of Rob. of Brunne, in order to verify the passage as printed by Hearne from the Inner Temple MS. we were not a little surprised to ascertain a fact hitherto overlooked, and indeed unknown, viz. that the Lambeth MS. (which is a folio, written on paper, and imperfect both at the beginning and close)[1] does not correspond with the Edition, but has evidently been revised by a later hand, which has abridged the Prologues, omitted some passages, and inserted others. The strongest proof of this exists in the passage before us, in which the Lambeth MS. entirely omits the lines of Rob. of Brunne respecting the authenticity of the story of Havelok, and in their place substitutes an abridged outline of the story itself, copied apparently from the French Chronicle of Gaimar. The interpolation is so curious, and so connected with our inquiry, as to be a sufficient apology for introducing it here."

'¶ Forth wente Gounter & his folk, al in to Denemark,
Sone fel ther hym vpon, a werre styth & stark,
Thurgh a Breton kyng, th$^t$ out of Ingeland cam,
& asked the tribut of Denmark, th$^t$ Arthur whylom nam.
They wythseide hit schortly, & non wolde they ȝelde,
But rather they wolde dereyne hit, wyth bataill y the felde.
Both partis on a day, to felde come they stronge,
Desconfit were the danes, Gounter his deth gan fonge.
When he was ded they schope brynge, al his blod to schame,
But Gatferes doughter the kyng, *Eleyne* was hure name,
Was kyng Gounteres wyf, and had a child hem bytwene,
Wyth wham scheo scapede vnethe, al to the se with tene.
The child hym highte HAUELOK, th$^t$ was his moder dere,
Scheo mette with grym atte hauene, a wel god marinere,

---

[1] The writing in the earlier portion (concerning Havelok) is hardly later than A.D. 1400.

He hure knew & highte hure wel, to helpe hure with his might,
To bryng hure saf out of the lond, wythinne th$^t$ ilke night.
When they come in myd se, a gret meschef gan falle,
They metten wyth a gret schip, lade wyth outlawes alle.
Anon they fullen hem apon, & dide hem Mikel peyne,
So th$^t$ wyth strengthe of their assaut, ded was quene Eleyne.
But ʒyt ascapede from hem Grym, wyth Hauelok & other fyue,
& atte the hauene of Grymesby, ther they gon aryue.
Ther was brought forth child Hauelok, wyth Grym & his fere,
Right als hit hadde be ther own, for other wyste men nere.
Til he was mykel & mighti, & man of mykel cost,
Th$^t$ for his grete sustinaunce, nedly serue he most.
He tok leue of Grym & Seburc, as of his sire & dame,
And askede ther blessinge curteysly, ther was he nought to blame.
Thenne drow he forth northward, to kynges court Edelsie,
Th$^t$ held fro Humber to Rotland, the kyngdam of Lyndesye.
Thys Edelsy of Breton kynde, had Orewayn his sister bright
Maried to a noble kyng, of Northfolk Egelbright.
Holly for his kyngdam, he held in his hand,
Al the lond fro Colchestre, right in til Holand.
Thys Egelbright th$^t$ was a Dane, & Orewayn the quene,
Hadden gete on Argill, a doughter hem bytwene.
Sone then deyde Egelbright, & his wyf Orewayn,
& therfore was kyng Edelsye, bothe joyful & fayn.
Anon their doughter & here Eyr, his nece dame Argill,
& al the kyngdam he tok in hande, al at his owene will.
Ther serued Hauelok as quistron, & was y-cald Coraunt,
He was ful mykel & hardy, & strong as a Geaunt.
He was bold Curteys & fre, & fair & god of manere,
So th$^t$ alle folk hym louede, th$^t$ auewest hym were.
But for couetise of desheraison, of damysele Argill,
& for a chere th$^t$ the kyng sey, scheo made Coraunt till,
He dide hem arraye ful symplely, & wedde togydere bothe,
For he ne rewarded desparagyng, were manion ful wrothe.
A while they dwelt after in court, in ful pore degre,
The schame & sorewe th$^t$ Argill hadde, hit was a deol to se.
Then seyde scheo til hure maister, of whenne sire be ʒe ?
Haue ʒe no kyn ne frendes at hom, in ʒoure contre ?
Leuer were me lyue in pore lyf, wythoute schame & tene,
Than in schame & sorewe, lede the astat of quene.
Thenne wente they forth to Grymesby, al by his wyues red,
& founde th$^t$ Grym & his wyf, weren bothe ded.
But he fond ther on Aunger, Grymes cosyn hend,
To wham th$^t$ Grym & his wyf, had teld word & ende.

How th$^t$ hit stod wyth Hauelok, in all manere degre,
& they hit hym telde & conseilled, to drawe til his contre,
Tasaye what grace he mighte fynde, among his frendes there,
& they wolde ordeyne for their schipynge, and al th$^t$ hem nede were.
When Aunger hadde y-schiped hem, they seilled forth ful swythe,
Ful-but in til Denemark, wyth weder fair & lithe.
Ther fond he on sire Sykar, a man of gret pousté,
Th$^t$ hey styward somtyme was, of al his fader fe.
Ful fayn was he of his comyng, & god help him behight,
To recouere his heritage, of Edulf kyng & knyght.
Sone asembled they gret folk, of his sibmen & frendes,
Kyng Edulf gadered his power, & ageyn them wendes.
Desconfyt was ther kyng Edulf, & al his grete bataill,
& so conquered Hauelok, his heritage saunz faille.
Sone after he schop him gret power, in toward Ingelond,
His wyues heritage to wynne, ne wolde he nought wonde.
Th$^t$ herde the kyng of Lyndeseye, he was come on th$^t$ cost,
& schop to fighte wyth hym sone, & gadered hym gret host.
But atte day of bataill, Edelsy was desconfit,
& after by tretys gaf Argentill, hure heritage al quit.
& for scheo was next of his blod, Hauelokes wyf so feyr,
He gaf hure Lyndesey after his day, & made hure his Eyr.
& atte last so byfel, th$^t$ vnder Hauelokes schelde,
Al Northfolk & Lyndeseye, holy of hym they helde.'

MS. Lamb. 131. leaf 76.

§ 12. We now come to the prose Chronicle called The Brute, which became exceedingly popular, and was the foundation of " Caxton's Chronicle," first printed by Caxton A. D. 1480, but of which Caxton was not the author, though he may have added some of the last chapters. The original is in French, and was probably compiled a few years *before* Robert of Brunne's translation of Langtoft was made, as it concludes with the year 1331, or, in some copies, with 1332. The author of it is not known, but it was probably only regarded as a compilation from the Chronicles of the earlier Historians. " In this Chronicle, in all its various shapes, is contained the Story of Havelock, *engrafted on the British History of Geoffrey of Monmouth*, and in its detail, following precisely the French text of the Romance. The only variation of consequence is the substitution of the name of Birkabeyn (as in the English text) for that of Gunter, and in some copies, both of the French and English MSS. of the Chronicle, the name of

*Goldeburgh* is inserted instead of *Argentille;* which variations are the more curious, as they prove the absolute identity of the story. For the sake of a more complete illustration of what has been advanced, we are induced to copy the passage at length, as it appears in the French Chronicle, taken from a well-written MS. of the 14th century, MS. Reg. 20 A 3, fol. 165 b."[1]

'*Des Rois Adelbright & Edelfi*, Cap. iiij$^{xx.}$ xix.'

Apres le Roi Constantin estoient deux Rois en graunt Brutaigne, dount li vns out a noun Aldelbright, & fust Danois, & [tint] tut le pais de Norff' & de Suffolk, & ly altre out a noun Edelfi, q*e* fust Brittone, & tint Nicol & Lindesey, & tote la terre desqes a Humber. Ceux deux Rois soi entreguerroierent, [& moult s'entrehaierent] mais puis furent il entre acordez & soi entreamerent, taunt com s'il vssent estee freres de vn ventre neez. Le Roi Edelfi out vne soer, Orewenne par noun, & la dona par grant amour al Roi Aldelbright a femme. Et il engendra de ly vne fille q*e* out a noun Argentille. En le tiercz an apres vne greue Maladie ly suruint, si deuereit morrir, & maunda par vn iour al Roi Edelfi, soun frere en lei, q'il venist a ly parler, & cil ly emparla volenters. Donqe ly pria le Roi Aldelbright et ly coniura en le noun [de] Dieu, q'il apres sa mort preist Argentille sa fille, & sa terre, & q'il la feist honestement garder [& nurrir] en sa chambre, & quant ele serreit de age, q'il la feist marier al plus fort hom & plus vaillaunt q'il porroit trouer, & q*e* a donqe ly rendist sa terre. Edelfi ceo graunta, & par serment afferma sa priere. Et quant Adelbright fust mort, & enterree, Edelfi prist la damoyscle, & la norrist en sa chambre, si deuynt ele la plus beale creature q*e* hom porreit trouer.

*Coment le Roi Edelfi Maria la damoisele Argentille a vn quistroun de sa quisine.* Cap$^{m.}$ C.

Le Roi Edelfi, q*e* fust vncle a la Damoysele Argentille, pensa fausement coment il porreit la terre sa Nece auoir pur touz iours, & malueisement countre soun serment pensa a deceiure la pucelle, si la maria a vn quistroun de sa quisyne q*e* fust apellée Curan, si esteit il le plus haut, le plus fort, & le plus vaillaunt de corps, q*e* hom sauoit nulle part a cel temps, & la quidoit hountousement marier, pur auoir sa terre a remenaunt, Mais il fust deceu. Car

---

[1] Sir F. Madden adds—" collated with another of the same age, MS. Cott. Dom. A. x, and a third, of the 15th century, MS. Harl. 200." I omit the collations; the words within square brackets are supplied from these other copies.

PREFACE. XV

cest Curan fust [le Roi] Hauelok, filz le Roi Kirkebain de
Denemarche, & il conquist la terre sa femme [en Bretaigne], &
occist le Roi Edelfi, vncle sa femme, & conquist tote la terre, *si com
aillours est trouée plus pleinement [en l'estorie]*, & il ne regna qe
treis auuz. Car Saxsouns & Danoys le occirent, & ceo fust grant
damage a tote la grant Brutaigne. Et les Brutouns le porterent
a Stonhenge, & illoeqes ly enterrerent a grant honour.'

§ 13. "With the above may be compared the English version,
as extant in MS. Harl. 2279, which agrees with the Ed. of Caxton,
except in the occasional substitution of one word for another." [1]

' MS. Harl. 2279, f. 47. *Of the kinges Albright & of Edelf.*
Ca' IIII$^{xx.}$ XI$^o$.

After kyng Constantinus ueth, ther were .ij. kynges in Britaigne,
that one men callede Adelbright, that was a Danoys, and helde the
cuntray of Northfolk and Southfolk, that other hight Edelf, and
was a Britoun & helde Nichole, Lindeseye, and alle the lande vnto
Humber. Thes ij. kynges faste werred togeders, but afterward
thei were acorded, and louede togedere as thei had ben borne of o
bodie. The kyng Edelf had a suster that men callede Orewenne,
and he yaf here thurghe grete frenshipe to kyng Adelbright to wif,
and he begate on here a doughter that men callede Argentille, and
in the .iij. yeer after him come vppon a strong sekenesse that nedes
he muste die, and he sent to kyng Edelf, his brother in lawe, that
he shulde come and speke with him, and he come to him with good
wille. Tho prayed he the kyng and coniurede also in the name of
God, that after whan he were dede, he shulde take Argentil his
doughter, and the lande, and that he kepte hir wel, and noreshed
in his chambre; and whan she were of age he shulde done here be
mariede to the strongest and worthiest man that he myȝt fynde,
and than he shulde yelde vp her lande ayen. Edelf hit grauntid,
and bi othe hit confermede his prayer. And whan Adelbright
was dede and Enterede, Edelfe toke the damesel Argentil, and
noreshid her in his chambre, and she become the fayrest creature
th$^t$ myȝt lif, or eny man finde.

*How kyng Edelf mariede the damysel Argentil to a knaue of his
kichyn.* Ca$^o$ IIII$^{xx.}$ XII.

This kyng Edelf, that was vncle to the damesel Argentil,
bithought how that he myȝte falsliche haue the lande from his nece

[1] I omit the collations with MSS. Harl. 24 and 753. Sir F. Madden proves
that this English version was made A. D. 1435, by *John Maundevile*, rector of
Burnham Thorp in Norfolk.

for euermore, and falsly ayens his othe thouȝte to desceyue the damysel, and marie here to a knave of his kichon, that men callede Curan, and he become the worthiest and strengest man of bodie that eny man wist in eny lande that tho leuede. And to him he thouȝt here shendfully haue mariede, for to haue had here lande afterward; but he was clene desceyuede. For this Curan that was Hauelokis son that was kyng of Kirkelane in Denmark, and this Curan Conquerede his wifes landes, and slow kyng Edelf, that was his wifes vncle, and had alle here lande, as in a-nother stede hit [MS. but] telleth more oponly, and he ne regnede but iij. yeer, for Saxones and Danoys him quelde, and that was grete harme to al Britaigne, and Britouns bere him to Stonehenge, and ther thei him interede with mochel honour and solempnite.'

"It must not be concealed, that in some copies, viz. in MSS. Harl. 1337, 6251, Digby 185, Hatton 50, Ashmole 791 and 793, the story is altogether omitted, and Conan made to succeed to Arthur. In those copies also of the English Polychronicon, the latter part of which resembles the above Chronicle, the passage is not found." "Among the Harl. MSS. (No. 63) is a copy of the same Chronicle in an abridged form, in which the name of *Goldesburghe* is substituted for that of Argentille." Sir F. Madden now adds—that "the story occurs also in some interpolated copies of Higden (the Latin text, viz. MSS. Harl. 655, Cott. Jul. E. 8, Reg. 13 E. 1. In an earlier form it is found in a Latin Chronicle of the 13th century, MS. Cott. Dom. A. 2, fol. 130."

§ 14. "It was, in all probability, to this Chronicle also, in its original form, that Thomas Gray, the author of the *Scala Cronica* (or *Scale Cronicon*), a Chronicle in French prose, composed between the years 1355 and 1362, is indebted for his knowledge of the tale." The original MS. is No. 132 in the library of Corpus Christi College, Cambridge, and was edited by Stevenson for the Maitland Club in 1836. The passage relative to Havelok is translated by Leland, *Collectanea*, vol. i. pt. 2, p. 511. This account resembles the others, and involves no new point of interest.

§ 15. I may here introduce the remark, that the story is also to be found in the *Eulogium Historiarum*, ed. Haydon, 1860, vol. ii. p. 378. I here quote the passage at length, as it is not referred to in Sir F. Madden's edition. The date of the Chronicle is about 1366. For various readings, see Haydon's edition.

Non enim est prætermittendum de quodam Dano generoso ætate juvenili florente, qui tempore regis Edelfridi casualiter Angliam adiit, qui a propria patria expulsus per quendam ducem falsissimum, cui pater ejus illum commiserat ipso moriente et ducem rogavit ut puerum nutriret usque dum posset Denemarchiæ regnum viriliter gubernare. Dux vero malitiam machinans juvenem hæredem rectum, Hauelok nomine, voluit occidisse. Puer vero comperiens aufugit per latibula usque dum quidam Anglicus et mercator in illis partibus adventaret; nomen autem mercatoris Grym vocitabatur. Hauelok autem, Grym rogans ut ipsum in Angliam transvectaret, ipse autem annuens, puerum secum conduxit et cum eo per aliquot tempus apud Grymesby morabatur. Tandem ipsum ad curiam regis Edelfridi conduxit et ibi in coquina regis moratus est.

Rex autem Edelfridus quamdam habuit sororem nomine Orwen et illam maritavit regi Athelberto, quod conjugium inter duos reges vinculum amoris catenavit. Rex autem Athelbert terram citra Trentam cum regio diademate occupavit, cum terra de Northfolk' et de Southfolk' et eis adjacentibus. Rex vero Edelfrid comitatum Lincolniæ et Lyndeseye et eis spectantibus. Ante maritagium puellæ Orwen illi duo reges semper debellabant, post matrimonium factum nulla fuit divisio, nec in familia inter eos nec in dominio.

Rex vero Ethelbert de uxore sua quamdam filiam genuit, nomine Argentile, pulcherrimam valde. Athelberto obiente, vel ante mortem ejus, regem rogavit Edelfridum ut filiam suam homini fortissimo ac validiori totius sui regni in conjugium copularet, nihil doli vel mali machinans.

Rex autem Adelfrid omnem malitiam ingeminans de conjugio puellæ malitiose disponens, cogitans se habere unum lixam in coquina sua qui omnes homines regni sui in vigore et fortitudine superabat, et juxta votum patris puellæ ad illum hominem fortissimum illam generosam juvenculam toro maritali copulavit, ob cupiditatem regni puellæ ipsam ita enormiter maritabat. Hauelok in patria Danemarchiæ et Argentile in Britannia æquali sorte ad custodiendum deputati sunt, totum tamen nutu Divino cedebat eis in honorem. Nam Hauelok post paucos annos regnum Britanniæ adoptus est, et a Saxonibus tandem occisus et apud le Stonhenge est sepultus. Pater ejus Kirkeban vocabatur.

This agrees closely with the accounts given above (§ 12 and § 13). The chief point to be noticed is that this account identifies Edelfrid with the Æthelfrith son of Æthelric who was king of the Northumbrians from A.D. 593 to 617, according to the computation of the A. S. Chronicle, and who was succeeded by Eadwine son of Ælle, who drove out the æthelings or sons of Æthelfrith. It may be remarked further, that the same Æthelfrith is called Æluric by Laʒamon, who gives him a very bad character; see Laʒamon, ed. Madden, vol. iii. p. 195.

§ 16. The story is also mentioned by Henry de Knyghton, a canon of Leicester abbey, whose history concludes with the year 1395. But his is no fresh evidence, as it is evidently borrowed from the French Chronicle of Rauf de Boun; see § 7. It is also alluded to in a blundering manner in a short historical compilation extending from the time of Brutus to the reign of Henry VI., and preserved in MS. Cotton Calig. A. 2. At fol. 107 *b* is the passage—" Ethelwolde, qui generavit filiam de (*sic*) Haueloke de Denmarke, per quem Danes per cccc. annos postea fecerunt clameum Anglie." Some omission after the word *de* has turned the passage into nonsense; but it is noteworthy as expressing the claim of the Danes to the English crown by right of descent from Havelok; a claim which is more clearly expressed in MS. Harl. 63, in which the King of Denmark is represented as sending a herald to Æthelstan (A.D. 927)—" to witte wheder he wold fynde a man to fight w*ith* Colbrande[1] for the righ[t]e of the kyngdom Northumb*re*, that the Danes had claymed byfore by the title of kyng Haueloke, that wedded Goldesburghe the kyngis daughter of Northumb*re* "—fol. 19.[2] Four hundred years before this date would intimate some year early in the sixth century. Finally, the story is found at a later period in Caxton's Chronicle (A.D. 1480) as above intimated in § 12; whence it was adopted by Warner, and inserted into his poem entitled Albion's England; book iv. chap. 20, published in 1586. Warner called it the tale of " Argentile and Curan; " and in this ballad-shape it was reprinted in Percy's Reliques of Ancient Poetry (vol. ii. p. 261; ed. 1812) with the same title. Not long after, in 1617, another author, William Webster, published a larger poem in six-line stanzas; but this is a mere paraphrase of Warner. The title is—" The most

[1] Colbrande is the giant defeated by Guy in the Ballad of "Guy and Colebrande." See *Percy Folio MS.*; ed. Hales and Furnivall, vol. ii. p. 528, where *Auelocke* means *Anlaf*.

[2] Quoted in a note in Sir F. Madden's preface, p. xxiii.

pleasant and delightful historie of Curan, a prince of Danske, and the fayre princesse Argentile," &c. John Fabyan, in his Concordance of Historyes, first printed in 1516, alludes to the two kings Adelbryght and Edill, only to dismiss the " longe processe " concerning them, as not supported by sufficient authority. See p. 82 of the reprint by Ellis, 4to, 1811.

§ 17. The only other two sources whence any further light can be thrown upon our subject are the traditions of Denmark and Grimsby. A letter addressed by Sir F. Madden to Professor Rask elicited a reply which was equivalent to saying that next to nothing is known about it in Denmark. This seems to be the right place to mention a small book of 80 pages, published at Copenhagen in the present year (1868), and entitled " Sagnet om Havelok Danske ; fortalt af Kristian Köster." It contains (1) a version, in Danish prose, of the English poem ; (2) a version of the same story, following the French texts of the Arundel and Royal MSS. ; and (3) some elucidations of the legend. The author proposes a theory that Havelok is really the Danish king Amlet, i. e. Hamlet ; but I have not space here to state all his arguments. As far as I follow them, some of the chief ones are these ; that Havelok ought to be found in the list of Danish kings ;[1] that Hamlet's simulation of folly or madness is paralleled by Havelok's behaviour, as expressed in ll. 945—954 of our poem ; and that both Hamlet and Havelok succeeded in fulfilling the revenge which they had long cherished secretly. But I am not much persuaded by these considerations, for, even granting some resemblance in the names,[2] the resemblance in the stories is very slight. But I must refer the reader to the book itself.

§ 18. Turning however to local traditions, we find that Camden briefly alludes to the story in a contemptuous manner

---

[1] So then ought Hamlet ; but the editor of Saxo Grammaticus says, " in antiquioribus regum Daniæ genealogiis Amlethus non occurrit." See Saxo Gram. ed. Müller, Havniæ, 1839 ; end of lib. iii. and beginning of lib. iv. ; also the note on p. 132 of the Notæ Uberiores. The idea that Havelock is Amlet is to be found in Grundtvig, North. Myth. 1832, p. 565.

[2] Havelok [or Hanelock, as it is sometimes read] is quite as like Anlaf, whence the blunder noticed in note 1, p. xviii. In the form Hablok, it is not unlike Blecca, who was a great man in Lindesey soon after the days of Æthelberht of Kent ; see Saxon Chronicle, An. DCXXVII.

(p. 353; ed. 8vo, Lond. 1587); but Gervase Holles is far from being disposed to regard it as fabulous. "In his MSS. collections for Lincolnshire, preserved in MS. Harl. 6829, he thus speaks of the story we are examining.[1]

"And it will not be amisse, to say something concerning y<sup>e</sup> Common tradition of her first founder Grime, as y<sup>e</sup> inhabitants (with a Catholique faith) name him. The tradition is thus. *Grime* (say they) a poore Fisherman (as he was launching into y<sup>e</sup> Riuer for fish in his little boate vpon Humber) espyed not far from him another little boate, empty (as he might conceaue) which by y<sup>e</sup> fauour of y<sup>e</sup> wynde & tyde still approached nearer & nearer vnto him. He betakes him to his oares, & meetes itt, wherein he founde onely a Childe wrapt in swathing clothes, purposely exposed (as it should seeme) to y<sup>e</sup> pittylesse [rage] of y<sup>e</sup> wilde & wide Ocean. He moued with pitty, takes itt home, & like a good foster-father carefully nourisht itt, & endeauoured to nourishe it in his owne occupation: but y<sup>e</sup> childe contrarily was wholy deuoted to exercises of actiuity, & when he began to write man, to martiall sports, & at length by his signall valour obteyned such renowne, y<sup>t</sup> he marryed y<sup>e</sup> King of England's daughter, & last of all founde who was his true Father, & that he was Sonne to y<sup>e</sup> King of Denmarke; & for y<sup>e</sup> comicke close of all; that *Haueloke* (for such was his name) exceedingly aduanced & enriched his foster-father Grime, who thus enriched, builded a fayre Towne neare the place where Hauelocke was founde, & named it Grimesby. Thus say some: others differ a little in y<sup>e</sup> circumstances, as namely, that Grime was not a Fisherman, but a Merchant, & that Hauelocke should be preferred to y<sup>e</sup> King's kitchin, & there liue a longe tyme as a Scullion: but however y<sup>e</sup> circumstances differ, they all agree in y<sup>e</sup> consequence, as concerning y<sup>e</sup> Towne's foundation, to which (sayth y<sup>e</sup> story) Hauelocke y<sup>e</sup> Danish prince, afterward graunted many immunityes. This is y<sup>e</sup> famous Tradition concerning Grimsby w<sup>ch</sup> learned Mr. Cambden gives so little creditt to, that he thinkes it onely *illis dignissima, qui anilibus fabulis noctem solent protrudere.*"

And again, after shewing that *by* is the Danish for *town*, and quoting a passage about Havelock's father being named Gunter, which may be found in Weever (Ancient Funeral Monuments, fol. Lond. 1631, p. 749), he proceeds: " that Hauelocke did sometymes reside in Grimsby, may be gathered from a great blew

---

[1] His account has been printed in the *Topographer*, V. i. p. 241. sq. 8vo, 1789. We follow, as usual, the MS. itself, p. 1.

Boundry-stone, lying at yᵉ East ende of Briggowgate, which retaines yᵉ name of *Hauelock's-Stone* to this day. Agayne yᵉ great priuiledges & immunityes, that this Towne hath in Denmarke aboue any other in England (as freedome from Toll, & yᵉ rest) may fairely induce a Beleife, that some preceding favour, or good turne called on this remuneration. But lastly (which proofe I take to be *instar omnium*) the Common Seale of yᵉ Towne, & that a most auncient one," &c. [Here follows a description of the Seal.]

"The singular fact," adds Sir F. Madden, "alluded to by Holles, of the Burgesses of Grimsby being free from toll at the Port of Elsineur, in Denmark, is confirmed by the Rev. G. Oliver, in his Monumental Antiquities of Grimsby, 8vo, Hull, 1825, who is inclined from that, and other circumstances, to believe the story is not so totally without foundation." There is also an absurd local story that the church at Grimsby, which has now but one turret, formerly had four, three of which were kicked down by Grim in his anxiety to destroy some hostile vessels. The first fell among the enemy's fleet; the second dropped in Wellowgate, and is now Havelock's stone; the third fell within the churchyard, but the fourth his strength failed to move. Perhaps amongst the most interesting notices of the story are the following words by Sir Henry Havelock, whose family seems to have originally resided in Durham. His own account, however, is this. "My father, William Havelock, descended from a family which formerly resided at Grimsby in Lincolnshire, and was himself born at Guisborough in Yorkshire."[1] And it may at least be said with perfect truth, that if the name of *Havelock* was not famous formerly, it is famous now.

§ 19. The last evidence for the legend is the still-existing seal of the corporation of Great Grimsby. The engraving of this seal, as it appears in the present edition, was made from a copy kindly furnished to the E. E. T. S. by the Mayor of Grimsby, and I here subjoin a description of it, communicated to me by J. Hopkin, Esq., Jun., of Grimsby, which was first printed, in a slightly different form, in Notes and Queries, 2nd Series, vol. xi. p. 41 ; see also p. 216.

---

[1] Quoted in Brock's Biography of Sir H. Havelock, 1858 ; p. 9.

## PREFACE.

"The ancient Town Seal of Great Grimsby is engraven on a circular piece of brass not very thick; and on the back, which is rather arched, is a small projecting piece of brass, placed as a substitute for a handle, in order when taking an impression the more easily to detach the matrix from the Wax. This seal is in an excellent state of preservation, and is inscribed in Saxon characters 'Sigillvm Comunitatis Grimebye' and represents thereon Gryme ('Gryem') who by tradition is reported to have been a native of Souldburg in Denmark, where he gained a precarious livelihood by fishing and piracy; but having, as is supposed, during the reign of Ethelbert,[1] been accidentally driven into the Humber by a furious storm, he landed on the Lincolnshire Coast near Grimsby, he being at this time miserably poor and almost destitute of the common necessaries of life; for Leland represents this 'poor fisschar' as being so very needy that he was not 'able to kepe his sunne Cuaran for poverty.' Gryme, finding a capacious haven adapted to his pursuits, built himself a house and commenced and soon succeeded in establishing a very lucrative Trade with Norway, Sweden, and Denmark. Other Merchants having in process of time settled near him, attracted by the commercial advantages offered by this excellent Harbour, they jointly constructed convenient appendages for extensive Trade, and the colony soon rose into considerable importance, and became known at an early period by the name of Grimsby. For not only was Grimsby constituted a borough so early as the seventh century, but Peter of Langtoft speaks of it as a frontier Town and the boundary of a Kingdom erected by the conquests of Egbert in the year 827, which he states included all that portion of the Island which lay between 'the maritime Towns of Grymsby and Dover.' So that even at that period, Grimsby must have been a place of peculiar strength and importance. Gryme is represented on the seal as a man of gigantic stature with comparatively short hair, a shaven chin, and a moustache, holding in his right hand a drawn sword and bearing on his left arm a circular shield with an ornate boss and rim. The sleeveless tunic above his under vest is most probably the panzar or panzara of the Danes. Between his feet is a Conic object, possibly intended for a helmet, as it resembles the chapelle-de-fer worn by William Rufus on his Great Seal, and which in the laws of Gula is distinguished as the Steel hufe. On the right hand of Gryme stands his protégé Haveloc ('Habloc'), whom, during one of his mercantile excursions soon after his arrival in Lincolnshire, Gryme had the good fortune to save

---

[1] Æthelberht of Kent reigned from A.D. 560—616 (56 years).

from imminent danger of Shipwreck, and who proved to be the Son of Gunter, King of Denmark, and who was therefore conveyed to the British Court, where he subsequently received in marriage Goldburgh, the Daughter of the British Sovereign. Above Gryme is represented a hand, being emblematical of the hand of providence by which Haveloc was preserved, and near the hand is the star which marks the point where the inscription begins and ends. Haveloc made such a favourable representation of his preserver at the British and Danish Courts, that he procured for him many honours and privileges. From the British Monarch Gryme, who had already realised an abundance of wealth, received a charter, and was made the chief governor of Grimsby; and the Danish Sovereign granted to the Town an immunity (which is still possessed by the Burgesses of Grimsby) from all Tolls at the Port of Elsineur. Gryme afterwards lived in Grimsby like a petty prince in his Hereditary Dominions. Above Haveloc is represented a crown and in his right hand is a battle axe, the favourite weapon of the Northmen, and in his right hand is a ring which he is presenting to the British Princess Goldburgh ('Goldebvrgh'), who stands on the left side of Gryme and whose right hand is held towards the Ring. Over her head is a Regal Diadem, and in her left hand is a Sceptre. Sir F. Madden states that it is certain that this seal is at least as old as the time of Edward I. (and therefore contemporaneous with the MS.) as the legend is written in a character which after the year 1300 fell into disuse, and was succeeded by the black letter, or *Gothic*."

§ 20. SKETCH OF THE STORY OF " Le Lai d'Aueloc." [1]

It is my intention to offer some remarks on the probable sources of the legend, and to fix a conjectural date for the existence of Havelok. But it is obviously convenient that a sketch of the story should first be given. It appears, however, that the resemblance between the French and English versions is by no means very close, and it will be necessary to give separate abstracts of them. I begin with the French version, in which I follow the Norfolk MS. rather than the abridgment by Gaimar. I have already said that the former is printed in Sir F. Madden's edition, and that it was reprinted by M. Michel with the title "Lai d'Havelok le Danois," Paris, 1833, and by Mr Wright for the Caxton Society in 1850.

[1] For this latter portion of the Preface I am entirely responsible.

The Britons made a lay concerning King Havelok, who is surnamed Cuaran. His father was Gunter, King of the Danes. Arthur crossed the sea, and invaded Denmark. Gunter perished by the treason of Hodulf, who gained the kingdom, and held it of Arthur. Gunter had a fine castle, where his wife and son were guarded, being committed to the protection of Grim. The child was but seven years old; but ever as he slept, an odorous flame issued from his mouth. Hodulf sought to kill him, but Grim prepared a ship, and furnished it with provisions, wherein he placed the queen and the child, and set sail from Denmark. On their voyage they encountered pirates ("outlaghes"), who killed them all after a hard fight, excepting Grim, who was an acquaintance of theirs, and Grim's wife and children. Havelok also was saved. They at last arrived at the haven, afterwards named "Grimesbi" from Grim. Grim there resumed his old trade, a fisherman's, and a town grew up round his hut, which was called Grimsby. The child grew up, and waxed strong. One day Grim said to him, "Son, you will never thrive as a fisherman; take your brothers with you, and seek service amongst the King's servants." He was soon well apparelled, and repaired with his two foster-brothers to Nicole [Lincoln].[1] Now at that time there was a king named Alsi, who ruled over all Nicole and Lindesie;[2] but the country southward was governed by another king, named Ekenbright, who had married Alsi's sister Orewen. These two had one only daughter, named Argentille. Ekenbright, falling ill, committed Argentille to the care of Alsi, till she should be of age to be married to the strongest man that can be found. At Ekenbright's death, Alsi reigned over both countries, holding his court at Nicole. Havelok, on his arrival there, was employed to carry water and cut wood, and to perform all menial offices requiring great strength. He was named Cuaran, which means—in the British language—a scullion. Argentille soon arrived at marriageable age, and Alsi determined to marry her to Cuaran, which would sufficiently fulfil her father's wish—Cuaran being confessedly the strongest man in those parts. To this marriage he compelled her to consent, hoping thereby to disgrace her for ever. Havelok was unwilling that his wife should perceive the marvellous flame, but soon forgot this, and ere long fell asleep. Then had Argentille a strange vision—that a savage bear and some foxes attacked Cuaran, but dogs and boars defended him. A boar having killed the bear, the foxes cried for quarter from Cuaran,

---

[1] *Nicole* is a French inversion of Lincoln. It is not uncommon.
[2] The northern part of Lincolnshire is called *Lindsey*.

who commanded them to be bound. Then he would have put to sea, but the sea rose so high that he was terrified. Next she beheld two lions, at seeing which she was frightened, and she and Cuaran climbed a tree to avoid them; but the lions submitted themselves to him, and called him their lord. Then a great cry was raised, whereat she awoke, and beheld the miraculous flame. "Sir," she exclaimed, "you burn!" But he reassured her, and, having heard her dream, said that it would soon come true. The next day, however, she again told her dream to a chamberlain, her friend, who said that he well knew a holy hermit who could explain it. The hermit explained to Argentille that Cuaran must be of royal lineage. "He will be king," he said, "and you a queen. Ask him concerning his parentage. Remember also to repair to his native place." On being questioned, Cuaran replied that he was born at Grimsby; that Grim was his father, and Saburc his mother. "Then let us go to Grimsby," she replied. Accompanied by his two foster-brothers, they came to Grimsby; but Grim and Saburc were both dead. They found there, however, a daughter of Grim's, named Kelloc, who had married a tradesman of that town. Up to this time Havelok had not known his true parentage, but Kelloc thought it was now time to tell him, and said: "Your father was Gunter, the King of the Danes, whom Hodulf slew. Hodulf obtained the kingdom as a grant from Arthur. Grim fled with you, and saved your life; but your mother perished at sea. Your name is HAVELOK. My husband will convey you to Denmark, where you must inquire for a lord named 'Sigar l'estal;' and take with you my two brothers." So Kelloc's husband conveyed them to Denmark, and advised Havelok to go to Sigar and show himself and his wife, as then he would be asked who his wife is. They went to the city of the seneschal, the before-named Sigar, where they craved a night's lodging, and were courteously entertained. But as they retired to a lodging for the night, six men attacked them, who had been smitten with the beauty of Argentille. Havelok defended himself with an axe which he found, and slew five, whereupon the sixth fled. Havelok and his party fled away for refuge to a monastery, which was soon attacked by the townsmen who had heard of the combat. Havelok *mounted the tower*, and defended himself bravely, *casting down a huge stone on his enemies*.[1] The news soon reached the ears of Sigar, who hastened to see what the uproar was about. Behold-

---

[1] Hence the obvious origin of the legend of "Havelok's stone," and the local tradition about Grim's casting down stones from the tower of Grimsby church.

ing Havelok fixedly, he called to mind the form and appearance of Gunter, and asked Havelok of his parentage. Havelok replied that Grim had told him he was by birth a Dane, and that his mother perished at sea; and ended by briefly relating his subsequent adventures. Then Sigar asked him his name. "My name is Havelok," he said, "and my other name is Cuaran." Then the seneschal took him home, and determined to watch for the miraculous flame, which he soon perceived, and was assured that Havelok was the true heir. Therefore he gathered a great host of his friends, and sent for the horn which none but the true heir could sound, promising a ring to any one who could blow it. When all had failed, it was given to Havelok, who blew it loud and long, and was joyfully recognized and acknowledged to be the true King. Then with a great army he attacked Hodulf the usurper, whom he slew with his own hand. Thus was Havelok made King of Denmark.

But after he had reigned four years, his wife incited him to return to England. With a great number of ships he sailed there, and arrived at Carleflure;[1] and sent messengers to Alsi, demanding the inheritance of Argentille. Alsi was indeed astonished at such a demand as coming from a scullion, and offered him battle. The hosts met at Theford,[2] and the battle endured till nightfall without a decisive result. But Argentille craftily advised her lord to support his dead men by stakes, to increase the apparent number of his army; and the next day Alsi, deceived by this device, treated for peace, and yielded up to his former ward all the land, from Holland[3] to Gloucester. Alsi had been so sorely wounded that he lived but fifteen days longer. Thus was Havelok king over Lincoln and Lindsey, and reigned over them for twenty years. Such is the lay of Cuaran.

§ 21. The chief points to be noticed in Gaimar's abridgment are the few additional particulars to be gleaned from it. We there find that Havelok's mother was *Alvive*, a daughter of King *Gaifer;* that the King of Nicole and Lindeseie was a *Briton*, and was named Edelsie; that his sister, named Orwain, was married to Adelbrit, a *Dane*, who ruled over Norfolk; and that Edelsie and Adelbrit lived in the days of Costentin (Constantine), who

---

[1] Possibly Saltfleet, suggests Mr Haigh. Such, at least, is the position required by the circumstances.

[2] In the Durham MS. it is Tiedfort, i. e. Tetford, not far from Horncastle, in Lincolnshire.

[3] A name given to the S.E. part of Lincolnshire.

succeeded Arthur. It is also said that the usurper Hodulf was brother to Aschis, who is the Achilles of Geoffrey of Monmouth. Another statement, that Havelok's kingdom extended from Holland to *Colchester,* seems to be an improvement upon "from Holland to *Gloucester.*"

The words of Mr Petrie, in his remarks upon the lay in Monumenta Historica Britannica, vol. i., may be quoted here. "Although both [French versions] have the same story in substance, and often contain lines exactly alike, yet, besides the different order in which the incidents are narrated, each has occasionally circumstances wanting in the other, and such too, it should seem, as would leave ae story incomplete unless supplied from the other copy. Thus, the visit to the hermit, which is omitted in Gaimar, was probably in the original romance; for without it Argentille's dream tells for nothing; and in the Arundel copy there is a particular account of Haveloc's defence of a tower by hurling stones on his assailants, which in Gaimar is so obscurely alluded to as to be hardly intelligible. On the other hand, instead of the description of the extraordinary virtues of Sygar's ring in Gaimar, it is merely said in the Arundel copy that Sygar would give his *anel d'or* to whoever could sound the horn; and, to omit other instances, a festival is described in Gaimar on the authority of *l'Estorie,* of which no notice whatever occurs in the Arundel MS."

### § 22. SKETCH OF THE ENGLISH POEM.

The "Lay of Havelok" has been admirably paraphrased by Professor Morley, in his "English Writers," vol. i. pp. 459—467, a book which should be in every reader's hands, and which should by all means be consulted. I only intend here to give a briefer outline, for the sake of comparing the main features of our poem with those of the French *Lai.*

Hear the tale of Havelok! There was once a good king in England, named Athelwold, renowned and beloved for his justice. He had but one child, a daughter named Goldborough. Knowing that his end was approaching, he sent for all his lords to assemble at Winchester, and there committed Goldborough to the care of Godrich, the earl of Cornwall; directing him to see her married to the strongest and fairest man whom he could find. But Godrich imprisoned her at Dover, and resolved to seize her inheritance for his own son. At that time there was also a King of Denmark, named Birkabeyn, who had one son, Havelok, and two daughters, Swanborough and Helfled. At the approach of death, he committed these to the care of Earl Godard. But Godard killed the two girls, and only spared Havelok because he did not like to kill him with his own hand. He therefore hired a fisherman, named Grim, to drown Havelok at sea. But Grim perceived, as Havelok slept, a miraculous light shining round the lad, whereby he knew that the child was the true heir, and would one day be king. In order to avoid Godard, Grim fitted up a ship, and provisioned it, and with his wife Leve, his three sons, his two daughters, and Havelok, put out to sea. They landed in Lindesey at the mouth of the Humber, at a place afterwards named Grimsby after Grim. Grim worked at his old trade, a fisherman's, and Havelok carried about the fish for sale. Then arose a great dearth in the land, and Havelok went out to seek his own livelihood, walking to Lincoln barefoot. He was hired as a porter by the earl of Cornwall's cook, and drew water and cut wood for the earl's kitchen. One day some men met to contend in games and to " put the stone." At the cook's command, Havelok also put the stone, hurling it further than any of the rest.[1] Godrich, hearing the praises of Havelok's strength, at once resolved to perform his oath by causing him to marry Goldborough; and carried his design into execution. As soon as the pair were married, Havelok suddenly quitted Lincoln with his wife, and returned to Grimsby, where he found that Grim was dead, but that his five children are yet alive. At night, Goldborough perceived a light shining round about Havelok, and observed a cross upon his shoulder. At the same time she heard an angel's voice, telling her of good fortune to come. Then he awoke, and told her a dream; how he had dreamt that all Denmark and England became his own. She encouraged him, and urged him to set sail for Denmark at once. He accordingly called to him Grim's three sons, and narrated to them his own history, and Godard's treachery, asking them to accompany him to Denmark. To this they assented, and sailed with him and Goldborough to Denmark. There he sought out a former friend of his father's, Earl Ubbe, who invited him and his friends to a sumptuous feast. After the feast, Havelok and Goldborough and Grim's sons went to the house of one Bernard Brown, whose house was that night attacked by sixty thieves. By dint of

---

[1] Here again is an allusion to " Havelok's stone."

great prowess, the friends at length slew all their sixty assailants, and Ubbe was so amazed at Havelok's valour that he resolved to dub him a knight, and invited him to sleep in his own castle. At night, he peeped into Havelok's chamber, and beheld the marvellous light, and saw a bright cross on his neck. Rejoiced at heart, he did homage to Havelok, and commanded all his friends and dependents to do the same. He also dubbed him knight, and proclaimed him King. With six thousand men he set out to attack Godard, whom he defeated and made prisoner, and afterwards caused to be flayed, drawn, and hung. Then Havelok swore that he would establish at Grimsby a priory of black monks, to pray for Grim's soul; and Godrich, having heard that Havelok has invaded England, raised a great army against him. An indecisive combat took place between Ubbe and Godrich, but a more decisive one between Godrich and Havelok; for Havelok cut off his foe's hand and made him prisoner. Then the English submitted to Goldborough, and acknowledged her as queen; but Godrich was condemned and burnt. Havelok rewarded both his own friends and the English nobles; for he caused Earl Reyner of Chester to marry Gunild, Grim's daughter, and Bertram, formerly Godrich's cook, to marry Levive, another of Grim's daughters; bestowing upon Bertram the earldom of Cornwall. Then were Havelok and Goldborough crowned at London, and a feast was given that lasted forty days. The kingdom of Denmark was bestowed upon Ubbe, who held it of King Havelok. Havelok and Goldborough lived to the age of a hundred years, and their reign lasted for sixty years in England. They had fifteen children, who were all kings and queens. Such is the *geste* of Havelok and Goldborough.

### § 23. POSSIBLE DATE OF HAVELOK'S REIGN.

The various allusions to the story of Havelok already cited naturally lead us to consider the question as to what date we should refer such circumstances of the story as may have some foundation in truth, or such circumstances as may have originated the story. I do not look upon this as altogether a hopeless or profitless inquiry, for it seems to me that a theory may be constructed which will readily and easily fit in with most of the statements of our authorities. In the first place, to place Havelok's father in the time of Alfred, as is done by Peter de Langtoft and his translators, is absurd, and evidently due to the confusion between the names of Gunter and Godrum or Guthrum. We may even adduce Langtoft's evidence against himself, as he alludes to Grimsby as being the boundary of Egbert's kingdom; and indeed, the mere fact of its being a British lay points to a time before the establishment of the Heptarchy. As already suggested in § 16, some of the authorities point to the sixth century. But the evidence of the French poem and of Gaimar points still more steadily to a similar early date. There we find Gunter appearing as the enemy, not of Alfred, but of Arthur. The French prose chronicle of the Brute places Adelbright and Edelfi after the death of Constantine, and it is clear that there is some close connection between the British lay of Havelok and the British Chronicle. The *Godrich* of the English version is the *Alsi* of the French poem, the *Edelsi* of Gaimar, the *Adelfrid*[1] or *Edelfrid* of the Eulogium Historiarum, the *Elfroi* of Wace, the *Æluric* of Laʒamon, the *Æthelfrith* who succeeded to the throne of Northumbria A. D. 593, according to the Saxon Chronicle. The *Athelwold* of the English version is the *Adelbrict* of Gaimar, the *Ekenbright* of the French poem, the *Athelbert* of the Eulogium Historiarum, the *Aldebar* of Wace, and the *Æthelbert* of Laʒamon, i. e. no other than the celebrated *Æthelberht* of Kent, who was baptized by St Augustine A. D. 596, according to the Saxon Chronicle. This is the right clue to the *names*, from which, when once obtained, the rest follows easily. The variations between the English and French versions are very great, and it is clear that each poet proceeded much as poets are accustomed to do. Taking a legend as the general guide or thread of a narrative, it is the simplest and easiest plan to dress it up after one's own fashion, and to draw upon the materials that are supplied by the *general surroundings* of the story. I feel confident that the narrators of the Lay of Havelok must have used materials not much unlike those used by Laʒamon, and a mere comparison of the French and English lays with Laʒamon will amply suffice to elucidate this. Æluric is first mentioned at p. 195 of vol. iii. of Laʒamon, as edited by Sir F. Madden; if we allow ourselves a margin on both sides of this, we may find many things akin to the lay of Havelok

[1] Hence, by confusion, the placing of Havelok's father in the time of *Ælfred*.

between pages 150 and 282 of that volume, as I will now shew.
The character of the good king Athelwold is taken from that of
Æthelberht of Kent, and his love of justice may remind us of the
ancient collection of laws which are still extant as having been
made by that king. His extensive rule, such as is also attributed
to Godrich and Havelok, may point to the title of *Bretwalda*,
which Æthelberht so long coveted, and at last obtained. Our
poet, in describing Birkabeyn, repeats this character so exactly,
and makes the circumstances of the deaths of Athelwold and
Birkabeyn so similar, that they are almost indistinguishable; a
fault which he doubles by repeating the character of Godrich in
describing that of Godard. Both of these answer to Laȝamon's
Æluric, who was "the wickedest of all kings" (Laȝ. iii. 195). So
far, perhaps, the connection of the various stories is not very evident, but I will now mention an obvious coincidence. The quarrel
and reconciliation between Athelbert and Edelfrid, as told in the
Eulogium Historiarum, &c., exactly answers to the quarrel and
reconciliation between Cadwan and Æluric as told in Laȝamon
(vol. iii. p. 205); where Cadwan has come forward in place of
Æthelbert, who has by this time dropped out of Laȝamon's
narrative. Again, the Gunter or Gurmond who was Havelok's
father reminds us of the Gurmund of Laȝamon (p. 156), who is
curiously described as king of Africa; but the name is Danish.
The character of Grim is fairly paralleled by that of Brian, who
makes sea-voyages, and goes about as a merchant (Laȝamon, iii.
232). In several respects Havelok may have been drawn from
Cadwalan, whose gallant attempts to gain the king of Northumber-
land are recorded in Laȝamon (iii. 216—254); his opponent
being Edwin, who has replaced Ethelfrid as Laȝamon's narrative
proceeds. At last he overthrows him and slays him in the great
battle of Heathfield or Hatfield, which took place, according to
the Saxon Chronicle, A. D. 633. This great battle resembles the
decisive one between Havelok and Godrich. As Cadwalan was
well supported by his liegeman Penda (Laȝamon, iii. 251), so was
Havelok by Ubbe. Again, Cadwalan marries Helen, whom he
found at

—þan castle of Deoure
on þere sæ oure; (Laȝamon, iii. 250),

which reminds us of Havelok's wife Goldborough, who was imprisoned at

—doure
þat standeth on þe seis oure ; (l. 320).

The very name Helen, though not the name of Havelok's wife, was that of his mother, who was killed by the pirates. For the connection between Laȝamon's Helen and pirates, see Sir F. Madden's note, vol. iii. p. 428. There is a most curious contradiction in the English lay about Havelok's religion; in l. 2520 he is a devout Christian, but in l. 2580 Godrich speaks of him as being a cruel pagan. Now it was just about this very time that Paulinus preached in Lindsey, " where the first that believed was a powerful man called *Blecca*, with all his followers " (A.S. Chron. ed. Thorpe, vol. ii. p. 21 ; A. D. 627). Havelok, according to some, was buried at Stonehenge ; but so was Constantine (Laȝamon, iii. 151). A dearth is mentioned in the English lay (l. 824); cf. Laȝamon, iii. 279. And I may here add another coincidence, of an interesting but certainly of a very circuitous nature. A close examination of the Lay of King Horn shews that there is no real connection between the story therein contained and that of Havelok. Yet there is a connection after a sort. Though by different authors, and in different metre, both lays are found in English in the same MS. ; both versions belong to the same date ; both are from French versions, written by Englishmen from British sources; and now, if we compare King Horn with the very part of Laȝamon now under consideration, there is at once seen to be a most exact resemblance in one point. The story of the ring given by Horn to Rymenhild (K. Horn, ed. Lumby, ll. 1026—1210) is remarkably like that of the ring whereby Brian is recognized by his sister (Laȝamon, iii. 234—238). But it is hardly worth while to pursue the subject further. It may suffice to suppose that the period of the existence of Havelok and Grim may be referred to the times of Æthelberht of Kent and Æthelfrith and Eadwine of Northumbria.[1] It is exceedingly probable that Havelok was never more than a chief or a petty prince, and

---

[1] Or, as I should prefer to say, earlier than those times. The two kings spoken of in the Lay may have had names somewhat similar to these, which may have been replaced by the more familiar names here mentioned.

whether he was a Danish or only a British enemy of the Angles is not of very great importance. If, however, more exact dates be required, they may be found in " The Conquest of Britain by the Saxons," by Daniel P. Haigh, London, 8vo, 1861, pp. 363—367; where the following dates are suggested. Havelok's father slain, A. D. 487; his expedition to Denmark, A. D. 507; his reign in England, A. D. 511—531, or a little later. These dates follow a system which is here about 16 years earlier than the dates in the A.S. Chronicle. His results are obtained from totally different considerations. On the whole, let us place Havelok in the *sixth* century, at *some* period of his life.

§ 24. It is, perhaps, worthy of a passing remark that some of the circumstances in the Lay may have been suggested by the romantic story of Eadwine of Northumbria, who was also born at the close of the sixth century. For he it was who really married the *daughter of Æthelberht*, and it was the *archbishop of York*, Paulinus, who performed the ceremony. The relation of how Eadwine was persecuted by *Æthelfrith*, how he fled and was protected by Rædwald, king of the East Angles, how he saw a vision of an angel who promised his restoration to the throne and that his rule should exceed that of his predecessors, how, with the assistance of Rædwald, he overthrew and *slew Æthelfrith* in a terrible battle beside the river Idle, may be found in Beda's Ecclesiastical History, bk. II. ch. 9—16.[1] In the last of these chapters there is again mention of *Blecca, the governor of the city of Lincoln.* Sir F. Madden, in his note to l. 45, speaks of the extraordinary proofs of the peaceable state of the country in the reign of Ælfred; but Beda uses similar language in speaking of the reign of Eadwine; and the earlier instance is even more remarkable. "It is reported that there was then such perfect peace in Britain, wheresoever the dominion of King Edwin extended, that, as *is still proverbially said*, a woman with her new-born babe might walk throughout the island, from sea to sea, without receiving any harm. That king took such care for the good of his nation, that in several places where he had seen clear springs near the highways, he caused stakes to be fixed, with brass dishes hanging

[1] Cf. Lappenberg's History of England, tr. by Thorpe, vol. i. pp. 145—154.

at them, for the conveniency of travellers; nor durst any man touch them for any other purpose than that for which they were designed, either through the dread they had of the king, or for the affection which they bore him, &c."[1] Readers who are acquainted with the pleasing poem of "Edwin of Deira," by the late Alexander Smith, will remember his adventures; and it may be noted, as an instance of the manner in which poets alter names at pleasure, that Mr Smith gives to Æthelfrith the name of Ethelbert, to Eadwine's wife Æthelburh, that of Bertha, and to his father Ælle, that of Egbert. My theory of the Lay of Havelok is then simply this, that I look upon it as the general result of various narratives connected with the history of Northumbria and Lindesey at the close, or possibly the beginning, of the sixth century, gathered round some favourite local (i. e. Lincolnshire) tradition as a nucleus. A similar theory may be true of the Lay of Horn.

### § 25. On the names "Curan" and "Havelok."

The French version tells us that *Coaran, Cuaran,* or *Cuheran* is the British word for a scullion. This etymology has not hitherto been traced, but it may easily have been perfectly true. A glance at Armstrong's Gaelic Dictionary shews us that the Gaelic *cearn* (which answers very well to the Old English *hirne,* a corner) has the meaning of a *corner,* and, secondly, of a *kitchen;* and that *cearnach* is an adjective meaning *of or belonging to a kitchen.* But we may come even nearer than this; for by adding the diminutive ending *-an* to the Gaelic *cocaire,* a cook, we see that *Cuheran* may really have conveyed the idea of *scullion* to a British ear, and this probably further gave rise to the story of Havelok's degradation. It is a common custom—one which true etymologists must always deplore—to invent a story to account for a derivation; and such a practice is invariably carried out with greater boldness and to a greater extent if the said derivation chances to be false. For it is possible that Curan may be simply the Gaelic *curan,* a brave man, and the Irish *curanta,* brave. The derivation of Havelok is certainly puzzling.

---

[1] See the same statement in Fabyan's Chronicles, p. 112; ed. Ellis, 1811.

Professor Rask declared it to have no meaning in Danish. It bears, however, a remarkable resemblance to the Old English *gavelok*, which occurs in Weber's *Kyng Alisaunder*, l. 1620, and which is the A.S. *gafeluc*, Icel. *gaflak*, Welsh *gaflach*, a spear, dart, or javelin. This is an appropriate name for a warrior, and possibly reappears in the instance of Hugh *Kevelock*, earl of Chester (Bp. Percy's Folio MS., ed. Hales and Furnivall, i. 128). It is remarkable that the Gaelic and Irish *corran* has the same sense, that of *a spear*, whilst *curan*, as above-mentioned, means *a brave man*. It is best, perhaps, to stop here; for etymology, when pursued too far, is wont to beguile the pursuer into every possible quagmire of absurdity.

## § 26. Description of the MS., &c.

The MS. from which the present poem is printed is in the Laudian collection in the Bodleian Library, where its old mark is K 60, and its present one Misc. 108. Being described in the old printed catalogue merely as *Vitæ Sanctorum*, the romance was in consequence for a long time overlooked. The Lives of the Saints occupy a large portion of the volume, and are probably to be ascribed to the authorship of Robert of Gloucester. "These Lives or Festivals," says Sir F. Madden, "are [here] 61 in number, written in long Alexandrine verse. Then succeed the Sayings of St Bernard and the Visions of St Paul, both in six-line stanzas; the *Disputatio inter Corpus et Animam*, the English Romance of Havelok, the Romance of Kyng Horn, and some additions in a hand of the 15th century, including the lives of St Blaise, St Cecilia, and St Alexius, and an alliterative poem intitled *Somer Soneday*, making in all the Contents of the Volume to amount to 70 pieces." The lays of Havelok and Horn are written out in the same handwriting, of an early date, certainly not later than the end of the thirteenth century. The Havelok begins on fol. 204, and is written in double columns, each column containing 45 lines. A folio is lost between fol. 211 and 212, but no notice of this has been taken in numbering the folios; hence the catchword which should have been found at the bottom of fol. 215 *b*, appears at the bottom of fol. 214 *b* (see l. 2164). The poem terminates at the

27th line on fol. 219 *b*, and is immediately followed by Kyng Horn in the same column. The character of the handwriting is bold and square, but the words are very close together. The initial letter of every line is written a little way apart from the rest, as in William of Palerne, and other MSS. Both the long and short *s* (ſ *and* s) are used. The long *s* is in general well distinguished from *f*, and on this account I have taken the liberty of printing both *esses* alike, as my experience in printing the Romans of Partenay proved that the difficulty of avoiding misprints is greater than the gain of representing the difference between them. The chief point of interest is that, as in *early* MSS., the long *s* is sometimes found at the *end* of a word, as in " uſ " in l. 22, and "iſ " in l. 23. The following are all the examples of the use of this letter in the first 26 lines; ſo (4), wicteſte (9), ſtede (10), criſt, ſchilde (16), Kriſt, ſo (17), ſo (19), ſchal (21), Kriſt, uſ (22), iſ (23), ſtalworþi (24), ſtalworþeſte (25), ſtede (26). With this exception, the present reprint is a faithful representation of the original; for, as the exact fidelity of a text is of the first importance, I have been careful to compare the proof-sheets with the MS. twice throughout; besides which, the original edition is itself exceedingly correct, and had been re-read by Sir F. Madden with the MS. His list of errata (nearly all of them of minor importance) agreed almost exactly with my own. A great difficulty is caused by the use of the Saxon letter *w* (ƿ). This letter, the thorn-letter (þ), and *y*, are all three made very nearly alike. In general, the *y* is dotted, but the dot is occasionally omitted. Wherever the letter really appears to be a *w*, I have denoted it by printing the *w* as an italic letter. The following are, I believe, the *only* examples of it. *W*it-drow = withdrew, l. 502 ; *w*e, 1058 ; *w*as, 1129 (cf. " him was ful wa," *Sir Tristr.* f. iii. st. 43) ; ber*w*en, 1426 (written " berwen " in l. 697) ; *w*at = known, 1674 ; *w*e, miswritten for *w*o = who, 1914 ; to which perhaps we may add *w*it, 997. This evidence is interesting as shewing that this letter was then fast going out of use, and I think that we may safely date the final disappearance of this letter from MSS. at about the year 1300. As regards the *th*, we may remark that at the end of a word both þ and *th* are used, as in " norþ and suth,"

l. 434; sometimes *th* occurs in the middle of a word, as "sithen," l. 1238, which is commonly written "siþen," as in l. 399. The words þe, þat, þer, &c., are hardly ever written otherwise. But the reader will remark many instances in which *th* final seems to have the hard sound of *t*, as in *brouth*, 57, *nouth*, 58, *lith*, 534, *þouth*, 1190, &c.; cf. § 27. The letter *t* is sometimes shortened so as nearly to resemble *c*, and *c* is sometimes lengthened into *t*. The letters *n* and *u* are occasionally alike, but the difference between them is commonly well marked. The *i* has a long stroke over it when written next to *m* or *n*. On the whole, the writing is very clear and distinct, after a slight acquaintance with it. The poem is marked out into paragraphs by the use of large letters. I have introduced a slight space at the end of each paragraph, to shew this more clearly.

§ 27. ON THE GRAMMATICAL FORMS OCCURRING IN THE POEM.

The following peculiarities of spelling may be first noted. We frequently find *h* prefixed to words which it is usual to spell without one. Examples are: *holde* for *old, hete* for *ete* (eat), *het* for *et* (ate), *heuere* for *euere, Henglishe* for *Englishe*, &c.; see the Glossary, under the letter H. This enables us to explain some words which at first appear puzzling; thus *her* = *er*, ere; *hayse* = *ayse*, ease; *helde* = *elde*, old age; *hore* = *ore*, grace; *hende* = *ende*, which in one passage means *end*, but in another *a duck*. The forms *hof, hus, hure,* for *of, us, ure* are such as we should hardly have expected to find. On the other hand, *h* is omitted in the words *auelok, aueden, osed,* and in *is* for *his* (l. 2254). These instances, and other examples such as follow, may readily be found by help of the Glossarial Index. Again, *d* final after *l* or *n* was so slightly sounded as to be omitted even in writing. Examples are: *lon* for *lond, hel* for *held, bihel* for *biheld, shel* for *sheld, gol* for *gold*. But a more extraordinary omission is that of *r* final in *the, neythe, othe, douthe,* which does not seem to be satisfactorily explained even by the supposition that the scribe may have omitted the small upward curl which does duty for *er* so frequently in MSS. For we further find the omission of *l* final, as in *mike* for *mikel, we* for *wel,* and of *t* final, as in *bes* for *best;* from which instances we should rather infer some peculiarity of pronunciation rendering final letters indistinct, of which there are numerous examples, as *fiel* for *field*, in modern provincial English. Cf. *il* for *ilk*, in ll. 818, 1740; and *twel* for *twelf*. " From the same license," says Sir F. Madden, " arises the frequent repetition of such rhythm as *riden* and *side*, where the final *n* seems to have been suppressed in pronunciation. Cf. ll. 29, 254, 957, 1105, 1183, 2098, &c., and hence we perceive how readily the infinitive verbal Saxon termination glided into its subsequent form. The broad pronunciation of the dialect in which the poem was written is also frequently discernible, as in *slawen*, l. 2676, and *knaue*, l. 949, which rhyme to *Rauen* and *plawe*.[1] So likewise, *bothe* or *bethe* is, in sound, equivalent to *rede*, ll. 360, 694, 1680." Other peculiarities will be noticed in discussing the Metre. Observe also the Anglo-Saxon *hw* for the modern *wh*, exemplified by *hwo*, 368, *hwan*, 474, *hweþer*, 294, *hwere*, 549, *hwil*, 301 ; compare also *qual, qui, quan*, meaning *whale, why, when*.[2] The letter *w* (initial) is the modern provincial 'oo, as in *wlf, wluine, wman*; cf. *hw, w*, both forms of *how*; and *lowerd* for *louerd*. In particular, we should notice the hard sound of *t* denoted by *th* in the words *with, rithe, brouth, nouth, ricth, knicth*, meaning *white, right, brought, naught, right, knight*; so too *douther*, daughter, *neth*, a net, *uth*, out, *woth*, wot, *leth*, let, *lauthe (laught)*, caught, *nither-tale (nighter-tale)*, night-time.[3] On the other hand, *t* stands for *th* in *hauet*, 564, *seyt*, 647, *herknet*, 1, *wit*, 100. When *th* answers to the modern sound, it seems equivalent to A.S. ð rather than to A.S. þ; examples are *mouth*, 433, *oth*, 260, *loth*, 261. *Y* and *g* are interchangeable, as in *yaf, gaf, youen, gouen*; *g* even occurs for *k*, as in *rang*, 2561. In MSS., *e* is not uncommonly written by

[1] " Cf. K. Horn, 1005, where *haue* rhymes with plawe."—M. Mr A. J. Ellis would consider *slawen, knaue*, &c., as assonances—" Do not think of the pronunciation of modern *drawen*. Read *sla-wen, kna-ue*, an assonance. *Beþe* does *not* rhyme to *reden*; it is only an assonance."— Ellis. On the other hand, we find the spellings *rathe, rothe* instead of *rede* in ll. 1335 and 2817.

[2] " *Qual = quhal*, the aspirate being omitted ; and *quhal = whal*."— Ellis.

[3] The use of *th* for *t* is not uncommon. In the *Romans of Partenay*, we have *thown, thaken, thouchyng*, &c., for *town, taken, touching*; see Preface, p. xvi. In the copy of Piers Plowman in MS. Camb. Univ. Lib. Dd 1. 17, I have observed several similar examples. Cf. Eng. *tea*, Ital. *tè*, Span. *té*, with Fr. *thé*, Swed. *the*, G. Du. Dan. *thee*.

PREFACE.   xxxix

mistake for *o;* this may perhaps account for *helde*, 2472, *meste*, 233, *her*, 1924, which should rather be *holde*, 30, *moste*, and *hor*, 235; there is a like confusion of *weren* and *woren;* and perhaps *grotinde* should be *gretinde*.[1] The vowel *u* is replaced by the modern *ou* in the words *prud*, 302, *suth*, 434, *but*, 1040, *hus*, 740, *spusen*, 1123; cf. *hws* in l. 1141. Mr Ellis shews, in his Early English Pronunciation, chap. v, that in pure specimens of the *thirteenth* century, there is no *ou* in such words, and in the *fourteenth* century, no simple *u*. This furnishes a ready explanation of the otherwise difficult *sure*, in l. 2005; it is merely the adverb of *sour, sourly* being used in the sense of *bitterly;* to *bye it bitterly*, or *bye it bittre*, is a common phrase in Piers Plowman. Other spellings worth notice occur in *ouerga*, 314, *stra*, 315 (spelt *strie* in l. 998), *hawe*, 1188, *plawe*, 950, *sal*, 628 (commonly spelt *shal*). Note also *arum* for *arm*, *harum* for *harm*, *boren* for *born*, 1878, and *koren* for *corn*, 1879. There are several instances of words joined together, as *haui*, 2002, *biddi*, 484; *shaltu*, 2186, *wiltu*, 905, *wenestu*, 1787; *wilte*, 528, *thenkeste*, 578, *shaltou*, 1800; *thouthe*, 790, *hauedet, youenet, hauenet; sawe*, 338; *latus*, 1772; where the personal pronouns *i, þu, he, it, we, us* are added to the verb. Hence, in l. 745, it is very likely that *calleth* is written for *callet*, i. e. call it; and on the same principle we can explain *dones;* see *Es* in the Glossary. In like manner *goddot* is contracted from *God wot;* and *þerl* from *þe erl*.

*Nouns.* As regards the nouns employed, I may remark that the final *e* is perhaps always sounded in the oblique cases, and especially in the dative case; as in *nedè, stedè*, &c. (see ll. 86—105), *willè*, 85, *gyuè*, 357, *blissè*, 2187, *cricè*, 2450; cf. the adjectives *longè*, 2299, *wisè*, 1713; also the nominatives *rosè*, 2919, *newè*, 2974. *Frend* is a pl. form; cf. *hend*, which is both a plural (2444) and a dat. sing. (505). In the plural, the final *e* is fully pronounced in the adjectives *allè*, 2, *hardè*, 143, *starkè*, 1015, *fremdè*, 2277, *bleikc*, 470, and in many others; cf. the full form *boþen*, 2223. Not only does the phrase *none kines*, of no kind, occur in ll. 861, 1140, but we find the unusual phrase *neuere kines*, of

---

[1] " Is *e* for *o* a mistake, or may it be compared with *preue* for *proue*, &c. ?"— Ellis. I would observe that *greting* is the spelling of the *substantive* in l. 166.

never a kind, in l. 2691. Among the numerals, we find not only þre, but þrinne.

*Pronouns.* The first personal pronoun occurs in many forms in the nominative, as *i, y, hi, ich, ic, hic,* and even *ihc;* the oblique cases take the form *me.* For the second person, we have þu, þou, in the nominative, and also *tu,* when preceded by þat, as in l. 2903. We may notice also *hijs* for *his,* l. 47; *he* for *they; sho,* 112, *scho,* 126, *sche,* 1721, for *she;* and, in particular, the dual form *unker,* of you two, 1882. The most noteworthy possessive pronouns are *minè,* pl. 1365, þinè, pl. 620; *his* or *hise,* pl. *hisè,* 34; *ure,* 606; *youres,* 2800; *hirè,* 2918, with which cf. the dat. sing. *hirè* of the personal pronoun, 85, 300. þis is plural, and means *these,* in l. 1145. As in other old English works, *men* is frequently an impersonal pronoun, answering to the French *on,* and is followed by a singular verb; as in *men ringes,* 390, *men seyt and suereth,* 647, *men fetes,* 2341, *men nam,* 900, *men birþe,* 2101, *men dos,* 2434; cf. *folk sau,* 2410; but there are a few instances of its use with a plural verb, as *men haueden,* 901, *men shulen,* 747. The former is the more usual construction.

*Verbs.* The infinitives of verbs rarely have *y-* prefixed; two examples are *y-lere,* 12, *y-se,* 334. Nor is the same prefix common before past participles; yet we find *i-gret,* 163, *i-groten,* 285, and *i-maked,* 5, as well as *maked,* 23. Infinitives end commonly in *-en* or *-e,* as *riden,* 26, *y-lere;* also in *-n,* as *don,* 117, *leyn,* 718; and even in *-o,* as *flo,* 612, *slo,* 1364. The present singular, 3rd person, of the indicative, ends both in *-es* or *-s,* and *-eth* or *-th,* the former being the more usual. Examples are *longes,* 396, *leues,* 1781, *haldes,* 1382, *fedes,* 1693, *bes,* 1744, *comes,* 1767, *glides,* 1851, þarnes, 1913, *haues,* 1952, *etes,* 2036, *dos,* 1913; also *eteth,* 672, *haueth,* 804, *bikenneth,* 1269, *doth,* 1876, *li*þ, 673. The full form of the 2nd person is *-est,* as *louest,* 1663; but it is commonly cut down to *-es,* as *weldes,* 1359, *slepes,* 1283, *haues,* 688, *etes,* 907, *getes,* 908; cf. *dos,* 2390, *mis-gos,* 2707, *slos,* 2706. The same dropping of the *t* is observable in the past tense, as in *reftes,* 2394, *feddes and claddes,* 2907. Still more curious is the ending in *.t* only, as in þu *bi-hetet,* 677, þou *mait,* 689; cf. ll. 852, 1348. In the subjunctive mood the *-st* disappears as in Anglo-Saxon, and hence the forms *bute þou gonge*, 690, *þat þu fonge*, 856, &c.; cf. *bede*, 668. In the 3rd person, present tense, of the same mood, we have the *-e* fully pronounced, as in *shildè*, 16, *yeuè*, 22, *leuè*, 334, *rede*, 687; and in l. 544, *wreken* should undoubtedly be *wrekè*, since the *-en* belongs to the plural, as in *moten*, 18. The plural of the indicative present ends in *-en*, as, *we hauen*, 2798, *ye witen*, 2208, *þei taken*, 1833; or, very rarely, in *-eth*, as *ye bringeth*, 2425, *he* (they) *strangleth*, 2584. Sometimes the final *-n* is lost, as in *we haue*, 2799, *ye do*, 2418, *he* (they) *brenne*, 2583. There is even a trace of the plural in *-es*, as in *haues*, 2581. The *present* tense has often a *future* signification, as in *etes*, 907, *eteth*, 672, *getes*, 908.

*Past tense.* Of the third person singular and plural of the past tense the following are selected examples. WEAK VERBS: *hauede*, 770, *sparedè*, 898, *yemedè*, 975, *semedè*, 976, *sparkëdè*, 2144, *þankedè*, 2189; pl. *loueden*, 955, *leykeden*, 954, *woundeden*, 2429, *starden*, 1037, *yemede* (rather read *yemeden*), 2277, *makeden*, 554, *sprauleden*, 475; also *calde*, 2115, *gredde*, 2417, *herde*, 2410, *kepte*, 879, *fedde*, 786, *ledde*, 785, *spedde*, 756, *clapte*, 1814, *kiste*, 1279; pl. *herden, brenden*, 594, *kisten*, 2162, *ledden*, 1246; and, thirdly, of the class which change the vowel, *aute*, 743, *laute*, 744, *bitauhte*, 2212. Compare the past participles *osed*, 971, *mixed*, 2533, *parred*, 2439, *gadred*, 2577; *reft*, 1367, *wend*, 2138, *hyd*, 1059; *told*, 1036, *sold*, 1638, *wrouth* = *wrout*, 1352. There are also at least two past participles in *-et*, as *slenget*, 1923, *grethet*, 2615, to which add *weddeth, beddeth*, 1127. In l. 2057, *knawed* seems put for *knawen*, for the rime's sake.

STRONG VERBS: third person singular, past tense, *bar*, 815, *bad*, 1415, *yaf*, or *gaf*, *spak*; *kam*, 766 (spelt *cham*, 1873), *nam, knew, hew*, 2729, *lep*, 1777, *let*, 2447 (spelt *leth*, 2651), *slep*, 1280, *wex*, 281; *drou*, 705, *for*, 2943, *low*, 903, *slow*, 1807, *hof*, 2750, *stod*, 986, *tok*, 751, *wok*, 2093; pl. *beden*, 2774, *youen*, or *gouen*; *comen*, 1017 (spelt *keme*, 1208), *nomen*, 2790 (spelt *neme*, 1207), *knewen*, 2149, *lopen*, 1896, *slepen*, 2128; *drowen*, 1837, *foren*, 2380, *lowen*, 1056, *slowen*, 2414, &c. And secondly, of the class which more usually change the vowel in the *plural* of the preterite, we find the singular forms *bigan*, 1357, *barw*, 2022, *karf*, 471, *swank*, 788, *warp*, 1061, *shon*, 2144, *clef*, 2643, *sau*, 2409, *grop*, 1965, *drof*, 725, *shof*,

892; pl. *bigunnen*, 1011, *sowen*, 1055, *gripen*, 1790, *driue*, for *driuen*, 1966; also *bunden*, 2436, *scuten*, 2431 (spelt *schoten*, 1864, *shoten*, 1838), *leyen*, 2132, &c. Compare the past participles *boren*, 1878, *youen* or *gouen*, *cumen*, 1436, *nomen*, 2265 (spelt *numen*, 2581), *laten*, 1925, *waxen*, 302, *drawen*, 1925, *slawen*, 2000, which two last become *drawe*, *slawe* in ll. 1802, 1803.

We should also observe the past tenses *spen*, 1819, *stirt*, 812, *fauth* for *faut* or *fauht*, 1990, *citte*, 942, *bere*, 974, *kipte*, 1050, *flow*, 2502, *plat*, 2755; and the past participles *demd* for *demed*, 2488, *giue* for *giuen*, 2488, *henged*, 1429, *keft*, 2005.

*Imperative Mood.* Examples of the imperative mood singular, 2nd person, are *et*, *sit*, 925, *nim*, 1336, *yif*, 674; in the plural, the usual ending is *-es*, as in *liþes*, 2204, *comes*, 1798, *folwes*, 1885, *lokes*, 2292, *bes*, 2246, to which set belong *slos*, 2596, *dos*, 2592; but there are instances of the ending *-eth* also, as in *cometh*, 1885, *yeueþ*, 911, to which add *doth*, 2037, *goth*, 1780. Indeed both forms occur in one line, as in *Cometh swiþe, and folwes me* (1885). Instead of *-eth* we even find *-et*, as in *herknet*, 1. These variations afford a good illustration of the unsettled state of the grammar in some parts of England at this period; we need not suppose the scribe to be at fault in all cases where there is a want of uniformity.

Of reflexive verbs, we meet with *me dremede*, 1284, *me met*, 1285, *me þinkes*, 2169, *him hungrede*, 654, *him semede*, 1652, *him stondes*, 2983, *him rewede*, 503. The present participles end most commonly in *-inde*, as *fastinde*, 865, *grotinde* (? *gretinde*), 1390, *lauhwinde*, 946, *plattinde*, 2282, *starinde*, 508; but we also find *gangande*, 2283, *driuende*, 2702. Compare the nouns *tiþande*, 2279, *offrende*, 1386, which are Norse forms, *tiðindi* (pl.) being the Icelandic for *tidings*, and *offrandi* the present participle of *offra*, to offer. But the true Icelandic equivalent of the substantive *an offering* is *offran*, and the old Swedish is *offer*; and hence we see at how very early a date the confusion between the noun-ending and the ending of the present participle arose; a confusion which has bewildered many generations of Englishmen. Yet this very poem in other places has *-ing* as a noun-ending *only*, never (that I remember) for the present participle. Examples of it are *greting*, 166, *dreping*, i. e. slaughter, 2684, *buttinge*, *skirming*, *wrastling*, *putting*, *harping*, *piping*, *reding*; see ll. 2322—2327. Such words are frequently called *verbal nouns*, but the term is very likely to mislead. I have found that many suppose it to imply *present participles used as nouns*, instead of *nouns of verbal derivation*. If such nouns could be called by some new name, such as *nouns of action*, or by any other title that can be conventionally restricted to signify them, it would, I think, be a gain. Amongst the auxiliary verbs, may be noted the use of *cone*, 622, as the subjunctive form of *canst*; *we mone*, 840, as the subjunctive of *mowen*; cf. *ye mowen*, 11; but especially we should observe the use of the comparatively rare verbs *birþe*, it behoves, pt. t. *birde*, it behoved, and *þurte*, he need, the latter of which is fully explained in the Glossary to William of Palerne, s. v. *þort*.

The prefix *to-* is employed in *both* senses, as explained in the same Glossary, s. v. *To-*. In *to-brised*, *to-deyle*, &c., it is equivalent to the German *zer-* and Mœso-Gothic *dis-*; of its *other* and *rarer* use, wherein it answers to the German *zu-* and Mœso-Gothic *du-*, there is but *one* instance, viz. in the word *to-yede*, 765, which signifies *went to*; cf. Germ. *zugehen*, to go to, *zugang* (A.S. *togang*), access, approach. There are some curious instances of a peculiar syntax, whereby the infinitive mood active partakes of a passive signification, as in *he made him kesten, and in feteres festen*, he caused him to be cast in prison (*or perhaps*, overthrown), and to be fastened in fetters; l. 81. But it is probable that this is to be explained by considering it as a phrase in which we should *now* supply the word *men*, and that we may interpret it by "he caused [men] to cast him in prison, and to fasten him with fetters;" for in ll. 1784, 1785, the phrase is repeated in a less ambiguous form. See also l. 86. So also, in ll. 2611, 2612, I consider *keste*, *late*, *sette*, to be in the infinitive mood. Such a construction is at once understood by comparing it with the German *er liess ihn binden*, he caused him to be bound. In l. 2352, appears the most unusual form *ilker*, which is literally *of each*, and hence, *apiece*; cf. *unker*, which also is a genitive plural. It will be observed that the verb following is in the plural, the real nominative to it being *þei þre*. In l. 2404, the expression *þat þer þrette*, "that there threat," recalls a colloquialism

*d*

which is still common. The word þrie, 730, is, apparently, the O.E. adverb thrie, thrice; liues, 509, is an adverb ending in -es, originally a genitive case. þus-gate is, according to Mr Morris, unknown to the Southern dialect; it occurs in ll. 785, 2419, 2586. I may add that Havelok contains as many as five expressions, which seem to refer to *proverbs* current at the time of writing it. See ll. 307, 648, 1338, 1352, 2461.

## § 28. On the Metre of Havelok.

The poem is written in the familiar rhythm of which I have already spoken elsewhere, viz. at p. xxxvii of the Preface to Mr Morris's edition of Genesis and Exodus. The metre of Havelok is rather more regular, but many of the remarks there made apply to it. The chief rule is that every line shall contain four accents,[1] the two principal types being afforded (1) by the eight-syllable and nine-syllable lines—

(*a*) For hém | ne yé|dë góld | ne fé, 44 ;
(*b*) It wás | a kíng | bi á|rë dáwës, 27 ;

and (2) by the seven-syllable and eight-syllable lines—

(*c*) Hérk|net tó | me gó|dë men, 1 ;
(*d*) Al|lë thát | he mícth|ë fyndë, 42.

To one of these four forms every line can be reduced, by the use of that slighter utterance of less important syllables which is so very common in English poetry. It is not the number of *syllables*, but of *accents*, that is essential. In *every* line throughout the poem there are four accents, with only two or three excep-

---

[1] "This *four accents* I consider to be a wrong way of stating the fact. . . The metre consists of four measures, each generally, not always, of *two* syllables, the first often *one* syllable, the others often of *three* syllables, and each measure has generally more stress on the last than on any other, but the accents or principal stresses in the verse are usually 2, sometimes 3, perhaps never 4."— A. J. Ellis. I need hardly add that such a statement is more exact, and that I here merely use the word *accent* in the loose sense it often bears, viz. as denoting the "stress," more or less heavy, and sometimes imperceptible, which is popularly supposed to belong to the last syllable in a measure. I must request the reader to remember that this present sketch of the metre is very slight and imperfect, and worded in the usual not very correct popular language. For more strict and careful statements the reader is referred to Mr A. J. Ellis's work on Early English Pronunciation. Until readers have made themselves acquainted with that work, they will readily understand what I *here* mean by "accents;" afterwards, they can easily adopt a stricter idea of its meaning.

tions, viz. ll. 1112, 1678, &c., which are defective. In a similar manner, we may readily scan any of the lines, as e. g. ll. 2—4;

(c) Wi|ues, mayd|nës, and al|lë men
(b) Of a ta|lë þat | ich you | wile tellë[1]
(b) Wo-so | 't wil' her' | and þer|to duellë, &c.

Here the syllables -*nes and* in l. 3, *of a* in l. 4, and *it wile* in l. 5, are so rapidly pronounced as to occupy only the room of one unaccented syllable in lines of the strict type. However awkward this appears to be in theory, it is very easy in practice, as the reciter readily manages his voice so as to produce the right rhythmical effect; and, indeed, this variation of arrangement is a real improvement, preventing the recitation from becoming monotonous. Those who have a good ear for rhythm will readily understand this, and it seems unnecessary to dwell upon it more at length. But it may be remarked, that the three lines above quoted are rather *more irregular than usual*, and that the metre is such as to enable us to fix the instances in which the final *-e* is pronounced with great accuracy, on which account I shall say more about this presently. I would, however, first enumerate the rimes which seem to be more or less inexact or peculiar, or otherwise instructive.

I. *Repetitions.* Such are *men, men; holden, holde,* 29; [2] *erþe, erþe,* 739; *heren, heren,* 1640; *nithes, knithes,* 2048; *youres, youres,* 2800. To this class belong also *longe, londe,* 172, *heye, heie,* 1151, 2544; where *longe, londe* is, however, only an assonance.

II. *Assonant rimes.* Here the rime is in the vowel-sound; the consonantal endings differ. Such are *rym, fyn,* 21; *yeme, quene,* 182; *shop, hok,* 1101 (where *shop* is probably corrupt); *odrat, bad,* 1153; *fet, ek,* 1303; *yer, del,* 1333; *maked, shaped,* 1646; *beþe, rede,* 1680; *riche, chinche,* 1763, 2940; *feld, swerd,* 1824, 2634; *seruede, werewed,* 1914; *wend, gent,* 2138; *þank, rang,* 2560; *boþen, ut-drowen,* 2658. To the same class belong *name, rauen,*

---

[1] "You cannot scan this line in any way. This method of doing it is quite impossible; it is a mere chopping to make a verse like this. The line is corrupt. Omit þat, and you have

Of | a tal' | ich you | wile telle

or better,

Of | a tal' | ich wil|e telle."—Ellis.

[2] The number is that of the *first* line of the pair.

1397, *grauen, name,* 2528 ; *slawen, rauen,* 2676. *Henged, slenget,* 1922, should rather be called an imperfect rime.¹ There is also found the exact opposite to this, viz., an agreement or *consonance* at the end, preceded by an apparent diversity in the vowel; as *longe, gange,* 795 (but see *longe, gonge,* 843), *bidde, stede,* 2548, *open, drepen,* 1782, *gres, is,* 2698, *boþe, rathe,* 2936 (but see *rathe, bathe,* 1335, 2542), *fet* (long *e*), *gret,* 2158 ; and not unlike these are some instances of loose rimes, as *beþe, rede,* 360, *knaue, plawe,* 949, *sawe, hawe* (where *hawe* is written for *haue*), 1187, *sawe, wowe,* 1962 (but see *wowe, lowe,* 2078, *lowe, sawe,* 2142, *wawe, woc,* 2470). Observe also *bouth, oft* (read *vt* or *ut = out ?*), 883, *tun, barun,* 1001 (cf. *toun, brun,* 1750, *championus, barouns,* 1032) ; *plattinde, gangande,* 2282, &c. *Eir, toþer,* 410, *harde, crakede,* 567, are probably due to mistakes.²

III. Rimes which shew that the final *-en* was pronounced so slightly as to be nearly equivalent to *-e.* Examples : *holden, holde,* 29 ; *gongen, fonge,* 855 ; *bringe, ringen,* 1105 ; *mouthen, douthe,* 1183 ; *riden, side,* 1758 ; *wesseylen, to-deyle,* 2098 ; *slawen, drawe,* 2476. In the same way ... rimes to *lond,* 1341, owing to the slight pronunciation of the final *d.*³

IV. Rimes which appear imperfect, but may be perfect. *Riche* answers to *like,* 132, but the true spelling is *rike,* answering to *sike,* 290. *Mithe,* 196, should probably be *moucte,* as in l. 257, and it would thus rime with *þoucte. Blinne,* 2670, should certainly be *blunne;* cf. A.S. *blinnan,* pt. t. s. *ic blan,* pt. t. pl. *we blunnon;* and thus it rimes to *sunne. Misdede,* 993, is clearly an error for

---

¹ "You have omitted the curious *harde, krakede,* 567, here ; it is only an assonance, not a mistake, I believe."—Ellis. But see note to l. 567.

² "On *i, e* rhymes, see p. 271, last line and following, of my Chap. IV. The *o, a* depend on a provincialism, and this applies to *sawe, wowe, beþe, rede, knaue, plawe, sawe, hawe,* &c. *Bouth, oft* is a case of assonance, *bouth* being *bought,* where properly the *ugh* is the voiced sound of Scotch *quh,* and easily passes into *f.* The assonance is therefore nearly a rhyme. *Plattinde, gangande* is probably a scribal error. *Eir, toþer* is certainly a mistake ; read

Swanborow, helfled, his sistres fair."—Ellis.

We may then perhaps alter *gangande* to *ganginde.* I do not quite like writing the modern form *fair* instead of the old plural *fayre* in order to gain a rime to *eir.* Cf. ll. 1095, 2300, 2538, 2768.

³ " *Hon, lond* may arise from a Danism, or from an English custom at that time of not pronouncing *d* after *n* in *nd* final ; Danish *Mand* and German *Mann* are identical."—Ellis. I prefer to call it Danish ; we English, now at least, often *add* a *d,* as in *sound, gownd,* from *soun, gown.*

PREFACE.           xlvii

*misseyde*, as appears from the parallel passage in ll. 49, 50 ; and it then rimes with *leyde*. So in l. 1736, for *deled* read *deyled*, as in l. 2098. *Boþe*, 430, has no line answering to it, and a line may have been lost. *Nicth*, *lict*, 575, is a perfect rime. *Halde*, *bolde*, 2308, may also be perfect. *For-sworen* answers to *for-lorn* (pronounced *for-loren*), 1423 ; *bitawte* to *authe* (pronounced *aute*), 1409 ; *yemede* (pronounced *yem-dè*) is not an improper rime to *fremde*, 2276 ; *anon* rimes with *iohan* (if pronounced *ion* or *John*, as indicated by the spelling *ion* in l. 177), 2562, 2956. Yet in another instance it seems to be two syllables, *Jo-han ;* see *wimman, iohan*, 1720.[1] *Speche* should be *speke*, and thus rimes to *meke*, 1065. *Sreden* should perhaps be *stradden*, or some such form, rightly riming to *ladden*, 1037. Under this head we may notice some rimes which throw, possibly, some light on the pronunciation. Thus, for the sound of *ey, ei*, observe *hayse, preyse*, 60 ; *leyke, bleike*, 469 ; *laumprei, wei*, 771 ; *deye* rimes to *preye*, 168 ; *day* to *wey*, 663 ; *seyd* to *brayd*, 1281 ; but we also find *hey, fri*, 1071 ; *hey, sley*, 1083, *heye, heie*, 1151 ; *heye, eie*, 2544 ; *leye, heye*, 2010 ; *heye, fleye*, 2750. *Fram* rimes to *sham*, 55 ; yet the latter word is really *shame*, 83 ; *gange* is also spelt *gonge*, *halde* rimes with *bolde*, 2308. The pronunciation of *ware, were,* or *wore*, seems ambiguous ; we find *sore, wore*, 236 ; *wore, more*, 258 ; *ware, sare*, 400 ; *wore, sore*, 414 ; *were, þere*, 741 ; *more, þore*, 921. For the sound of *e*, observe *suere, gere*, 388 ; *suereth, dereth*, 648 ; *eten, geten*, 930 ; *yet, fet*, 1319 ; *stem, bem*, 592 ; *glem, bem*, 2122 ; also *yeue, liue*, 198 ; *liue, gyue*, 356 ; *lyue, yeue*, 1217 ; *her, ther*, 1924 ; *fishere, swere*, 2230. For that of *i*,

[1] " *Johan* is almost *Jon* in Chaucer, however written, but l. 177 wants a measure ; read— Bi [Jhesu] crist, and bi seint ion.
In l. 1720 also the verse is defective ; omit *al*, and read—
In denemark nis wimman [non]
So fayr so sche, bi *seint* Johan,
where *seint* is a dissyllable ; see p. 264 of my Early English Pronunciation. *Hey, fri*, 1071, is an error ; read *hy*, and see p. 285 of my book. The other instances of *ei, ai* are all regular, the confusion of *ei, ai* being perfect in the thirteenth century. *Shame*, l. 83, is dative, and would prove nothing, but *shame* in Ormrin is conclusive. Hence in *sham'*, 56, we have an *e* omitted; compare p. 323 of my book, and the German *Ruh'*." — Ellis. In other places, the spelling *heye* occurs, rather than *hy ;* see ll. 719, 987, 1071, 1083, 1289 1685, 2431. 2471, 2544, 2724, 2750, 2945, &c.

observe *cri, merci,* 270; *sire, swire,* 310; *swiþe, vnbliþe,* 140; *fir, shir,* 587; *sire, hire,* 909; *rise, bise,* 723; *fyr, shir,* 915; *lye, strie,* 997; *hey, fri,* 1071; *for-þi, merci,* 2500. For that of *o*, observe *two, so,* 350; *do, so,* 713; *shon, on,* 969; *hom, grom,* 789; *lode, brode,* 895; *anon, ston,* 927; *ston, won,* 1023; *do, sho* (shoe), 1137; *do, sho* (she), 1231; *stod, mod,* 1702; *ilkon, ston,* 1842; *shon* (shoon), *ston,* 2144; *croud, god,* 2338; *don, bon,* 2354; *sone* (soon), *bone,* 2504; *bole, hole,* 2438.[1] Only in a few of these instances would the words rime in modern standard English. For the *ou* and *u* sounds, observe *coupe, moupe,* 112; *yow, now,* 160; *wolde, fulde,* 354; *yw, nou,* 453; *bounden, wnden,* 545; *sowel, couel,* 767; *low, ynow,* 903; *sowen, lowe,* 957; *strout, but,* 1039; *þou, nou,* 1283; *doun, tun,* 1630; *crus, hous,* 1966; *wounde, grunde,* 1978; *bowr, tour,* 2072; *spuse, huse,* 2912. *Lowe,* 1291, 2431, 2471, should rather be *lawe,* as in l. 2767. These hints will probably suffice for the guidance of those who wish to follow up the subject. It is evident that full dependence cannot be placed upon the *exactness* of the rimes.

## § 29. On the final -e, &c.

There can be little doubt that the final -*e* is, in general, fully pronounced in this poem wherever it is written, with but a very few exceptions; but at the same time it is liable to be elided when followed by a vowel or (sometimes) by the letter *h*, as is usual in old English poetry. In the following remarks, I shall use an apostrophe to signify that *e is written, but not pronounced;* thus "wil' " signifies that "wile" is the MS. form, but "wil" the apparent pronunciation. I shall use an italic *e* to signify that the *e* is elided because followed by a vowel or *h*, as "cupp*e*" (l. 14); and in the same way, "rid*en*," "lit*el*," &c., signify that the syllables -*en*, -*el* are slurred over in a like manner. It will be seen that such syllables are, in general, slurred over when they occur before a vowel or *h* ; under the same circumstances, that is, as the final -*e*. When I simply write the word in the form "gode" as in the MS., I mean that the -*e* is *fully pronounced;* so that "gode" stands for "godë."

---

[1] "The instances of *o* are all regular, except *croud, god,* 2338, which is a false rhyme altogether ; *ou* = modern *oo.*"—Ellis.

The following, then, are instances. I follow the order in Mr Morris's Introduction to Chaucer's Prologue, &c. (Clarendon Press Series).

(*A*) In nouns and adjectives (of A.S. origin) the final -*e* represents one of the final vowels *a, u, e*, and hence is fully sounded even in the nominative case in such instances. Examples; gome (A.S. *goma*), 7, blome (A.S. *bloma*), 63, trewe (A.S. *treowe*), 179, knaue (A.S. *cnafa*), 308, 450, sone (A.S. *sunu*), 394.

(*B*) In words of French origin it is sounded as in French verse. Such words are scarce in Havelok. Examples: hayse, 59, beste, 279, mirácle, 500, rose, 2919, curtesye (*miswritten* curteyse), 2876, cf. 194, drurye, 195, male, 48, larg*e*, 97, noble, 1263.

(*C*) It is a remnant of various grammatical inflexions :—(1) it is a sign of the *dative* case in nouns ; as, nede, 9, stede, 10, trome, 8, wronge, 72, stede, 142, dede (not elided, because of the cæsura), 167, arke, 222, erþe, 248, lite þrawe, 276. It also sometimes marks the accusative, or the genitive of feminine nouns : *accusatives*, cupp*e*, 14, wede, 94, brede, 98, shrede, 99, mede, 102, quiste, 219, sorwe, 238 (cf. sorw' in l. 240), son*e*, 308, knaue, 308, sone, 350, wille, 441 : *genitives*, messe, 186, 188, helle, 405.

(2) In adjectives it marks—

(*a*) the *definite form* of the adjective; as, þe meste, 233, þe riche (not elided[1]), 239, te beste, 87, þe hexte [man], 1080, þat wicke, 1158, þat foule, 1158, þe firste, 1333, þe rede, 1397. This rule is most often violated in the case of *dissyllabic* superlatives; as, þe wictest', 8, þe fairest, þe strangest, 1081, 1110 ; cf. 199, 200.

(*b*) the *plural* number. Examples abound, as, gode, 1, alle, 2, are, 27, yung = yung*e*, 30, holde, 30, gode, 34, 55, harde, 143, gren*e*, 470, bleike, 470, halte, 543, doumbe, 543, &c.

The same use is often extended to possessive pronouns ; we find the plurals mine, 385, 514 (but min', 392), þine, 620, hise, 34, 67, hure, 1231 ; and even the singulars hire, 84, 85, hure, 338, yure, 171. But the personal pronoun feminine is often hir', 172, 209 ; yet see l. 316.

(*c*) the *vocative* case, as, dere, 839, 2170 ; leue, 909.

---

[1] *Riche* being both A.S. and French, has the *e* even when indefinite; a riche king, 341 ; a riche man, 373.

# PREFACE.

(3) In verbs it marks—

(*a*) the infinitive mood; as, telle, 3, duelle, 4, falle, 39, beye, 53, swere, 254, be-bedde, 421, bere, 549, &c. On this point there cannot be a moment's doubt, for the form *-en* is found quite as often, and they rime together, as in 254, 255, cf. 29, 30. But it is well worth remarking that *-en* is slurred over exactly where *-e* would be, with much regularity. Examples are: rid*en*, 10, biginn*en*, 21, mak*en*, 29, heng*en*, 43, lurk*en*, 68, crep*en*, 68, rid*en*, 88, hau*en*, 270. Other examples are very numerous. But we sometimes find *-en* not slurred over, as, drinken, 15; and the same is true even of *-e*, but such cases are exceptional and rare.

(*b*) the gerund; as, to preyse, 60.

(*c*) the past participle of a strong verb; as, drawe, 1802, slawe, 1803. But these are rare, as they are commonly written drawen, slawen, 2224.

(*d*) the past tense of weak verbs, where the *-e* follows *-ed*, *-t*, or *-d*. Examples are very numerous; as, louede = lov'de, 30, 35 (not elided), 37, hauede = hav'de, 343; cf. haued = havd', 336; þurte, 10, durst*e*, 65, reft*e*, 94; dede, 29, sende, 136, seyde, 228, herde, 286. Observe hated = hated*e*, 40  The plurals of these tenses are rarely in *-e*, generally in *-en*, as, haueden, 241, ded*en*, 242, sprauleden = spraul'den, 475.

(*e*) the subjunctive or optative mood, or the 3rd person of the imperative mood, which is really the 3rd person of the subjunctive. This rule seems to be carefully observed. Examples are yeue, 22, thaue, 296, yerne, 299, leue, 406, were, 513, wit*e*, 517, &c. So for the *first* person, as, lat*e*, 509, lepe (not elided), 2009, spek*e*, 2079; and for the *second* person, as, understonde, 1159, fare, 2705, cone, 622, 623.

(*f*) other parts of a *few* verbs; thus, the 1st person singular present, as, liue, 301, ete, 793, rede, 1660, wille, 388, where *wille* is equivalent to *wish*.

(*g*) present participles: thus, plattínde, 2282, is a half-rime to gangánde. In other places, the author is careful to place them before a vowel, as gretind*e*, 1390, lauhwind*e*, 946, starind*e*, 508, driuend*e*, 2702, fastind*e*, 865.

(4) In adverbs the final *-e* denotes—

(*a*) an older vowel-ending; as, son*e* (A.S. *sóna*), 136, sone, 218,

251, yete (A.S. *géta*, as well as *gét*), 495, ofte (Swed. *ofta*, Dan. *ofte*), 227.

(*b*) an adverb as distinguished from its corresponding adjective, as, yerne, 153, loude, 96, longe, 241, more, 301, softe, 305, heye, 335, swiþe, 455, harde, 639. Hence, in l. 640, we should read *neye*.

(*c*) an older termination in -*en* or -*an*; as, þer-hinne, 322, 709, 712, henne, 843, inne, 855. Cf. A.S. *heonan, innan*.

(*d*) It is also sounded in the termination -*like*, as, sikerlike, 422. Hence, in baldelike, 53, *both* the *ees* are sounded; cf. feblelike, 418. When the final -*e* is slurred over before an *h* in *Chaucer*, *h* is found commonly to begin the pronoun *he*, or its cases, the possessive pronouns *his, hire*, or their cases, a part of the verb to *have*, or else the adverbs *how* or *heer*. The same rule seems to hold in *Havelok*. Observe, that *e* often forms a syllable in the *middle* of a word, as, bondeman, 32, engelondes, 63, pourelik*e*, 322.

With regard to the final -*en*, it is most commonly slurred over before a vowel or the *h* in *he* or *haue*, not only when it is the termination of the infinitive mood, but in *many other cases*. One striking example may suffice:

He gret*en* and gouled*en* and gou*en* hem ille, 164.

A still more striking peculiarity is that *the same rule often holds* for the ending -*es*. We find it, of course, forming a distinct syllable in plurals; as, limes, 86; and in adverbs, as, liues, 509. But observe such instances as maydn*es*, 2, prest*es*, 33, vtlaw*es*, 41, siþ*es*, 213, &c.

In the same way, when rapid final syllables such as -*el*, -*er*, -*ere*, &c., are slurred over, it will *generally* be found *that a vowel or* h *follows them*. Examples: lit*el*, 6, won*eth*, 105, bed*els*, 266, bod*i*, 345, deu*el*, 446, hung*er*, 449. Compare oue*ral*, 38, 54. There are many other peculiarities which it would take long to enumerate, such as, that *sworn* is pronounced *sworen*, 204; that the final -*e* is sometimes preserved before a vowel, as in *dedë am*, 167; that the word *ne* is very frequently not counted, as it were, in the scansion, as in 57, 113, 220, 419, the second *ne* in l. 547, and in several other places. But it must suffice to state merely, that when the above rules (with allowance of a few exceptions) are carefully observed, it will be found that the metre of Havelok is *very regular*, and *valuable on account of its regularity*.

It would therefore be easy to correct the text in many places by help of an exact analysis of the rhythm. But this, except in a very few places, has not been attempted, because the imperfect, but unique, MS. copy is more instructive as it stands. In l. 19, e. g. *wit* should be *wite;* in l. 47, *red* should be *rede;* in l. 74, *his soule* should be *of his soule*, &c. The importance of attending to the final *-e* may be exemplified by the lines—

> Allë greten swiþë sore, 236 ;
> But sonë dedë hirë fetë, 317 ;
> þinë cherlës, þinë hinë, 620.
> Grimës sonës allë þre, 1399 ;
> Hisë sistres herë lif, 2395.

Mr Ellis writes—" These final examples suggested to me to compose the following German epitaph, which contains just as many final *e*'s, and which I think no German would find to have anything peculiar in the versification:

### GRABSCHRIFT.

> Diese alte reiche Frau
> Hasste jede eitle Schau,
> Preiste Gottes gute Gabe,
> Mehrte stets die eig'ne Habe,
> Liegt hier unbeweint im Grabe.

I think Havelok may be well compared with Goethe's ballad,

> Es war ein Kön*ig in Thu*le,
> Gar treu bis an das Grab,
> Dem, sterbend, seine Buhle
> *Einen gold*enen Becher gab.

> Es ging ihm nichts darüber,
> Er leert' ihn jeden Schmaus,
> Die Augen gin*gen ihm* über
> So oft er trank daraus.

> Und als er kam zu sterben,
> Zählt' er *seine Städt'* im Reich,
> Gönnt' alles seinem Erben,
> Den Becher nicht zugleich:—

and the end :—
> Die Augen thä*ten ihm sink*ēn,
> Trank nie *einen Trop*fen mehr.

The *italicised* trisyllabic measures are fine. Observe also the elisions of final *-e* before a following vowel (*Städt'* being very unusual), and the omission of the dative *-e* in *im Reich*, to rhyme with *zugleich*."

I have only to add that my special thanks are due to Sir F. Madden for his permission to make use of his valuable notes, glossary, and preface, and for his assistance; as also to Mr Ellis for his notes, which, however, reached me only at the last moment, when much alteration of the proofs was troublesome. There are many things probably which Mr Ellis does not much approve of in this short popular sketch of the metre, in which attention is drawn only to some of the *principal* points. In particular, he disapproves of the term *slurring over*, though I believe that I mean precisely the same thing as he does, viz. that these light syllables are really *fully pronounced*, and not in any way forcibly suppressed; but that, owing to their being light syllables, and occurring before vowel sounds, the full pronunciation of them does not cause the verse to halt, but merely imparts to it an agreeable vivacity. As I have already said elsewhere [1]—" A poet's business is, in fact, to take care that the syllables which *are* to be rapidly pronounced are such as easily *can* be so; and that the syllables which are to be heavily accented are naturally those that *ought* to be. If he gives attention to this, it does not much matter whether each foot has *two* or *three* syllables in it."

[1] Preface to Mr Morris's Genesis and Exodus, p. xxxviii.

# EMENDATIONS, ETC.

Some emendations have been made in the text by inserting letters and words within square brackets. A few more may be noticed here.

p. 2, l. 47. The MS. has *red ;* but it should be *rede.*

p. 3, l. 66. For the MS. reading *here* Mr Garnett proposed to read *othere,* which is clearly right.

p. 3, l. 74. For *his soule* (as in the MS.) we should probably read *of his soule.*

p. 3, l. 79. For *wo diden* (as in the MS.) we should read *wo so dide.*

p. 6, l. 177. *Read*—"Bi [ihesu] crist," &c., to fill up ; but this is doubtful ; see l. 1112.

p. 18, l. 560. For *with,* Mr Garnett proposed to read *wilt.*

p. 20, l. 60. For *ney* (as in MS.) read *neye,* the adverbial form.

p. 21, l. 660. Perhaps there should be a comma after *Slep,* making the sense to be *sleep, son,* not *sleep soon.*

p. 23, l. 746. For *alle,* Mr Garnett proposed to read *shalle.*

p. 24, l. 784. Perhaps we should, however, read *se-weren,* and the note on the line (p. 93) may be wrong. See *Weren* in the Glossary.

p. 32, l. 1037. For *stareden* we should perhaps read *stradden ;* see the Glossary.

p. 33, l. 1080. For *hexte* we should rather read *hexte* [*man*] ; cf. l. 199.

p. 38, l. 1233. Mr Garnett suggested that *cloþen* may mean *clothes*. If so, dele the comma after it.

p. 43, l. 1420. For *wolde* we should rather read [*he*] *wolde*.

p. 46, l. 1687. *parned* is an error of the scribe for *poled;* see the Glossary.

p. 47, l. 1720. Perhaps we should rather read—*is womman* [*non*].

p. 47, l. 1733. *Bidde* must mean *offer*, rather than *bid* (as in the Glossary); unless it be miswritten for *bide* = tarry.

p. 47, l. 1736. The MS. reading *deled* should be *deyled;* cf. l. 2099.

p. 76, l. 2670. The MS. reading *blinne* should clearly be *blunne*. A few other suggestions of emendations will be found in the Glossarial Index. See the words *Arwe, Birþe, Felde, Sor, Tauhte, þenne, Thit, Werewed, Wreken,* &c. See also the suggestions in the preface, pp. xxxix, xli, xlvi, xlvii.

p. 132, s. v. *Loken*. The reference to the Ancren Riwle is to MS. Titus D 18, fol. 17; cf. the edition by Morton (Camd. Soc. 1853), p. 56.

In the Glossary, *Dunten* is wrongly placed after *Dint*.

Also, *Greting* is wrongly placed before *Gres*.

*Hal*, more probably, is shortened from *half*, like *twel* from *twelue*.

*Shoten*, in l. 1838, means *rushed, darted, flew*.

*Teyte* may mean *lively*. My explanation is not generally accepted.

*Bise* occurs in l. 724.

# Incipit vita Havelok, quondam Rex Anglie et Denemarchie.

---

Herknet to me, gode men,     [Fol. 204, col. 1.]
  Wiues, maydnes, and alle men,     Hearken!
Of a tale þat ich you wile telle,
Wo so it wile here, and þer-to duelle.    4   I will tell you the tale of Havelok.
Þe tale is of hauelok i-maked;
Wil he was litel he yede ful naked:
Hauelok was a ful god gome,
He was ful god in eueri trome,    8
He was þe wicteste man at nede,     a wight man at need.
Þat þurte riden on ani stede.
Þat ye mowen nou y-here,
And þe tale ye mowen y-lere.    12
At the beginning[1] of vre tale,     First, fill me a cup of ale.
Fil me a cuppe of ful god ale;
And [y] wile drinken her y spelle,
Þat crist vs shilde alle fro helle!    16
Krist late vs heuere so for to do,     Christ grant we may do right!
Þat we moten comen him to,
And wit[e][2] þat it mote ben so!
*Benedicamus domino!*    20
Here y schal biginnen a rym,
Krist vs yeue wel god fyn!

---

[1] MS. Beginnig.     [2] *See* ll. 517, 1316.

## THE GOOD KING ATHELWOLD

*The rime is about Havelok.*

The rym is maked of hauelok,
A stalworþi man in a flok; 24
He was þe stalworþeste man at nede,
þat may riden on ani stede.

*There was once a king who made good laws.*

IT was a king bi are dawes,
That in his time were gode lawes 28
He dede maken, an ful wel holden;
Hym louede yung, him louede holde,
Erl and barun, dreng and kayn,
Knict, bondeman, and swain, 32

*All loved him.*

Wydues, maydnes, prestes and clerkes,
And al for hise gode werkes.
He louede god with al his micth,
And holi kirke, and soth, ant ricth; 36
Ricth-wise[1] men he louede alle,
And oueral made hem forto calle;

*He hated traitors and robbers.*

Wreieres and wrobberes made he falle,
And hated hem so man doth galle; 40
Vtlawes and theues made he bynde,
Alle that he micthe fynde,
And heye hengen on galwe-tre;
For hem ne yede gold ne fe. 44

*At that time, men could carry gold about safely,*
[Fol. 204, col. 2.]

In that time a man þat bore
[Wel fyfty pund, y woth, or more,][2]
Of red gold up-on hijs bac,
In a male with or blac, 48
Ne funde he non that him misseyde,
N[e] with iuele on [him] hond leyde.
þanne micthe chapmen fare
þuruth englond wit here ware, 52

*and boldly buy and sell.*

And baldelike beye and sellen,
Oueral þer he wilen dwellen,

---

[1] MS. "Rirth wise."
[2] Supplied from conjecture. Cf. v. 653, 787. A few more instances will be found where a similar liberty has been taken, for the purpose of completing the sense.

In gode burwes, and þer-fram
Ne funden he non þat dede hem sham,                56
Þat he ne weren sone to sorwe brouth,
An pouere maked, and browt to nouth.
Þanne was engelond at hayse ;[1]                    *Then was*
Michel was svich a king to preyse,                  60 *England at ease.*
Þat held so eng[e]lond in grith !
Krist of heuene was him with.
He was engelondes blome ;
Was non so bold lond to rome,                       64
Þat durste upon his [menie] b·˙nghe
Hunger, ne here wicke þinghe
Hwan he felede hise foos,                           *The king made*
He made hem lurken, and crepen in wros :        68 *his foes hide*
Þe hidden hem alle, and helden hem stille,          *themselves.*
And diden al his herte wille.
Ricth he louede of alle þinge,
To wronge micht him no man bringe,                  72
Ne for siluer, ne for gold :—
So was he his soule hold.
To þe faderles was he rath,                         *He befriended*
Wo so dede hem wrong or lath,                   76  *the fatherless.*
Were it clerc, or were it knicth,
He dede hem sone to hauen ricth ;
And wo [so] diden widuen wrong,
Were he neure knicth so strong,                     80
Þat he ne made him sone kesten,
And in feteres ful faste festen ;
And wo so dide maydne shame                         *Them who*
Of hire bodi, or brouht in blame,               84  *wrought shame*
Bute it were bi hire wille,                         *he punished.*
He[2] made him sone of limes spille.
He was te[3] beste knith at nede,
Þat heuere micthe riden on stede,                   88
Or wepne wagge, or folc vt lede ;

[1] MS. athayse.    [2] MS. Ke.    [3] MS. Ke waste.

Of knith ne hauede he neuere drede,
þat he ne sprong forth so sparke of glede,
And lete him [knawe] of hise hand-dede, 92
Hw he couþe with wepne spede;
And oþer he refte him hors or wede,
Or made him sone handes sprede,
And "louerd, merci!" loude grede. 96
He was large, and no wicth gnede;
Hauede he non so god brede,
Ne on his bord non so god shrede,
þat he ne wolde þorwit fede, 100
Poure þat on fote yede;
Forto hauen of him þe mede
þat for vs wolde on rode blede,
Crist, that al kan wisse and rede, 104
þat euere woneth in ani þede.

¶ þe king was hoten aþelwold,
Of word, of wepne he was bold;
In engeland was neure knicth, 108
þat betere hel þe lond to ricth.
Of his bodi ne hauede he eyr
Bute a mayden swiþe fayr,
þat was so yung þat sho ne couþe 112
Gon on fote, ne speke wit mouþe.
þan him tok an iuel strong,
þat he we[l] wiste, and under-fong,
þat his deth was comen him on: 116
And seyde, "crist, wat shal y don!
Louerd, wat shal me to rede!
I woth ful wel ich haue mi mede.
W shal nou mi douhter fare? 120
Of hire haue ich michel kare;
Sho is mikel in mi þouth,
Of me self is me rith nowt.
No selcouth is, þou me be wo; 124

Sho ne kan speke, ne sho kan go.
Yif scho couþe on horse ride,   *Were she but of age,*
And a thousande men bi hire syde ;
And sho were comen intil helde,   128
And engelond sho couþe welde ;
And don hem of þar hire were queme,
An hire bodi couþe yeme ;
No wolde me neuere iuele like   132  *I would not care for myself."*
Me þou ich were in heuene-riche !"

Quanne he hauede þis pleinte maked,
  þer-after stronglike [he] quaked.
He sende writes sone on-on   136
After his erles euere-ich on ;   *[Fol. 204 b, col. 2.]*
And after hise baruns, riche and poure,   *He summons his lords, from Roxburgh to Dover.*
Fro rokesburw al into douere,
That he shulden comen swiþe   140
Til him, that was ful vnbliþe ;
To þat stede þe[r] he lay,
In harde bondes, nicht and day.
He was so faste wit yuel fest,   144
þat he ne mouthe hauen no rest ;
He ne mouthe no mete hete,   *He can no longer eat.*
Ne he ne mouchte no lyþe gete ;
Ne non of his iuel þat couþe red ;   148
Of him ne was nouth buten ded.

Alle þat the writes herden,   *All sadly obey his summons.*
  Sorful an sori til him ferden ;
He wrungen hondes, and wepen sore,   152
And yerne preyden cristes hore,
þat he [wolde] turnen him
Vt of þat yuel þat was so grim !
þanne he weren comen alle   156
Bifor þe king into the halle,   *They come to Winchester.*
At winchestre þer he lay :

## ATHELWOLD SELECTS EARL GODRICH

"Welcome," he seyde, "be ye ay!
Ful michel þank[e] kan [y] yow          160
That ye aren comen to me now!"

*They all mourn and lament.*

Quanne he weren alle set,
    And þe king aueden i-gret,
He greten, and gouleden, and gouen hem ille,   164
And he bad hem alle ben stille;
And seyde, "þat greting helpeth nouth,
For al to dede am ich brouth.
Bute nov ye sen þat i shal deye,         168

*He prays them to tell him who can guard his daughter best.*

Nou ich wille you alle preye
Of mi douther þat shal be
Yure leuedi after me,
Wo may yemen hire so longe,              172
Boþen hire and engelonde,
Til þat she [mowe] winan of helde,
And þa she mowe yemen and welde?"
He ansuereden, and seyden an-on,         176

*They answer, "Earl Godrich of Cornwall."*

Bi crist and bi seint ion,
That þerl Godrigh of cornwayle
Was trewe man, wit-uten faile;
Wis man of red, wis man of dede,         180
And men haueden of him mikel drede.

[Fol. 205, col. 1.]  "He may hire alþer-best[e] yeme,
Til þat she mowe wel ben quene."

Þe king was payed of that Rede;          184

*The king sends for chalice and paten,*

    A wol fair cloth bringen he dede,
And þer-on leyde þe messebok,
Þe caliz, and þe pateyn ok,
Þe corporaus, þe messe-gere;             188
Þer-on he garte þe erl suere,

*for the earl to swear upon.*

Þat he sholde yemen hire wel,
With-uten lac, wit-uten tel,
Til þat she were tuelf¹ winter hold,     192

¹ *Qu.* tuenti. Cf. v. 259.

And of speche were bold;
And þat she covþe of curteysye,
Gon, and speken of luue-drurye;
And til þat she louen þoucte,[1]
Wom so hire to gode thoucte;
And þat he shulde hire yeue
þe beste man that micthe liue,
þe beste, fayreste, the strangest ok :—
Þat dede he him sweren on þe bok.
And þanne shulde he engelond
Al bitechen in-to hire hond.

Quanne[2] þat was sworn on his wise,
þe king dede þe mayden arise,
And þe erl hire bitaucte,
And al the lond he euere awcte;
Engelonde eueri del;
And preide, he shulde yeme hire wel.

Þe king ne mowcte don no more,
But yerne preyede godes ore;
And dede him hoslen wel and shriue,
I woth, fif hundred siþes and fiue;
An ofte dede him sore swinge,
And wit hondes smerte dinge;
So þat þe blod ran of his fleys,
Þat tendre was, and swiþe neys.
[3] And sone gaf it euere-il del;
He made his quiste swiþe wel.
Wan it was gouen, ne micte men finde
So mikel men micte him in winde,
Of his in arke, ne in chiste,

196 *His daughter is to marry the best and fairest man that can be found.*

200

204

*He gives up all England to the earl, to keep for her.*

208

212

*The king does penance.*

216

220 *He makes his will.*

---

[1] MS. mithe. But see l. 257.
[2] MS. Ouanne. And perhaps "his" should have been "þis."
[3] Some lines appear to be wanting here, such as—
"He þoucte his quiste þan to make,
His catel muste he wel bitake," &c.

## KING ATHELWOLD DIES.

In engelond þat noman wiste:
For al was youen, faire and wel, 224
þat him was leued no catel.

[Fol. 205, col. 2.]
Þanne he hauede ben ofte swngen,
Ofte shriuen, and ofte dungen,
"*In manus tuas*, lou[er]de," he seyde, 228
Her þat he þe speche leyde.

The king dies.
To ihesu crist bigan to calle,
And deyede biforn his heymen alle.
Þan he was ded, þere micte men se 232
þe meste sorwe that micte be;
þer was sobbing, siking, and sor,
Handes wringing, and drawing bi hor.

All mourn for him.
Alle greten swiþe sore, 236
Riche and poure þat þere wore;
An mikel sorwe haueden alle,
Leuedyes in boure, knictes in halle.

Quan þat sorwe was somdel laten, 240
And he haueden longe graten,

Masses are sung for him.
Belles deden he sone ringen,
Monkes and prestes messe singen;
And sauteres deden he manie reden, 244
þat god self shulde his soule leden
Into heuene, biforn his sone,
And þer wit-uten hende wone.

He is buried and the earl takes possession,
Þan he was to þe erþe brouth, 248
þe riche erl ne foryat nouth,
þat he ne dede al engelond
Sone sayse intil his hond;
And in þe castels leth he [1] do 252
þe knictes he micte tristen to;
And alle þe englis dede he swere[n],

---

[1] Sir F. Madden printed "lechhe"; but the MS. may be read "leth he."

þat he shulden him ghod fey beren ;
He yaf alle men, þat god þoucte,    256   *till the maiden is twenty years old.*
Liuen and deyen til þat him moucte,[1]
Til þat þe kinges dowter wore
Tuenti winter hold, and more.

Þanne he hauede taken þis oth    260
   Of erles, baruns, lef and loth,
Of knictes, cherles, fre and þewe,
Justises dede he maken newe,            *Earl Godrich appoints justices,*
Al engelond to faren þorw,    264   *sheriffs, &c.*
Fro douere into rokesborw.
Schireues he sette, bedels, and greyues,
Grith-sergeans, wit longe gleyues,
To yemen wilde wodes and paþes    268
Fro wicke men, that wolde don scaþes ;
And forto hauen alle at his cri,
At his wille, at his merci ;
þat non durste ben him ageyn,    272   [Fol. 205 b, col. 1.]
Erl ne barun, knict ne sweyn.
Wislike for soth, was him wel            *He grows very rich,*
Of folc, of wepne, of catel.
Soþlike, in a lite þrawe    276
Al engelond of him stod [in] awe ;
Al engelond was of him adrad,[2]            *and all England fears him.*
So his þe beste fro þe gad.

ÞE kinges douther bigan þriue,    280   *The maiden grows up very fair.*
   And wex þe fayrest wman on liue.
Of alle þewes w[as] she wis,
þat gode weren, and of pris.
Þe mayden Goldeboru was hoten ;    284   *Her name is Goldborough.*
For hire was mani a ter igroten.

---

   [1] So in MS. But the sense requires
      "He gaf alle men, þat god *him* þouchte,
         Liuen and deyen til þat *he* moucte," &c.
   [2] MS. "adred," altered to "adrad."

## GODRICH PLOTS AGAINST HIS WARD.

|   |   |
|---|---|
| | Quanne the Erl godrich him herde |
| | Of þat mayden, hw we[l s]he ferde ; |
| | Hw wis sho was, w chaste, hw fayr,     288 |
| | And þat sho was þe rithe eyr |
| | Of engelond, of al þe rike :— |
| Godrich is vexed. | Þo bigan godrich to sike, |
| | And seyde, " weþer she sholde be     292 |
| | Quen and leuedi ouer me ? |
| | Hweþer sho sholde al engelond, |
| | And me, and mine, hauen in hire hond ? |
| | Daþeit hwo it hire thaue !     296 |
| | Shal sho it neuere more haue. |
| "Shall I give England to a fool, a girl?" | Sholde ic yeue a fol, a þerne, |
| | Engelond, þou sho it yerne ? |
| | Daþeit hwo it hire yeue,     300 |
| | Euere more hwil i liue ! |
| | Sho is waxen al to prud, |
| | For gode metes, and noble shrud, |
| | Þat hic haue youen hire to offte ;     304 |
| | Hic haue yemed hire to softe. |
| | Shal it nouth ben als sho þenkes, |
| | ' Hope maketh fol man ofte blenkes.' |
| My son shall have England. | Ich haue a sone, a ful fayr knaue,     308 |
| | He shal engelond al haue. |
| | He shal [ben] king, he shal ben sire, |
| | So brouke i euere mi blake swire !" |

|   |   |
|---|---|
| | Hwan þis trayson was al þouth,     312 |
| He lets his oath go for nothing. | Of his oth ne was him nouth. |
| | He let his oth al ouer-ga, |
| | Þerof ne yaf he nouth a stra ; |
| | But sone dede hire fete,     316 |
| [Fol. 205 b, col. 2.] | Er he wolde heten ani mete, |
| | Fro winchestre þer sho was, |
| | Also a wicke traytur iudas ; |
| He sends the maiden to Dover. | And dede leden hire to doure,     320 |

## BIRKABEYN IS KING OF DENMARK.

þat standeth on þe seis oure;
And þerhinne dede hire fede
Pourelike in feble wede.
þe castel dede he yemen so,     324   He shuts her up in the castle.
þat non ne micte comen hire to
Of hire frend, with [hire] to speken,
þat heuere micte hire bale wreken.

Of Goldeboru shul we nou laten,     328
   þat nouth ne blinneth forto graten,
þet sho liggeth in prisoun:
Ihesu crist, that lazarun
To liue broucte fro dede bondes,     332   May Christ release Goldborough from prison!
He lese hire wit hise hondes;
And leue sho mo him y-se
Heye hangen on galwe tre,
þat hire haued in sorwe brouth,     336
So as sho ne misdede nouth!

Sawe nou forth in hure spelle;
   In þat time, so it bifelle,       At that time there was a king
Was in þe lon of denemark     340   of Denmark, called Birkabeyn.
A riche king, and swyþe stark.
þ[e] name of him was birkabeyn,
He hauede mani knict and sueyn;
He was fayr man, and wicth,     344
Of bodi he was þe beste knicth
þat euere micte leden uth here,
Or stede onne ride, or handlen spere,
þre children he hauede bi his wif,     348   He had three children.
He hem louede so his lif.
He hauede a sone [and] douhtres two,
Swiþe fayre, as fel it so.
He þat wile non forbere,     352
Riche ne poure, king ne kaysere,
Deth him tok þan he bes[t] wolde       Death came upon him.

|   |   |   |
|---|---|---|
| | Liuen, but hyse dayes were fulde; | |
| | þat he ne moucte no more liue, | 356 |
| | For gol ne siluer, ne for no gyue. | |
| He sends for the priests. | Hwan he þat wiste, raþe he sende<br>After prestes fer an hende, | |
| | Chanounes gode, and monkes beþe,[1] | 360 |
| | Him for to[2] wisse, and to Rede; | |
| [Fol. 206, col. 1.] | Him for to hoslon, an forto shriue, | |
| | Hwil his bodi were on liue. | |
| | Hwan he was hosled and shriuen, | 364 |
| | His quiste maked, and for him gyuen, | |
| | His knictes dede he alle site, | |
| | For þorw hem he wolde wite, | |
| He asks who will guard his children? | Hwo micte yeme hise children yunge, | 368 |
| | Til þat he kouþen speken wit tunge; | |
| | Speken and gangen, on horse riden, | |
| | Knictes an sweynes bi here siden. | |
| | He spoken þer-offe, and chosen sone | 372 |
| | A riche man was under mone, | |
| He chooses Godard. | Was þe trewest þat he wende, | |
| | Godard, þe kinges oune frende; | |
| | And seyden, he Moucthe hem best loke, | 376 |
| | Yif þat he hem vndertoke, | |
| | Til hise sone Mouthe bere | |
| | Helm on heued, and leden vt here, | |
| | In his hand a spere stark, | 380 |
| | And king ben maked of denemark. | |
| | He wel trowede þat he seyde, | |
| | And on Godard handes leyde; | |
| He commends the children to Godard. | And seyde, "Here bi-teche i þe | 384 |
| | Mine children alle þre, | |
| | Al denemark, and al mi fe, | |
| | Til þat mi sone of helde be; | |

[1] MS. "boþe." But "beþe" rimes to "Rede"; see l. 694.
[2] MS. forthm to, the hm being expuncted.

But þat ich wille, þat þo[u] suere  388  *He makes him swear to take care of them,*
On auter, and on messe-gere,
On þe belles þat men ri*n*ges,
On messe-bok þe prest on singes,
Þat þou mine children shalt we[l] yeme,  392
Þat hire kin be ful wel queme,
Til mi sone mowe ben knicth,
Þanne biteche him þo his Ricth,  *and to give up the kingdom to*
Denemark, and þat þertil lo*n*ges,  396  *the boy.*
Casteles and tunes, wodes and wo*n*ges."

Godard stirt up, an sw*or* al þat  *Godard swears to do so.*
   þe king him bad, and siþen sat
Bi the knictes, þat þer ware,  400
Þat wepen alle swiþe sare
For þe king þat deide sone:
Ihe*s*u cr*i*st, that makede mone  *Christ save the king's soul!*
On þe mirke nith to shine,  404
Wite his soule fro helle pine;
And leue þat it mote wone
In heuene-riche with godes sone!  [Fol. 206, col. 2.]

Hwan birkabeyn was leyd i*n* gr*a*ue,  408  *Godard shuts up the children, Havelok, Swanborough, and Helfled, in a castle.*
   þe erl dede sone take þe knaue,
Hauelok, þat was þe eir,
Swanborow, his sister, helfled, þe toþ*er*,[1]
And in þe castel dede he hem do,  412
Þer non ne micte hem come*n* to
Of here kyn, þer þei sperd wore;[2]
Þer he greten ofte sore,
Boþe for hunger and for kold.  416
Or he weren þre wint*er* hold.
Feblelike he gaf he*m* cloþes,
He ne yaf a note of hise oþes;  *He cares not for his oaths.*

---

[1] Corrupt? Lines 410, 411 do not rime well together.
[2] MS. were. But see l. 237.

## GODARD IMPRISONS THE THREE CHILDREN.

|     |     |
| --- | --- |
|                          | He hem [ne] cloþede rith, ne fedde, | 420 |
|                          | Ne hem ne dede richelike be-bedde. |  |
|                          | þanne godard was sikerlike |  |
| *He is a traitor.*       | Vnder god þe moste swike, |  |
|                          | þat eure in erþe shaped was, | 424 |
|                          | With-uten on, þe wike Iudas. |  |
| *May he be accursed!*    | Haue he þe malisun to-day |  |
|                          | Of alle þat eure speken may! |  |
|                          | Of patriark, and of pope! | 428 |
|                          | And of prest with loken kope! |  |
|                          | Of monekes, and hermites boþe!¹ |  |
|                          | And of þe leue holi rode, |  |
|                          | þat god him-selue ran on blode! | 432 |
| *Cursed be he by north and south!* | Crist warie him with his mouth! |  |
|                          | Waried wrthe he of norþ and suth! |  |
|                          | Offe alle man, þat speken kunne! |  |
|                          | Of crist, þat made² mone and sunne! | 436 |
|                          | þanne he hauede of al þe lond |  |
|                          | Al þe folk tilled in-til his hond, |  |
|                          | And alle haueden sworen him oth, |  |
|                          | Riche and poure, lef and loth, | 440 |
|                          | þat he sholden hise wille freme, |  |
| *He plots against the children.* | And þat he shulde[n] him nouth greme, |  |
|                          | He þouthe a ful strong trechery, |  |
|                          | A trayson, and a felony, | 444 |
|                          | Of þe children forto make: |  |
|                          | þe deuel of helle him sone take! |  |
| *He goes to the tower where they are.* | Hwan þat was þouth, onon he ferde |  |
|                          | To þe tour þer he woren sperde, | 448 |
|                          | þer he greten for hunger and cold: |  |
|                          | þe knaue þat was sumdel bold, |  |
|                          | Kam him ageyn, on knes him sette, |  |
| [Fol. 206 b, col 1.]     | And godard ful feyre he þer grette; | 452 |
|                          | And Godard seyde, "Wat is yw? |  |

¹ Lines 430, 431, 432 rime together. NB. The words *holi rode* are written over an erasure. ² MS. maude.

## GODARD KILLS SWANBOROUGH AND HELFLED.     15

Hwi grete ye and goulen nou ? "
" For us hungreth swiþe sore : "—   *Havelok says*
Seyden he wolden [haue] more,   456   *they are hungry*
" We ne haue to hete, ne we ne haue
Herinne neyther knith ne knaue
þat yeueth us drinken, ne no mete,
Haluendel þat we moun ete.   460
Wo is us þat we weren born!   *"Alas, that we*
Weilawei! nis it no korn,   *were born!"*
þat men micte maken of bred?
Vs¹ hungreth, we aren ney ded."   464

Godard herde here wa,   *Godard cares not.*
  Ther-offe yaf he nouth a stra,
But tok þe maydnes bothe samen,
Al-so it were up-on hiis gamen;   468
Al-so he wolde with hem leyke,
þat weren for hunger grene and bleike.
Of boþen he karf on two here þrotes,   *He cuts the*
And siþen [karf] hem alto grotes.   472   *throats of the two girls.*
Þer was sorwe, wo so it sawe!
Hwan þe children bi þ[e]² wawe
Leyen and sprauleden in þe blod :
Hauelok it saw, and þe[r] bi stod.   476   *Havelok sees it, and is afraid.*
Ful sori was þat seli knaue,
Mikel dred he mouthe haue,
For at hise herte he saw a knif,
For to reuen him hise lyf.   480
But þe knaue,³ þat litel was,
He knelede bifor þat iudas,   *He begs Godard to spare him,*
And seyde, " louerd, merci nov !
Manrede, louerd, biddi you !   484
Al denemark i wile you yeue,
To þat forward þu late me liue ;
Here hi wile on boke swere,
þat neure more ne shal i bere   488

¹ MS. þs; cf. l. 455.   ² MS. biþ; cf. l. 2470.   ³ MS. kaue.

| | | |
|---|---|---|
| *offering never to oppose him,* | Ayen þe, louerd, shel ne spere, | |
| | Ne oþer wepne [1] that may you dere. | |
| | Louerd, haue merci of me ! | |
| | To-day i wile fro denemark fle, | 492 |
| *and to flee from Denmark.* | Ne neuere more comen ageyn : | |
| | Sweren y wole, þat bircabein | |
| | Neuere yete me ne gat : "— | |
| | Hwan þe deuel he[r]de [2] that, | 496 |
| [Fol. 206 b, col. 2.] | Sum-del bigan him forto rewe ; | |
| | With-drow þe knif, þat was lewe | |
| *Godard has pity on him.* | Of þe seli children blod ; | |
| | þer was miracle fair and god ! | 500 |
| | þat he þe knaue nouth ne slou, | |
| | But fo[r] rewnesse him wit-drow.[3] | |
| | Of auelok rewede him ful sore, | |
| | And þoucte, he wolde þat he ded wore, | 504 |
| | But on þat he nouth wit his hend | |
| | Ne drepe him nouth,[4] þat fule fend ! | |
| | þoucte he, als he him bi stod, | |
| | Starinde als he were wod : | 508 |
| *But he reflects* | " Yif y late him liues go, | |
| | He micte me wirchen michel wo. | |
| | Grith ne get y neuere mo, | |
| | He may [me] waiten for to slo ; | 512 |
| *that, were Havelok dead, his children would be the heirs.* | And yf he were brouct of liue, | |
| | And mine children wolden thriue, | |
| | Louerdinges after me | |
| | Of al denemark micten he be. | 516 |
| | God it wite, he shal ben ded, | |
| | Wile i taken non oþer red ; | |

[1] MS. "wepue bere," where "bere" is redundant.
[2] MS. hede.
[3] Printed thus in the former edition :—" But to rewnesse him thit drow." But the MS. has *fo*, not *to*, where *fo* is corruptly written for *for*, as in l. 1318; and the initial letter of the last syllable but one may be read as a Saxon *w* (p), not a thorn-letter (þ). It merely repeats the idea in ll. 497, 498.    [4] Qu. mouth.

## GODARD TELLS GRIM TO DROWN HAVELOK.

I shal do casten him in þe se,[1]
þer i wile þat he drench[ed] be ;
Abouten his hals an anker god,
þat he ne flete in the flod."
þer anon he dede sende
After a fishere þat he wende,
þat wolde al his wille do,
And sone anon he seyde him to :
" Grim, þou wost þu art mi þral,
Wilte don mi wille al,
þat i wile bidden þe,
To-morwen [i] shal maken þe fre,
And aucte þe yeuen, and riche make,
With-þan þu wilt þis child[e] take,
And leden him with þe to-nicht,
þan þou sest se [2] Mone lith,
In-to þe se, and don him þer-inne,
Al wile [i] taken on me þe sinne."
Grim tok þe child, and bond him faste,
Hwil þe bondes micte laste ;
þat weren of ful strong line :—
Þo was hauelok in ful strong pine.
Wiste he neuere her wat was wo :
Ihesu crist, þat makede to go
þe halte, and þe doumbe speken,
Hauelok, þe of Godard wreken !

Hwan grim him hauede faste bounden,
And siþen in an eld cloth wnden
A keuel of clutes, ful, un-wraste,
þat he [ne] mouthe speke, ne fnaste,
Hwere he wolde him bere or lede.
Hwan he hauede don þat dede,
Hwan [3] þe swike him hauede hethede,[4]

520 — He determines to drown him.

524 — He sends for a fisherman,

528 — "Grim, I will make you free.

532

536 — Throw this child into the sea."

540 — Grim binds the child.

544 — [Fol. 207, col. 1.] Christ wreak thee of Godard, Havelok !

548 — Grim gags the child.

---

[1] MS. she.   [2] *So in* MS. *Qu.* þe.
[3] We should rather read "þan."   [4] MS. he þede.

|                                      |                                         |     |
|--------------------------------------|-----------------------------------------|-----|
|                                      | þat he shulde him forth [lede]          | 552 |
|                                      | And him drinchen in þe se;              |     |
|                                      | þat forwarde makeden he.                |     |
| He puts him in a bag, and takes him on his back. | In a poke, ful and blac,    |     |
|                                      | Sone he caste him on his bac,           | 556 |
|                                      | Ant bar him hom to hise cleue,          |     |
|                                      | And bi-taucte him dame leue,            |     |
| He puts him in charge of his wife.   | And seyde, " wite þou þis knaue,        |     |
|                                      | Al-so thou with mi lif haue;            | 560 |
|                                      | I shal dreinchen him in þe se,          |     |
|                                      | For him shole we ben maked fre,         |     |
|                                      | Gold hauen ynou, and oþer fe;           |     |
|                                      | þat hauet mi louerd bihoten me."        | 564 |
| She throws down Havelok violently.   | Hwan dame [leue] herde þat,             |     |
|                                      | Vp she stirte, and nouth ne sat,        |     |
|                                      | And caste þe knaue adoun so harde,      |     |
|                                      | þat hise croune he þer crakede          | 568 |
|                                      | Ageyn a gret ston, þer it lay:          |     |
|                                      | Þo hauelok micte sei, "weilawei!        |     |
|                                      | þat euere was i kinges bern!"           |     |
|                                      | þat him ne hauede grip or ern,          | 572 |
|                                      | Leoun or wlf, wluine or bere,           |     |
|                                      | Or oþer best, þat wolde him dere.       |     |
| The child lies there till midnight.  | So lay þat child to middel nicth,       |     |
|                                      | þat grim bad leue bringen lict,         | 576 |
|                                      | For to don on [him] his cloþes:         |     |
|                                      | " Ne thenkeste nowt of mine oþes        |     |
|                                      | þat ich haue mi louerd sworen?          |     |
|                                      | Ne wile i nouth be forloren.            | 580 |
|                                      | I shal beren him to þe se,              |     |
|                                      | þou wost þat [bi-]houes me;             |     |
|                                      | And i shal drenchen him þer-inne;       |     |
| Grim tells his wife to light the fire and a candle. | Ris up swiþe, an go þu binne, | 584 |
|                                      | And blou þe fir, and lith a kandel:"    |     |
|                                      | Als she shulde hise cloþes handel       |     |

## GRIM SEES THAT HAVELOK IS THE KING'S SON.       19

On forto don, and blawe þe ¹ fir,     [Fol. 207, col. 2.]
She saw þer-inne a lith ful shir,     588  *She sees a light shining round the lad.*
Also brith so it were day,
Aboute þe knaue þer he lay.
Of hise mouth it stod a stem,
Als it were a sunnebem ;     592
Also lith was it þer-inne,
So þer brenden cerges inne : ²
" Ihesu crist ! " wat dame leue,
" Hwat is þat lith in vre cleue !     596
Sir ³ up grim, and loke wat it enes,     *She bids Grim come and see.*
Hwat is þe lith as þou wenes
He stirten boþe up to the knaue,
For man shal god wille haue,     600
Vnkeueleden him, and swiþe unbounden,
And sone anon [upon] him funden,     *They find a mark on his shoulder.*
Als he tirneden of his serk,
On his rith shuldre a kyne merk ;     604
A swiþe brith, a swiþe fair :
" Goddot ! " quath grim, " þis [is] ure eir
þat shal [ben] louerd of denemark,
He shal ben king strong and stark ;     608  *Grim says the lad is to be king.*
He shal hauen in his hand
A[l] denemark and engeland ;
He shal do godard ful wo,
He shal him hangen, or quik flo ;     612
Or he shal him al quic graue,
Of him shal he no merci haue."
þus seide grim, and sore gret,
And sone fel him to þe fet,     616
And seide, " louerd, haue merci     *He prays Havelok to forgive him.*
Of me, and leue, that is me bi !
Louerd, we aren boþe þine,
þine cherles, þine hine.     620

¹ MS. þer.     ² *Qu.* þrinne. See ll. 716, 761, 2125.
³ *Qu.* stir, *or* stirt.

|   |   |   |
|---|---|---|
| | Lowerd, we sholen þe wel fede, | |
| | Til þat þu cone riden on stede, | |
| | Til þat þu cone ful wel bere | |
| | Helm on heued, sheld and spere. | 624 |
| Godard shall never know about this. | He ne shal neuere wite, sikerlike, Godard, þat fule swike. | |
| | Þoru oþer man, louerd, than þoru þe, | |
| | Sal i neuere freman be. | 628 |
| | Þou shalt me, louerd, fre maken, | |
| | For i shal yemen þe, and waken ; | |
| | Þoru þe wile i fredom haue : " | |
| [Fol. 207 b, col. 1.] | Þo was haueloc a bliþe knaue. | 632 |
| Havelok is glad, and asks for bread. | He sat him up, and craued bred. | |
| | And seide, " ich am [wel] ney ded, | |
| | Hwat for hunger, wat for bondes | |
| | Þat þu leidest on min hondes ; | 636 |
| | And for [þe] keuel at þe laste, | |
| | Þat in mi mouth was þrist faste. | |
| | y was þe[r]-with so harde prangled, | |
| | Þat i was þe[r]-with ney strangled." | 640 |
| | " Wel is me þat þu mayth hete : | |
| Dame Leve brings him bread and cheese, butter, &c. | Goddoth ! " quath leue, " y shal þe fete Bred an chese, butere and milk, | |
| | Pastees and flaunes, al with suilk | 644 |
| | Shole we sone þe wel fede, | |
| | Louerd, in þis mikel nede, | |
| | Soth it is, þat men seyt and suereth : | |
| | ' Þer god wile helpen, nouth no dereth.' " | 648 |
| | Þanne sho hauede brouth þe mete, | |
| Havelok eats all up greedily. | Haueloc anon bigan to ete | |
| | Grundlike, and was ful bliþe ; | |
| | Couþe he nouth his hunger Miþe. | 652 |
| | A lof he het, y woth, and more, | |
| | For him hungrede swiþe sore. | |
| | Þre dayes þer-biforn, i wene, | |

Et he no mete, þat was wel sene. 656
Hwan he hauede eten, and was fed,
Grim dede maken a ful fayr bed ; *Grim puts him to bed.*
Vncloþede him, and dede him þer-inne,
And seyde, "Slep sone, with michel winne ; 660
Slep wel faste, and dred þe nouth,
Fro sorwe to ioie art þu brouth."
Sone so it was lith of day,
Grim it under-tok þe wey 664 *Grim tells Godard he has killed Havelok.*
To þe wicke traitour godard,
þat was denemak a [1] stiward,
And seyde, "louerd, don ich haue
þat þou me bede of þe knaue ; 668
He is drenched in þe flod,
Abouten his hals an anker god ;
He is witer-like ded,
Eteth he neure more bred ; 672
He liþ drenched in þe se :—
Yif me gold [and] oþer fe,[2] *and asks for his reward.*
þat y mowe riche be ;
And with þi chartre make [me] fre, 676
For þu ful wel bi-hetet me, [Fol. 207 b, col. 2.]
þanne i last[e] spak with þe."
Godard stod, and lokede on him *Godard bids him go home, and*
þoruth-like, with eyne grim ; 680 *remain a thrall ;*
And seyde, "Wiltu [nou] ben erl ?
Go hom swiþe, fule drit, cherl ;
Go heþen, and be euere-more
þral and cherl, als þou er wore. 684
Shal [þou] haue non oþer mede ;
For litel i [shal] [3] do þe lede
To þe galues, so god me rede !

[1] *Qu.* Denemarkes.
[2] Cf. l. 1225.
[3] The MS. has "ig," but the *g* is expuncted ; and it omits "shal."

| | | |
|---|---|---|
| *for he has done wickedly.* | For þou haues don a wicke dede. | 688 |
| | þou Mait stonden her to longe, | |
| | Bute þou swiþe eþen gonge." | |

Grim thoucte to late þat he ran
Fro þat traytour, þa wicke man; 692
*Grim fears that both himself and Havelok will be hung.*
And þoucte, "wat shal me to rede?
Wite he him onliue, he wile beþe
Heye hangen on galwe-tre:
Betere us is of londe to fle, 696
And berwen boþen ure liues,
And mine children, and mine wiues."
*Grim sells his live stock.*
Grim solde sone al his corn,
Shep wit wolle, neth wit horn, 700
Hors, and swin, [and gate] wit berd,
þe gees, þe hennes of þe yerd;
Al he solde, þat outh douthe,
That he eure selle moucte, 704
And al he to þe peni drou:
*He fits up his ship carefully.*
Hise ship he greyþede wel inow,
He dede it tere, an ful wel pike,
þat it ne doutede sond ne krike; 708
þer-inne dide a ful god mast,
Stronge kables, and ful fast,
Ores god, an ful god seyl,
þer-inne wantede nouth a nayl, 712
þat euere he sholde þer-inne do:
*He takes with him his wife, his three sons, his two daughters, and Havelok.*
Hwan he hauedet greyþed so,
Hauelok þe yunge he dide þer-inne,
Him and his wif, hise sones þrinne, 716
And hise two doutres, þat faire wore,
And sone dede he leyn in an ore,
And drou him to þe heye se,
þere he mith alþer-best[e] fle. 720
Fro londe woren he bote a mile,

## GRIM FOUNDS THE TOWN OF GRIMSBY.

Ne were neuere but ane hwile, [Fol. 208, col. 1.]
þat it ne bigan a wind to Rise                     A north wind arises, called the
Out of þe north, men calleth 'bise'    724  *bise*, and drives them to England.
And drof hem intil engelond,
þat al was siþen in his hond,
His, þat hauelok was þe name ;
But or he hauede michel shame,         728
Michel sorwe, and michel tene,
And prie he gat it al bidene ;
Als ye shulen nou forthwar lere,[1]
Yf that ye wilen þer-to here.          732

IN humber grim bigan to lende,                    Grim went up the Humber to Lindesey.
In lindeseye, Rith at þe north ende.
þer sat is ship up-on þe sond,
But grim it drou up to þe lond ;       736
And þere he made a litel cote,
To him and to hise flote.
Bigan he þere for to erþe,
A litel hus to maken of erþe,          740  There he built a house.
So þat he wel þore were
Of here herboru herborwed þere ;
And for þat grim þat place aute,
þe stede of grim þe name laute ;       744
So þat [hit] grimesbi calleth alle                 That place was called Grimsby, after Grim.
þat þer-offe speken alle,
And so shulen men callen it ay,
Bituene þis and domesday.              748

Grim was fishere swiþe god,                        Grim was a good fisherman.
And mikel couþe on the flod ;
Mani god fish þer-inne he tok,
Boþe with neth, and with hok.          752
He tok þe sturgiun, and þe qual,                   He caught sturgeons, turbot, &c.
And þe turbut, and lax with-al,

[1] MS. here; *read* lere. Cf. ll. 12, 1640.

## HAVELOK DOES NOT LIKE BEING IDLE.

He tok þe sele, and þe hwel;
He spedde ofte swiþe wel:                               756
Keling he tok, and tumberel,
Hering, and þe makerel,

*He had four panniers made for himself a:d his sons.*

Gode paniers dede he make                               760
Ontil him, and oþer þrinne,
Til hise sones to beren fish inne,
Vp o-londe to selle and fonge;
Forbar he neyþe[r] tun, ne gronge,                      764
Þat he ne to-yede with his ware;
Kam he neuere hom hand-bare,

[Fol· 208, col. 2.]

Þat he ne broucte bred and sowel,
In his shirte, or in his couel;                         768
In his poke benes and korn :—
Hise swink ne hauede he nowt forlorn.

*He used to sell lampreys at Lincoln,*

And hwan he tok þe grete laumprei,
Ful we[l] he couþe þe rithe wei                         772
To lincolne, þe gode boru;
Ofte he yede it þoru and þoru,
Til he hauede wol¹ wel sold,
And þer-fore þe penies told.                            776
Þanne he com, þenne he were bliþe,
For hom he brouthe fele siþe

*and bring home simnels, meal, meat, and hemp.*

Wastels, simenels with þe horn,
Hise pokes fulle of mele an korn,                       780
Netes flesh, shepes, and swines,
And hemp to maken of gode lines;
And stronge ropes to hise netes,
In þe se weren he ofte setes.²                          784

*Thus they lived for 12 years.*

Þus-gate grim him fayre ledde.
  Him and his genge wel he fedde
Wel twelf winter, oþer more:
Hauelok was war þat grim swank sore                     788

¹ *Qu.* ful *or* al.      ² *Sic* in MS.

For his mete, and he lay at hom :
Thouthe, "ich am nou no grom ;
Ich am wel waxen, and wel may eten
More þan euere Grim may geten.   792
Ich ete more, bi god on liue,
Þan grim an hise children fiue !
It ne may nouth ben þus longe,
Goddot ! y wile with þe gange,   796
For to leren sum god to gete ;
Swinken ich wolde for mi mete.
It is no shame forto swinken ;
Þe man þat may wel eten and drinken,   800
Þat nouth ne haue but on swink long,
To liggen at hom it is ful strong.
God yelde him þer i ne [1] may,
Þat haueth me fed to þis day !   804
Gladlike i wile þe paniers bere ;
Ich woth, ne shal it me nouth dere,
Þey þer be inne a birþene gret,
Al so heui als a neth.   808
Shal ich neuere lengere dwelle,
To morwen shal ich forth pelle."

On þe morwen, hwan it was day,
He stirt up sone, and nouth ne lay ;   812
And cast a panier on his bac,
With fish giueled als a stac ;
Also michel he bar him one,
So he foure, bi mine mone ! [2]   816
Wel he it bar, and solde it wel,
Þe siluer he brouthe hom il del ;
Al þat he þer-fore tok
With-held he nouth a ferþinges nok.   820
So yede he forth ilke day,
Þat he neuere at home lay.

[1] MS. ine.    [2] Cf. ll. 1711, 1972.

| | | |
|---|---|---|
| | So wolde he his mester lere; | |
| A great dearth arises. | Bifel it so a strong dere | 824 |
| | Bigan to rise of korn of bred, | |
| | That grim ne couþe no god red, | |
| | Hw he sholde his meine fede; | |
| | Of hauelok hauede he michel drede: | 828 |
| | For he was strong, and wel mouthe ete | |
| | More þanne heuere mouthe he gete; | |
| They have not enough to eat. | Ne he ne mouthe on þe se take | |
| | Neyþer lenge, ne þorn[e]bake,[1] | 832 |
| | Ne non oþer fish þat douthe | |
| | His meyne feden with he[r][2] mouthe. | |
| Grim is sorry for Havelok. | Of hauelok he hauede kare, | |
| | Hwilgat þat he micthe fare; | 836 |
| | Of his children was him nouth, | |
| | On hauelok was al hise þouth, | |
| | And seyde, " hauelok, dere sone, | |
| | I wene that we deye mone | 840 |
| | For hunger, þis dere is so strong, | |
| | And hure mete is uten long. | |
| He advises him to go to Lincoln, | Betere is þat þu henne gonge, | |
| | þan þu here dwelle longe; | 844 |
| | Heþen þow mayt gangen to late; | |
| | Thou canst ful wel þe ricthe gate | |
| | To lincolne, þe gode borw, | |
| | þou hauest it gon ful ofte þoru; | 848 |
| | Of me ne is me nouth a slo, | |
| | Betere is þat þu þider go, | |
| | For þer is mani god man inne, | |
| and work there. | þer þou mayt þi mete winne. | 852 |
| | But wo is me! þou art so naked, | |
| He makes him a coat of an old sail. | Of mi seyl y wolde þe were maked | |
| | A cloth, þou mithest inne gongen, | |
| | Sone, no cold þat þu ne fonge." | 856 |

[1] See l. 759.   [2] *Qu.* her, *i.e.* their. MS. he.

## HE HELPS THE EARL OF CORNWALL'S COOK.   27

He tok þe sh[e]res¹ of þe nayl,          [Fol. 208 b, col. 2.]
And made him a couel of þe sayl,
And hauelok dide it sone on ;
Hauede neyþer hosen ne shon,       860
Ne none kines oþe[r] wede ;
To lincolne barfot he yede.           *Havelok goes to Lincoln barefoot.*
Hwan he kam þe[r], he was ful wil,
Ne hauede he no frend to gangen til ;    864
Two dayes þer fastinde he yede,        *He fasts for two days.*
þat non for his werk wolde him fede ;
þe þridde day herde he calle :
"Bermen, bermen, hider forth alle!"    868
[Poure þat on fote yede]²
Sprongen forth so sparke on glede.
Hauelok shof dun nyne or ten,         *Havelok becomes the earl's cook's porter.*
Rith amidewarde þe fen,          872
And stirte forth to þe kok,
[þer the herles mete he tok,]
þat he bouthe at þe brigge : ҭ
þe bermen let he alle ligge,        876
And bar þe mete to þe castel,
And gat him þere a ferþing wastel.     *He gets a farthing cake.*

Þet oþer day kepte he ok           *Another day, he watches the earl's cook,*
Swiþe yerne þe erles kok,        880
Til þat he say him on þe b[r]igge,
And bi him mani fishes ligge.
þe herles mete hauede he bouth
Of cornwalie, and kalde oft :       884
"Bermen, bermen, hider swiþe!"      *who calls for a porter.*
Hauelok it herde, and was ful bliþe,
þat he herde "bermen" calle ;
Alle made he hem dun falle        888

---

¹ *Qu.* sheres. MS. shres.
² Cf. ll. 91, 101. Here and below an additional line seems requisite.

| | | |
|---|---|---|
| Havelok upsets 16 lads. | þat in his gate yeden and stode, | |
| | Wel sixtene laddes gode. | |
| | Als he lep þe kok [vn-]til, | |
| | He shof hem alle upon an hyl; | 892 |
| | Astirte til him with his rippe, | |
| He catches up the cook's fish, | And bigan þe fish to kippe. | |
| | He bar up wel a carte lode | |
| | Of segges, laxes, of playces brode, | 896 |
| | Of grete laumprees, and of eles; | |
| | Sparede he neyþer tos ne heles, | |
| and carries them to the castle. | Til þat he to þe castel cam, | |
| | þat men fro him his birþene nam. | 900 |
| | þan men haueden holpen him doun | |
| | With þe birþene of his croun, | |
| | þe kok [bi] stod, and on him low, | |
| [Fol. 209, col. 1.] | And þoute him stalworþe man ynow, | 904 |
| | And seyde, "wiltu ben wit me? | |
| The cook takes him into his service. | Gladlike wile ich feden þe; | |
| | Wel is set þe mete þu etes, | |
| | And þe hire þat þu getes." | 908 |
| | "Goddot!"[1] quoth he, "leue sire, | |
| | Bidde ich you non oþer hire; | |
| | But yeueþ me inow to ete, | |
| Havelok tells the cook what he can do. | Fir and water y wile yow fete, | 912 |
| | þe fir blowe, an ful wele maken; | |
| | Stickes kan ich breken and kraken, | |
| | And kindlen ful wel a fyr, | |
| | And maken it to brennen shir; | 916 |
| | Ful wel kan ich cleuen shides, | |
| | Eles to-turnen[2] of here hides; | |
| | Ful wel kan ich dishes swilen, | |
| | And don al þat ye euere wilen." | 920 |
| The cook is | Quoth þe kok, "wile i no more; | |

[1] Soddot, MS.
[2] MS. to turuen; *but the* u *and* n *are almost indistinguishable.* Cf. l. 603; and *William of Palerne*, 2590.

Go þu yunder, and sit þore,      con·ent to hire
And y shal yeue þe ful fair bred,      him.
And make þe broys in þe led.      924
Sit now doun and et ful yerne :
Daþeit hwo þe mete werne !"

Hauelok sette him dun anon,      Havelok eats
  Also stille als a ston,      a good dinner.
Til he hauede ful wel eten ;      928
Þo hauede hauelok fayre geten.
Hwan he hauede eten inow,
He kam to þe welle, water up-drow,      932
And filde þe[r] a michel so ;      He fills a
Bad he non ageyn him go,      large tub with
But bi-twen his hondes he bar it in,      water for the kitchen.
A[l] him one to þe kichin.      936
Bad he non him water to fete,
Ne fro b[r]igge to bere þe mete,
He bar þe turues, he bar þe star,
Þe wode fro the brigge he bar ;      940
Al that euere shulden he nytte,      He draws water,
Al he drow, and al he citte ;      and cuts wood.
Wolde he neuere hauen rest,
More þan he were a best.      944
Of alle men was he mest meke.
Lauhwinde ay, and bliþe of speke ;      He is always
Euere he was glad and bliþe,      laughing and blithe.
His sorwe he couþe ful wel miþe.      948
It ne was non so litel knaue,      [Fol. 209, col. 2.]
For to leyken, ne forto plawe,
Þat he ne wo[l]de with him pleye :
Þe children that y[e]den in þe weie      952 Children play
Of him he deden al he[r] wille,      with him.
And with him leykeden here fille.
Him loueden alle, stille and bolde.
Knictes, children, yunge and holde ;      956

| | | |
|---|---|---|
| All like him. | Alle him loueden þat him sowen, | |
| | Boþen heyemen and lowe. | |
| | Of him ful wide þe word sprong, | |
| | Hw he was mike, hw he was strong, | 960 |
| | Hw fayr man god him hauede maked, | |
| He has nothing to wear but the old sail. | But on þat he was almest naked: | |
| | For he ne hauede nouth to shride, | |
| | But a kouel ful unride, | 964 |
| | þat [was] ful, and swiþe wicke, | |
| | Was it nouth worth a fir sticke. | |
| The cook buys him new clothes. | þe cok bigan of him to rewe, | |
| | And bouthe him cloþes, al spannewe; | 968 |
| | He bouthe him boþe hosen and shon, | |
| | And sone dide him dones on. | |
| He looks very well in his new suit. | Hwan he was cloþed, osed, and shod, | |
| | Was non so fayr under god, | 972 |
| | þat euere yete in erþe were, | |
| | Non þat euere moder bere; | |
| | It was neuere man þat yemede | |
| | In kinneriche, þat so wel semede | 976 |
| | King or cayser forto be, | |
| | þan he was shrid, so semede he; | |
| Havelok is the tallest man in Lincoln, | For þanne he weren alle samen | |
| | At lincolne, at þe gamen, | 980 |
| | And þe erles men woren al þore, | |
| | þan was hauelok bi þe shuldren more | |
| | þan þe meste þat þer kam: | |
| | In armes him noman [ne] nam, | 984 |
| | þat he doune sone ne caste; | |
| | Hauelok stod ouer hem als a mast. | |
| | Als he was heie, al[1] he was long, | |
| | He was boþe stark and strong; | 988 |
| and the strongest in England. | In engelond [was] non hise per | |
| | Of strengþe þat euere kam him ner. | |
| | Als he was strong, so was he softe; | |

[1] *Qu.* so; see l. 991.

| | |
|---|---|
| Þey a man him misdede ofte, | 992 |
| Neuere more he him misdede, | |
| Ne hond on him with yuele leyde. | [Fol. 209 b, col. 1.] |
| Of bodi was he mayden clene, | *He is good-natured and pure.* |
| Neuere yete in game, ne in grene, | 996 |
| Þit[1] hire ne wolde leyke ne lye, | |
| No more þan it were a strie. | |
| In þat time al hengelond | |
| Þerl Godrich hauede in his hond, | 1000 *Godrich summons a parliament at Lincoln.* |
| And he gart komen into þe tun | |
| Mani erl, and mani barun; | |
| And alle [men] þat liues were | |
| In eng[e]lond, þanne wer þere, | 1004 |
| Þat þey haueden after sent, | |
| To ben þer at þe parlement. | |
| With hem com mani chanbioun, | *Some champions begin to contend in games.* |
| Mani with ladde, blac and brown; | 1008 |
| An fel it so, þat yunge men, | |
| Wel abouten nine or ten, | |
| Bigunnen þe[r] for to layke: | |
| Þider komen bothe stronge and wayke; | 1012 |
| Þider komen lesse and more, | |
| Þat in þe borw þanne weren þore; | |
| Chaunpiouns, and starke laddes, | *Strong lads and bondmen are there.* |
| Bondemen with here gaddes, | 1016 |
| Als he comen fro þe plow; | |
| Þere was sembling i-now! | |
| For it ne was non horse-knaue, | |
| Þo þei sholden in honde haue, | 1020 |
| Þat he ne kam þider, þe leyk to se: | |
| Biforn here fet þanne lay a tre, | |
| And putten[2] with a mikel ston | *They begin to "put the stone."* |
| Þe starke laddes, ful god won. | 1024 |

[1] *Qu.* wit = with: miswritten owing to confusion of þ with p (*w*)?

[2] MS. pulten. But see ll. 1031, 1033, 1044, 1051, &c.

    Þe ston was mikel, and ˙: greth,
    And al so heui so a neth;
    Grund stalwrthe man he sholde be,
    Þat mouthe liften it to his kne;    1028

*Few can lift it.* Was þer neyþer clerc, ne prest,
    Þat mithe liften it to his brest:
    Þerwit putten the chaunpiouns,
    Þat þider comen with þe barouns.  1032
    Hwo so mithe putten þore
    Biforn a-noþer, an inch or more,
    Wore ye yung, [or] wore he hold,
    He was for a kempe told.    1036

*Whils this is going on,* Al-so þe[i] stoden, an ofte stareden,
    Þe chaunpiouns, and ek the ladden,

[Fol. 208 b, col. 2.] And he maden mikel strout
    Abouten þe alþerbeste but,    1040

*Havelok looks on at them.* Hauelok stod, and lokede þer-til;
    And of puttingge he was ful wil,
    For neuere yete ne saw he or
    Putten the stone, or þanne þor.  1044

*His master tells him to try.* Hise mayster bad him gon þer-to,
    Als he couþe þer-with do.
    Þo hise mayster it him bad,
    He was of him sore adrad;    1048
    Þerto he stirte sone anon,
    And kipte up þat heui ston,
    Þat he sholde puten wiþe;

*He puts the stone 12 feet beyond the rest.* He putte at þe firste siþe,    1052
    Ouer alle þat þer wore,
    Twel fote, and sumdel more.
    Þe chaunpiouns þat [þat] put sowen,
    Shuldreden he ilc oþer, and lowen;  1056
    Wolden he no more to putting gange,
    But seyde, "*we*[1] dwellen her to longe!"

    [1] In the former edition—"ye". But the *y* is not dotted, and it may be "þe."

## GODRICH HEARS OF HAVELOK'S STRENGTH.

| | | |
|---|---|---|
| Þis selkouth mithe nouth ben hyd, | | This fent is everywhere |
| Ful sone it was ful loude kid | 1060 | talked about. |
| Of hauelok, hw he warp þe ston | | |
| Ouer þe laddes euerilkon; | | |
| Hw he was fayr, hw he was long, | | |
| Hw he was with, hw he was strong; | 1064 | |
| Þoruth england yede þe speke,[1] | | |
| Hw he was strong, and ek meke; | | |
| In the castel, up in þe halle, | | |
| Þe knithes speken þer-of alle, | 1068 | |
| So that Godrich it herde wel. | | Godrich hears the knights talking of it. |
| Þe[r] speken of hauelok, eueri del, | | |
| Hw he was strong man and hey, | | |
| Hw he was strong and ek fri, | 1072 | |
| And þouthte godrich, "þoru þis knaue | | |
| Shal ich engelond al haue, | | |
| And mi sone after me; | | |
| For so i wile þat it be. | 1076 | |
| The king aþelwald me dide swere | | "Athelwold said I was to marry his daughter to the strongest man alive. |
| Vpon al þe messe-gere, | | |
| Þat y shu[l]de his douthe[r] yeue | | |
| Þe hexte þat mithe liue, | 1080 | |
| Þe beste, þe fairest, þe strangest ok; | | |
| Þat gart he me sweren on þe bok. | | |
| Hwere mithe i finden ani so hey | | |
| So hauelok is, or so sley? | 1084 | [Fol. 210, col. 1.] |
| Þou y southe heþen in-to ynde, | | |
| So fayr, so strong, ne mithe y finde. | | |
| Hauelok is þat ilke knaue, | | |
| Þat shal goldeborw haue." | 1088 | That is Havelok. |
| Þis þouthe [he] with trechery, | | |
| With traysoun, and wit felony; | | |
| For he wende, þat hauelok wore | | |
| Sum cherles sone, and no more; | 1092 | |
| Ne shulde he hauen of engellond | | |

[1] MS. speche. Read "speke," as in l. 946.

> Onlepi forw in his hond,
> With hire, þat was þerof eyr,
> þat boþe was god and swiþe fair. 1096

*He thought Havelok was only a thrall.*
> He wende, þat hauelok wer a þral,
> þer-þoru he wende hauen al
> In engelond, þat hire rith was;
> He was werse þan sathanas, 1100
> þat ihesu crist in erþe shop:[1]
> Hanged worþe he on an hok!

*He sends for Goldborough to Lincoln.*
> After goldebo[r]w sone he sende,
> þat was boþe fayr and hende, 1104
> And dide hire to lincolne bringe,
> Belles dede he ageyn hire ringen,
> And ioie he made hire swiþe mikel,
> But neþeles he was ful swikel. 1108
> He seyde, þat he sholde hire yeue
> þe fayrest man that mithe liue.

*She says she will marry none but a king.*
> She answerede, and seyde anon,
> Bi crist, and bi seint iohan, 1112
> þat hire sholde noman wedde,
> Ne noman bringen to hire[2] bedde,
> But he were king, or kinges eyr,
> Were he neuere man so fayr. 1116

*Godrich is wrath at this.*
> Godrich þe erl was swiþe wroth,
> þat she swore swilk an oth,
> And seyde, "hwor þou wilt be
> Quen and leuedi ouer me? 1120
> þou shalt hauen a gadeling,
> Ne shalt þou hauen non oþer king;

*He says she shall marry his cook's servant.*
> þe shal spusen mi cokes knaue,
> Ne shalt þou non oþer louerd haue. 1124
> Daþeit þat þe oþer yeue
> Euere more hwil i liue!

[1] *Qu.* shok *or* strok.  [2] *Qu.* hise.

To-mo[r]we ye sholen ben weddeth,
And, maugre þin, to-gidere beddeth." 1128
Goldeborw gret, and was[1] hire ille, [Fol. 210, col. 2.]
She wolde ben ded bi hire wille.
On the morwen, hwan day was sprungen,
And day-belle at kirke rungen, 1132
After hauelok sente þat iudas, *He sends next day for Havelok, and says,*
þat werse was þanne sathanas:
And seyde, " mayster, wilte wif ?" *"Master, wilt wive?"*
"Nay," quoth hauelok, " bi my lif ! 1136
Hwat sholde ich with wif do ?
I ne may hire fede, ne cloþe, ꝫ sho.
Wider sholde ich wimman bringe ?
I ne haue none kines þinge. 1140 *Havelok refuses.*
I ne haue hws, y ne haue cote,
Ne i ne[2] haue stikke, y ne haue sprote,
I ne haue neyþer bred ne sowel,
Ne cloth, but of an hold with couel. 1144
þis cloþes, þat ich onne haue,
Aren þe kokes, and ich his knaue."
Godrich stirt up, and on him dong *Godrich beats him, and threatens to hang him.*
[With dintes swiþe hard and strong,] 1148
And seyde, " But þou hire take,
þat y wole yeuen þe to make,
I shal hangen þe ful heye,
Or y shal þristen vth þin heie." 1152
Hauelok was one, and was odrat,
And grauntede him al þat he bad. *Havelok consents.*
þo sende he after hire sone,
þe fayrest wymman under mone ; 1156
And seyde til hire, [false][3] and slike,
þat wicke þral, þat foule swike : *Godrich next threatens Goldborough.*
" But þu þis man under-stonde,

[1] The first letter of this word is either þ or a Saxon w (ƿ). I read it as the latter.
[2] MS. ine.
[3] Both sense and metre require this word.

## HAVELOK RESOLVES TO GO TO GRIMSBY.

|   |   |
|---|---|
| | I shal flemen þe of londe ;     1160 |

              I shal flemen þe of londe ;         1160
              Or þou shal to þe galwes renne,
              And þer þou shalt in a fir brenne."
              Sho was adrad, for he so þrette,
              And durste nouth þe spusing lette,     1164
              But þey hire likede swiþe ille,

*She consents, thinking it is God's will.*     þouthe it was godes wille :
              God, þat makes to growen þe korn,
              Formede hire wimman to be born.     1168
              Hwan he hauede don him for drede,
              þat he sholde hire spusen, and fede,
              And þat she sholde til him holde,

*A dowry is given her.*     þer weren penies þicke tolde,     1172
              Mikel plente upon þe bok :
              He ys hire yaf, and she as tok.

[Fol. 210 b, col. 1.]     He weren spused fayre and wel,
              þe messe he deden eueridel,     1176
              þat fel to spusing, and god cle[r]k,

*The archbishop of York marries them.*     þe erchebishop uth of yerk,
              þat kam to þe parlement,
              Als god him hauede þider sent.     1180

              Hwan he weren togydere in godes lawe,
              þat þe folc ful wel it sawe,
              He ne wisten hwat he mouthen,

*Havelok knows not what to do.*     Ne he ne wisten wat hem douthe ;     1184
              þer to dwellen, or þenne to gonge,
              þer ne wolden he dwellen longe,
              For he wisten, and ful wel sawe,
              þat godrich hem hatede, þe deuel him hawe !     1188
              And yf he dwelleden þer outh—
              þat fel hauelok ful wel on þouth—
              Men sholde don his leman shame,
              Or elles bringen in wicke blame.     1192
              þat were him leuere to ben ded,

*He determines*     For-þi he token anoþer red,

## GRIM'S CHILDREN WELCOME HAVELOK.

|   |   |
|---|---|
| þat þei sholden þenne fle | *to go to Grimsby.* |
| Til grim, and til hise sones þre ; | 1196 |
| þer wenden he alþer-best to spede, | |
| Hem forto cloþe, and for to fede. | |
| þe lond he token under fote, | |
| Ne wisten he non oþer bote, | 1200 |
| And helden ay the riþe [sti][1] | |
| Til he komen to grimesby. | |
| þanne he komen þere, þanne was grim ded, | *He finds that Grim is dead, but* |
| Of him ne haueden he no red ; | 1204 *his five children are alive.* |
| But hise children alle fyue | |
| Alle weren yet on liue ; | |
| þat ful fayre ayen hem neme, | |
| Hwan he wisten þat he keme, | 1208 |
| And maden ioie swiþe mikel, | |
| Ne weren he neuere ayen hem fikel. | |
| On knes ful fayre he hem setten, | |
| And hauelok swiþe fayre gretten, | 1212 |
| And seyden, " welkome, louerd dere ! | *They welcome Havelok very kindly.* |
| And welkome be þi fayre fere ! | |
| Blessed be þat ilke þrawe, | |
| þat þou hire toke in godes lawe ! | 1216 |
| Wel is hus we sen þe on lyue, | |
| þou mithe us boþe selle and yeue ; | |
| þou mayt us boþe yeue and selle, | |
| With þat þou wilt here dwelle. | 1220 [Fol. 210 b, col. 2.] |
| We hauen, louerd, alle gode, | |
| Hors, and neth, and ship on flode, | *They beg him to stay with them.* |
| Gold, and siluer, and michel auchte, | |
| þat grim ure fader us bitawchte. | 1224 |
| Gold, and siluer, and oþer fe | |
| Bad he us bi-taken þe. | |
| We hauen shep, we hauen swin, | |
| Bi-leue her, louerd, and al be þin ; | 1228 |
| þo shalt ben louerd, þou shalt ben syre, | *They will serve* |

[1] A word is here erased; but see l. 2618.

## 38 GOLDBOROUGH SEES THE WONDROUS LIGHT.

him and his wife.
And we sholen seruen þe and hire;
And hure sistres sholen do
Al that euere biddes sho; 1232
He sholen hire cloþen, washen, and wringen,
And to hondes water bringen;
He sholen bedden hire and þe,
For leuedi wile we þat she be." 1236
Hwan he þis ioie haueden maked,
Sithen stikes broken and kraked,

They make a fire, and spare neither goose nor hen.
And þe fir brouth on brenne,
Ne was þer spared gos ne henne, 1240
Ne þe hende, ne þe drake,
Mete he deden plente make;
Ne wantede þere no god mete,

They fetch wine and ale.
Wyn and ale deden he fete, 1244
And made[n] hem [ful] glade and bliþe,
Wesseyl ledden he fele siþe.

At night Goldborough lies down sorrowful.
On þe nith, als goldeborw lay,
Sory and sorwful was she ay, 1248
For she wende she were bi-swike,
Þat sh[e w]ere[1] yeuen un-kyndelike.

She sees a great light.
O nith saw she þer-inne a lith,
A swiþe fayr, a swiþe bryth, 1252
Al so brith, al so shir,
So it were a blase of fir.
She lokede no[r]þ,[2] and ek south,

It comes out of Havelok's mouth.
And saw it comen ut of his mouth, 1256
Þat lay bi hire in þe bed:
No ferlike þou she were adred.
Þouthe she, "wat may this bi-mene!
He beth heyman yet, als y wene, 1260
He beth heyman er he be ded:"—

She sees a red cross on his shoulder, and
On hise shuldre, of gold red
She saw a swiþe noble croiz,

[1] MS. shere, *evidently miswritten for* she were.  [2] MS. noþ.

## HAVELOK TELLS HER HIS STRANGE DREAM.

Of an angel she herde a uoyz :  1264  *hears an angel, saying,*

"Goldeborw, lat þi sorwe be,  [Fol. 211, col. 1.]
For hauelok, þat haueþ spuset þe,  *"Goldborough, be not sad.*
He¹ kinges sone, and kinges eyr,
þat bikenneth þat croiz so fayr.  1268
It² bikenneth more, þat he shal
Denemark hauen, and englond al;
He shal ben king strong and stark  *Havelok shall be a king,*
Of engelond and denemark;  1272
þat shal þu wit þin eyne sen,
And þo shalt quen and leuedi en !"  *and thou, queen."*

Þanne she hauede herd the steuene
Of þe angel uth of heuene,  1276
She was so fele siþes blithe,  *She rejoices, and kisses Havelok.*
þat she ne mithe hire ioie mythe;
But hauelok sone anon she kiste,
And he slep, and nouth ne wiste.  1280
Hwan þat aungel hauede seyd,
Of his slep a-non he brayd,  *He awakes, and says he has had a dream.*
And seide, "lemman, slepes þou?
A selkuth drem dremede me nou.  1284

Herkne nou hwat me haueth met:
Me þouthe y was in denemark set,  *He dreamt he was on a high hill in Denmark,*
But on on þe moste hil
þat euere yete kam i til.  1288
It was so hey, þat y wel mouthe
Al þe werd se, als me þouthe.
Als i sat up-on þat lowe,
I bigan denemark for to awe,  1292  *and began to possess all that country.*
þe borwes, and þe castles stronge;
And mine armes weren so longe,
That i fadmede, al at ones,

¹ *Qu.* Is.        ² MS. Iit.

|                                    | denemark, with mine lo*n*ge bones ;              | 1296 |
|                                    | And þa*n*ne y wolde mine armes drawe             |      |
|                                    | Til me, and hom for to haue,                     |      |
| All things in Denmark cleaved to his arms. | Al that euere in denemark liueden        |      |
|                                    | On mine armes faste clyueden ;                   | 1300 |
|                                    | And þe stronge castles alle                      |      |
|                                    | On knes bigunne*n* for to falle,                 |      |
|                                    | Þe keyes felle*n* at mine fet :—                 |      |
| He also dreamt that he went to England, | Anoþer drem dremede me ek,                   | 1304 |
|                                    | Þat ich fley ouer þe salte se                    |      |
|                                    | Til engeland, and al with me                     |      |
|                                    | Þat euere was in denemark lyues,                 |      |
|                                    | But bo*n*demen, and here wiues,                  | 1308 |
|                                    | And þat ich kom til engelond,                    |      |
| [Fol. 211, col. 2.] and that became his too. | Al closede it i*n*til min hond,          |      |
|                                    | And, goldeborw, y gaf [it] þe :—                 |      |
|                                    | Deus ! lem*m*an, hwat may þis be ? "             | 1312 |
|                                    | Sho answerede, and seyde sone :                  |      |
|                                    | " Ihe*s*u cr*i*st, þat made mone,                |      |
|                                    | Þine dremes tu*r*ne to ioye ;                    |      |
|                                    | Þat wite þw that sittes i*n* trone !             | 1316 |
| She says, he will be king of England and Denmark. | Ne non stro*n*g ki*n*g, ne caysere,    |      |
|                                    | So þou shalt be, fo[r] þou shalt bere            |      |
|                                    | In engelond coru*n*e yet ;                       |      |
|                                    | Denemark shal knele to þi fet ;                  | 1320 |
|                                    | Alle þe castles þat aren þer-inne,               |      |
|                                    | Shal-tow, lem*m*an, ful wel winne.               |      |
|                                    | I woth, so wel so ich it sowe,                   |      |
|                                    | To þe shole come*n* heye and lowe,               | 1324 |
| " All men in Denmark shall come to thee. | And alle þat in denemark wone,               |      |
|                                    | Em and broþer, fader and sone,                   |      |
|                                    | Erl and baroun, dre*n*g an kayn,                 |      |
|                                    | Knithes, and burgeys, and sweyn ;                | 1328 |
|                                    | And mad king heyelike and wel,                   |      |
|                                    | Denemark shal be þin euere-ilc del.              |      |

Haue þou nouth þer-offe douthe
Nouth þe worth of one nouthe;  1332
Þer-offe with-inne þe firste yer
Shalt þou ben king, of euere-il del.  *Thou shalt be*
But do nou als y wile rathe,  *king within the year.*
Nim in with þe to denema[r]k baþe,  1336
And do þou nouth onfrest þis fare,
Lith and selthe felawes are.
For shal ich neuere bliþe be
Til i with eyen denemark se;  1340
For ich woth, þat al þe lond
Shalt þou hauen in þin hon[d].
Prey grimes sones alle þre,  *Pray Grim's sons*
That he wenden forþ with þe;  1344 *to go with you to Denmark.*
I wot, he wilen þe nouth werne,
With þe wende shulen he yerne,
For he louen þe herte-like,
Þou maght til he aren quike,  1348
Hwore so he o worde aren;
Þere ship þou do hem swithe yaren,  *Go at once.*
And loke þat þou dwellen nouth:  *Delays are*
Dwelling haueth ofte scaþe wrouth."  1352 *dangerous."*


Hwan Hauelok herde þat she radde,
  Sone it was day, sone he him cladde,
And sone to þe kirke yede,
Or he dide ani oþer dede,  [Fol. 211 b, col. 1.]
And bifor þe rode bigan falle,  1356
Croiz and crist bi[gan] to kalle,
And seyde, "louerd, þat al weldes,  *Havelok prays for*
Wind and water, wodes and feldes,  1360 *success,*
For the holi milce of you,
Haue merci of me, louerd, nou!
And wreke me yet on mi fo,  *and for vengeance*
Þat ich saw biforn min eyne slo  1364 *on his foe,*
Mine sistres, with a knif,

|   |   |   |
|---|---|---|
| | And siþen wolde me mi lyf | |
| | Haue reft, for in the [depe] se | |
| | Bad he grim haue drenched me. | 1368 |
| | He [hath] mi lond with mikel vn-Rith, | |
| | With michel wrong, with mikel plith, | |
| | For i ne¹ misdede him neuere nouth, | |
| | And haued me to sorwe brouth. | 1372 |
| who had caused hiᴍ to be a beggar. | He haueth me do mi mete to þigge, | |
| | And ofte in sorwe and pine ligge. | |
| | Louerd, haue merci of me, | |
| | And late [me] wel passe þe se, | 1376 |
| He prays for a fair passage across the sea. | þat ihc haue ther-offe douthe and kare, | |
| | With-uten stormes ouer-fare, | |
| | þat y ne drenched [be] þer-ine, | |
| | Ne forfaren for no sinne. | 1380 |
| | And bringge me wel to þe lond, | |
| | þat godard haldes in his hond ; | |
| | þat is mi Rith, eueri del : | |
| | Ihesu crist, þou wost it wel !" | 1384 |
| He leaves his offering on the altar. | Þanne he hauede his bede seyd, | |
| | His offrende on þe auter leyd, | |
| | His leue at ihesu crist he tok, | |
| | And at his suete moder ok, | 1388 |
| | And at þe croiz, þat he biforn lay, | |
| | Siþen yede sore grotinde awey. | |
| He finds Grim's sons ready to fish. | ² Hwan he com hom, he wore yare, | |
| | Grimes sones, forto fare | 1392 |
| | In-to þe se, fishes to gete, | |
| | þat hauelok mithe wel of ete. | |
| | But auelok þouthe al anoþer, | |
| Havelok calls Grim's three sons. | First he ka[l]de þe heldeste broþer, | 1396 |
| | Roberd þe rede, bi his name, | |

¹ MS. ine.
² In the MS. the Capital letter is prefixed to the next line.

## HE ASKS THEM TO GO WITH HIM TO DENMARK.

Wiliam wenduth, and h[uwe r]auen,[1]
Grimes sones alle þre,
And sey[d]e, "liþes nou alle to me,    1400   [Fol. 211 b, col. 2.]
Louerdinges, ich wile you sheue,
A þing of me þat ye wel knewe.
Mi fader was king of denshe lond,           *He says, "My*
Denemark was al in his hond    1404   *father was king of Denmark.*
þe day þat he was quik and ded;
But þanne hauede he wicke red,
þat he me, and denemark al,
And mine sistres bi-tawte a þral:    1408   *He left me and my sisters in*
A deueles lime [he] hus bitawte,           *charge of a foul fiend,*
And al his lond, and al hise authe.
For y saw that fule fend
Mine sistres slo with hise hend;    1412
First he shar a-two here þrotes,           *who slew my sisters,*
And siþen [karf] hem al to grotes,
And siþen bad [he] in þe se
Grim, youre fader, drenchen me.    1416   *and bade Grim drown me.*
Deplike dede he him swere
On bok, þat he sholde me bere
Vnto þe se, an drenchen ine,
And wolde taken on him þe sinne.    1420
But grim was wis, and swiþe hende,        *But Grim was wise.*
Wolde he nouth his soule shende;
Leuere was him to be for-sworen,
þan drenchen me, and ben for-lorn;    1424
But sone bigan he forto fle
Fro denemark, forto berwen[2] me,        *He fled from Denmark with me,*
For yif[3] ich hauede þer ben funden,
Hauede ben slayn, or harde bunden,    1428
And heye ben henged on a tre,

---

[1] MS. hauen. Cf. ll. 1868, 2528. Only an assonance, not a rime, seems intended.
[2] MS. berpen, *the A.S. w being used here.* Cf. l. 697.
[3] MS. yif.

Hauede go for him gold ne fe.
For-þi fro denemark hider he fledde,
*and took care of me.* And me ful fayre and ful wel fedde,     1432
So þat vn-to þis [ilke] day,
Haue ich ben fed and fostred ay.
But nou ich am up to þat helde
Cumen, that ich may wepne welde,     1436
And y may grete dintes yeue,
*And now, I mus go to Denmark.* Shal i neuere hwil ich lyue
Ben glad, til that ich denemark se;
*Go with me, and I will make you rich men."* I preie you þat ye wende with me,     1440
And ich may mak you riche men,
Ilk of you shal haue castles ten,
And þe lond þat þor-til longes,
Borwes, tunes, wodes and wonges."[1]     1444

    \*   \*   \*   \*   \*
    \*   \*   \*   \*   \*

[Fol. 212, col. 1.] "With swilk als ich byen shal:
þer-of bi-seche you nou leue;
*Havelok asks Ubbe to give him leave to buy and sell there.* Wile ich speke with non oþer reue,
But with þe, þat iustise are,     1628
þat y mithe seken[2] mi ware
In gode borwes up and doun,
And faren ich wile fro tun to tun."
A gold ring drow he forth anon,     1632
An hundred pund was worth þe ston,
*He gives Ubbe a gold ring.* And yaf it ubbe for to spede:—
He was ful wis þat first yaf mede,
And so was hauelok ful wis here,     1636

---

[1] A folio has here been cut out of the MS., containing 180 lines. The missing portion must have been to this effect. "To this they gladly assented; and Havelok, accompanied by his wife Goldeborw and the sons of Grim, set sail for Denmark. Disembarking, they travel till they reach the castle of a great Danish earl, named Ubbe, who had formerly been a close friend to king Birkabeyn. Havelok begs that he will allow him to live in that part of the country, and to gain a livelihood by trading."

[2] *Qu.* sellen.

## UBBE INVITES HAVELOK TO A FEAST.

He solde his gold ring ful dere,      *Dearly he sells it,*
Was neuere non so dere sold,      *all the same.*
For chapmen, neyþer yung ne old :
þat sholen [1] ye forthward ful wel heren,      1640
Yif þat ye wile þe stórie heren.

Hwan ubbe hauede þe gold ring,      *Ubbe takes the ring,*
  Hauede he youenet for no þing,
Nouth for þe borw euere-il del :—      1644
Hauelok bi-hel he swiþe wel,
Hw he was wel of bones maked,      *admires*
Brod in þe sholdres, ful wel schaped,      *Havelok's make and strength,*
þicke in þe brest, of bodi long ;      1648
He semede wel to ben wel strong.
" Deus ! " hwat ubbe, " qui ne were he knith ?
I woth, þat he is swiþe with !
Betere semede him to bere      1652    *and think he*
Helm on heued, sheld and spere,      *ought to be a knight, not a*
þanne to beye and selle ware.      *pedlar.*
Allas ! þat he shal þer-with fare.
Goddot ! wile he trowe me,      1656
Chaffare shal he late be."
Neþeles he seyde sone :
" Hauelok, haue [þou] þi bone,      *" Havelok, bring*
And y ful wel rede þ[e]      1660    *your wife, and come and eat*
þat þou come, and ete with me      *with me."*
To-day, þou, and þi fayre wif,
þat þou louest also þi lif.
And haue þou of hire no drede,      1664
Shal hire no man shame bede.
Bi þe fey that y owe to þe,
þerof shal i me serf-borw be."

Hauelok herde þat he bad,      1668
  And thow was he ful sore drad,
With him to ete, for hise wif ;      *[Fol. 212, col. 2.]*

         [1] MS. shoren.

| | | |
|---|---|---|
| Havelok fears ill may come of it. | For him wore leuere þat his lif<br>Him wore reft, þan she in blame<br>Felle, or lauthe ani shame.<br>Hwanne he hauede his wille wat,[1]<br>þe stede, þat he onne sat, | 1672 |
| But Ubbe rides away, saying, | Smot ubbe with spures faste,<br>And forth awey, but at þe laste,<br>Or he fro him ferde,<br>Seyde he, þat his folk herde: | 1676 |
| "Mind that you come." | "Loke þat ye comen beþe,<br>For ich it wile, and ich it rede." | 1680 |
| Havelok dares not refuse. | Hauelok ne durste, þe he were adrad,<br>Nouth with-sitten þat ubbe bad;<br>His wif he dide with him lede,<br>Vn-to þe heye curt he y[e]de.[2] | 1684 |
| Robert the Red leads Goldborough. | Roberd hire ledde, þat was red,<br>Þat hau[ed]e þarned for hire þe ded<br>Or ani hauede hire misseyd,<br>Or hand with iuele onne leyd. | 1688 |
| William Wendut is on the other side of her. | Willam wendut was þat oþer<br>Þat hire ledde, roberdes broþer,<br>Þat was with at alle nedes:<br>Wel is him þat god man fedes!<br>Þan he weren comen to þe halle,<br>Biforen ubbe, and hise men alle, | 1692 |
| Ubbe starts up to welcome them. | Vbbe stirte hem ageyn,<br>And mani a knith, and mani a sweyn,<br>Hem for to se, and forto shewe;<br>Þo stod hauelok als a lowe | 1696 |
| Havelok is a head taller than any of them. | Aboven [þo] þat þer-inne wore,<br>Rith al bi þe heued more<br>Þanne ani þat þer-inne stod:<br>Þo was ubbe bliþe of mod,<br>Þat he saw him so fayr and hende, | 1700<br><br>1704 |

[1] MS. *either* þat *or* pat.  [2] MS. yde.

## UBBE SENDS HAVELOK TO BERNARD.

Fro him ne mithe his herte wende,
Ne fro him, ne fro his wif;
He louede hem sone so his lif.
Weren non in denemark, þat him þouthe,    1708   Ubbe loves Havelok better than any one else.
þat he so mikel loue mouthe;
More he louede hauelok one,
þan al denemark, bi mine wone!
Loke nou, hw god helpen kan    1712
O mani wise wif and man.

Hwan it was comen time to ete,
    Hise wif dede ubbe sone in fete,    [Fol. 212 b, col. 1.]
And til hire seyde, al on gamen:    1716
"Dame, þou and hauelok shulen ete samen,    Ubbe's wife is to eat with Havelok, and Goldeborough with Ubbe.
And goldeboru shal ete wit me,
þat is so fayr so flour on tre;
In al denemark nis¹ wimman    1720
So fayr so sche, bi seint iohan!"
þanne [he] were set, and bord leyd,
And þe beneysun was seyd,
Biforn hem com þe beste mete    1724   There were cranes, swans, venison, fish, and wines.
þat king or cayser wolde ete;
Kranes, swannes, ueneysun,
Lax, lampreys, and god sturgun,
Pyment to drinke, and god clare,    1728
Win hwit and red, ful god plente.
Was þer-inne no page so lite,
þat euere wolde ale bite.
Of þe mete forto tel,    1732
Ne of þe metes² bidde i nout dwelle;    No need to tell it all.
þat is þe storie for to lenge,
It wolde anuye þis fayre genge.
But hwan he haueden þe kiwing³ deled,    1736   When the feast is over,
And fele siþes haueden wosseyled,
And with gode drinkes seten longe,

---

¹ MS. is.    ² Qu. win.    ³ Uncertain in MS. See note.

And it was time for to gonge,
Il man to þer he cam fro,   1740
þouthe ubbe, "yf I late hem go,
þus one foure, with-uten mo,
So mote ich brouke finger or to,
For þis wimman bes mike wo!   1744
For hire shal men hire louerd slo."
He tok sone knithes ten,
And wel sixti oþer men,
Wit gode bowes, and with gleiues,   1748
And sende him unto þe greyues,
þe beste man of al þe toun,
þat was named bernard brun;
And bad him, als he louede his lif,   1752
Hauelok wel y[e]men,[1] and his wif,
And wel do wayten al þe nith,
Til þe oþer day, þat it were lith.
Bernard was trewe, and swiþe with,   1756
In al þe borw ne was no knith
þat betere couþe on stede riden,
Helm on heued, ne swerd bi side.
Hauelok he gladlike under-stod,   1760
With mike loue, and herte god,
And dide greyþe a super riche,
Also he was no with chinche,
To his bihoue euer-il del,   1764
þat he mithe supe swiþe wel.

Also he seten, and sholde soupe,
So comes a ladde in a ioupe,
And with him sixti oþer stronge,   1768
With swerdes drawen, and kniues longe,
Ilkan in hande a ful god gleiue,
And seyde, "undo, bernard þe greyue!
Vndo swiþe, and latus[2] in,   1772

[1] MS. ymen.   [2] *Sic* in MS.

Or þu art ded, bi seint austin!"
Bernard stirt up, þat was ful big,     *Bernard starts up, arms himself,*
And caste a brinie up-on his rig,
And grop an ax,[1] þat was ful god,     1776
Lep to þe dore, so he wore wod,
And seyde, "hwat are ye, þat are þer-oute,
Þat þus biginnen forto stroute?
Goth henne swiþe, fule þeues,     1780 *and tells them to go away.*
For, bi þe louerd, þat man on leues,
Shol ich casten þe dore open,
Summe of you shal ich drepen!
And þe oþre shal ich kesten     1784
In feteres, and ful faste festen!"
"Hwat haue ye seid," quoth a ladde,     *They defy him.*
"Wenestu þat we ben adradde?
We sholc at þis dore gonge     1788
Maugre þin, carl, or outh longe."
He gripen sone a bulder ston,     *They break the door open with a boulder.*
And let it fleye, ful god won,
Agen þe dore, þat it to-rof:     1792
Auelok it saw, and þider drof,
And þe barre sone vt-drow,     *Havelok seizes the bar of the door, and says,*
Þat was unride, and gret ynow,
And caste þe dore open wide,     1796
And seide, "her shal y now abide:
Comes swiþe vn-to me![2]     *"Come here to me."*
Datheyt hwo you henne fle!"
"No," quodh on, "þat shaltou coupe,"     1800
And bigan til him to loupe,
In his hond is swerd ut-drawe,     *Three men attack Havelok.*
Hauelok he wende þore haue slawe;
And with [him] comen oþer two,     1804
Þat him wolde of liue haue do.     [Fol. 213, col. 1.]

[1] MS. ar; *but see* l. 1894.
[2] MS. vnto me datheit,—evidently the repetition of the first word in the succeeding line.

|            |                                              |      |
|------------|----------------------------------------------|------|
|            | Hauelok lifte up þe dore-tre,                |      |
| He kills them all. | And at a dint he slow he*m* þre ;      |      |
|            | Was non of hem þat his he*r*nes              | 1808 |
|            | Ne lay þer-ute ageyn þe sternes.             |      |
| A fourth he knocks down with a blow on the head. | Þe ferþe þat he siþen mette, |      |
|            | Wit þe barre so he him grette,               |      |
|            | Bifor þe heued, þat þe rith eye              | 1812 |
|            | Vt of þe hole made he fleye,                 |      |
|            | And siþe clapte him on þe crune,             |      |
|            | So þat he stan-ded fel þor dune.             |      |
| A fifth he hits between the shoulders. | Þe fifte þat he ouer-tok,        | 1816 |
|            | Gaf he a ful sor dint[e] ok,                 |      |
|            | Bitwen þe sholdres, þer he stod,             |      |
|            | Þat he spen his herte blod.                  |      |
| A sixth he smites on the neck. | Þe sixte wende fcr to fle,           | 1820 |
|            | And he clapte him with þe tre                |      |
|            | Rith in þe fule necke so,                    |      |
|            | Þat he smot hise necke on to.                |      |
|            | Þa*n*ne þe sixe weren doun feld,             | 1824 |
| A seventh aims at Havelok's eye. | Þe seuenþe brayd ut his swerd,     |      |
|            | And wolde hauelok Riht i*n* the eye ;        |      |
|            | And haue*lok* le[t þe] ¹ barre fleye,        |      |
| Havelok kills him. | And smot him sone ageyn þe brest,    | 1828 |
|            | Þat hauede he neue*r*e sch[r]ifte of p*r*est ; |    |
|            | For he was ded on lesse hwile,               |      |
|            | Þan me*n* mouthe re*n*ne a mile.             |      |
| The rest divide into two parties, | Alle þe oþere were*n* ful kene,   | 1832 |
|            | A red þei taken hem bi-twene,                |      |
|            | Þat he sholde him bi-halue,                  |      |
|            | And brise*n* so, þat wit no salue            |      |
|            | Ne sholde him helen leche non :              | 1836 |
|            | Þey drowen ut swerdes, ful god won,          |      |
| and rush at him like dogs at a bear. | And shoten on him, so don on bere |    |
|            | Dogges, þat wolden him to-tere,              |      |

¹ *Qu.* Hauelok let the.  MS. " haue le."

## THE THIEVES SHOOT AT HIM FROM A DISTANCE. 51

Þanne men doth þe bere beyte :                    1840
Þe laddes were kaske and teyte,
And vn-bi-yeden him ilkon,
Sum smot with tre, and sum wit ston ;
Summe putten with gleyue, in bac and side,        1844
And yeuen wundes longe and wide ;                 *They wound Havelok in twenty places.*
In twenti stedes, and wel mo,
Fro þe croune til the to.
Hwan he saw þat, he was wod,                      1848
And was it ferlik hw he stod,
For the blod ran of his sides                     [Fol. 213, col. 2.]
So water þat fro þe welle glide ;
But þanne bigan he for to mowe                    1852
With the barre, and let hem shewe,
Hw he cowþe sore smite,
For was þer non, long ne lite,                    *He at last succeeds in killing twenty of them.*
Þat he Mouthe ouer-take,                          1856
Þat he ne garte his croune krake ;
So þat on a litel stund,
Felde he twenti to þe grund.

Þo bigan gret dine to rise,                       1860
   For þe laddes on ilke wise
Him asayleden wit grete dintes,                   *They throw stones at him.*
Fro fer he stoden, him with flintes
And gleyues schoten him fro ferne,                1864
For drepen him he wolden yerne ;
But dursten he newhen him no more,
Þanne he bor or leun wore.

Huwe rauen þat dine herde,                        1868  *Hugh Raven hears the noise,*
   And þowthe wel, þat men mis-ferde
With his louerd, for his wif,
And grop an ore, and a long knif,
And þider drof al so an hert,                     1872
And cham þer on a litel stert,                    *and comes to help.*

And saw how þe laddes wode
Hauelok his louerd umbistode,
And beten on him so doth þe smith                1876
With þe hamer on þe stith.

"Allas!" hwat hwe, "þat y was boren!
þat euere et ich bred of koren!
þat ich here þis sorwe se!                       1880

*Hugh calls out to Roberd! willam! hware ar ye?
Robert and
William.*
Gripeth eþer unker a god tre,
And late we nouth þise doges fle,
Til ure louerd wreke [we] ;                      1884
Cometh swiþe, and folwes me!
Ich haue in honde a ful god ore :
Datheit wo ne smite sore !"

*Robert comes to* "Ya! leue, ya!" quod roberd sone,     1888
*the rescue,* "We hauen ful god lith of þe mone."
Roberd grop a staf, strong and gret,
þat mouthe ful wel bere a net,

*and William too,* And willam wendut grop a tre         1892
*and Bernard.* Mikel grettere þan his þe,[1]
And bernard held his ax ful faste ;

[Fol. 213 b, col. 1.] I seye, was he nouth þe laste ;
And lopen forth so he weren wode                 1896
To þe laddes, þer he stode,
And yaf hem wundes swiþe grete ;

*They fight with* þer mithe men wel se boyes bete,
*the thieves.*
And ribbes in here sides breke,                  1900
And hauelok on hem wel wreke.
He broken armes, he broken knes,
He broken shankes, he broken thes.
He dide þe blode þere renne dune                 1904
To þe fet rith fro the crune,

*No head was* For was þer spared heued non :
*spared.* He leyden on heuedes, ful god won,

---

[1] MS. þre, *the* r *being caught from the word above.* Cf. l. 1903.

## ALL THE SIXTY THIEVES ARE SLAIN.

And made croune[s] breke and crake,     1908
Of þe broune, and of þe blake;
He maden here backes al so bloute     *He made their backs as soft as their bellies.*
Als h[er]e¹ wombes, and made hem rowte
Als he weren kradelbarnes:     1912
So dos þe child þat moder þarnes.

Daþeit wo² recke! for he it seruede,
   Hwat dide he þore weren he werewed;
So longe haueden he but and bet     1916
With neues under hernes set,
Þat of þo sixti men and on     *All sixty assailants are slain.*
Ne wente þer awey liues non.

On þe morwen, hwan³ it was day,     1920   *At morn, there they lay like dogs.*
   Ilc on other wirwed lay,
Als it were dogges þat weren henged,
And summe leye in dikes slenget,
And summe in gripes bi þe her     1924
Drawen ware, and laten ther.
Sket cam tiding intil ubbe,
Þat hauelok hauede with a clubbe
Of hise slawen sixti and on     1928
Sergaunz, þe beste þat mithen gon.
"Deus!" quoth ubbe, "hwat may þis be!     *Ubbe comes to see what is the matter.*
Betere his i nime⁴ miself and se,
Þat þis baret on hwat is wold,     1932
Þanne i sende yunge or old.
For yif i sende him un-to,
I wene men sholde him shame do,
And þat ne wolde ich for no þing:     1936

¹ *Qu.* here. MS. he.
² MS. "pe," clearly miswritten for "po" or "wo." See ll. 2047, 296, 300, &c.
³ MS. "hhan," miswritten for "hpan," from which it differs very slightly.
⁴ MS. inime.

## 54 UBBE ASKS BERNARD WHAT HAS HAPPENED.

        I loue him wel, bi heuene king!
        Me wore leuere i wore lame,
        þanne men dide him ani shame,
[Fol. 213 b, col. 2.]   Or tok, or onne handes leyde,            1940
        Vn-ornelike,[1] or same seyde."
        He lep up on a stede lith,
        And with him mani a noble knith,
        And ferde forth un-to þe tun,            1944
*He calls for Bernard Brown.*   And dide calle bernard brun
        Vt of his hus, wan he þer cam;
        And bernard sone ageyn [him] nam,
        Al to-tused and al to-torn,             1948
        Ner also naked so he was born,
        And al to-brised, bac and þe:
*Ubbe asks who has beaten him about so?*   Quoth ubbe, "bernard, hwat is þe?
        Hwo haues þe þus ille maked,        1952
        þus to-riuen, and al mad naked?"

        "Louerd,[2] merci," quot he sone,
        "To-nicht also ros þe mone
*"Sixty thieves attacked me last night.*   Comen her mo þan sixti þeues,       1956
        With lokene copes, and wide sleues,
        Me forto robben, and to pine,
        And for to drepe me and mine.
        Mi dore he broken up ful sket,        1960
        And wolde me binden hond and fet.
        Wan þe godemen þat sawe,
*Havelok and his friends drove them off.*   Hauelok, and he þat bi þe wowe
        Leye, he stirten up sone on-on,       1964
        And summe grop tre, and sum grop ston,
        And driue hem ut, þei he weren crus,
        So dogges ut of milne-hous.
        Hauelok grop þe dore-tre,           1968
        And [at] a dint he slow hem thre.

---

[1] MS. Vn ornelſke; *but ſ should certainly be* i.
[2] MS. Iouerd.

He is þe beste man at nede,
Þat euere mar shal ride stede!
Als helpe god, bi mine wone, 1972
A þhousend of men his he worth one! *He is worth a thousand men.*
Yif he ne were, ich were nou ded,
So haue ich don Mi soule red;
But it is hof him mikel sinne; 1976
He maden him swilke woundes þrinne,
Þat of þe alþer-leste wounde
Were a stede brouht to grunde.
He haues a wunde in the side, 1980 *He has some bad wounds, more than twenty.*
With a gleyue, ful un-ride,
And he haues on þoru his arum,
Þer-of is ful mikel harum,
And he haues on þoru his þhe, 1984 [Fol. 214, col. 1.]
Þe vn-rideste þat men may se,
And oþe[r] wundes haues he stronge,
Mo than twenti swiþe longe.
But siþen he hauede lauth þe sor 1988
Of þe wundes, was neuere bor
Þat so fauth so he fauth þanne;
Was non þat hauede þe hern-panne
So hard, þat he ne dede alto-cruhsse, 1992
And alto-shiuere, and alto-frusshe.
He folwede hem so hund dos hare, *He followed them like a dog does a hare.*
Daþeyt on he wolde spare,
Þat [he] ne made hem euerilk on 1996
Ligge stille so doth þe ston:
And þer nis he nouth to frie,
For oþer sholde he make hem lye
Ded, or þei him hauede slawen, 2000
Or alto-hewen, or al-to-drawen.


Louerd, haui no more plith
Of þat ich was þus greþed to-nith.
Þus wolde þe theues me haue reft, 2004

## THE OTHERS CONFIRM BERNARD'S STORY.

*But I fear Havelok is all but dead."*

But god-þank, he hauenet sure keft.
But it is of him mikel scaþe :
I woth þat he bes ded ful raþe."

Quoth ubbe, "bernard, seyst þou soth ?" 2008
" Ya, sire, that i ne¹ lepe oth.
Yif y, louerd, a word leye,
To-morwen do me hengen heye."

*The rest confirm Bernard's story.*

Þe burgeys þat þer-bi stode þore, 2012
Grundlike and grete oþes swore,
Litle and mikle, yunge and holde,
Þat was soth, þat bernard tolde.
Soth was, þat he wolden him bynde, 2016
And trusse al þat he mithen fynde
Of hise, in arke or in kiste,
Þat he mouthe in seckes þriste.

*"The thieves wanted to steal all he had.*

"Louerd, he haueden al awey born 2020
His þing, and him-self alto-torn,
But als god self barw him wel,
Þat he ne tinte no catel.
Hwo mithe so mani stonde ageyn, 2024
Bi nither-tale, knith or swein ?
He weren bi tale sixti and ten,
Starke laddes, stalworþi men,

*They were led on by one G[r]iffin Gall."*

And on, þe mayster of hem alle, 2028
Þat was þe name giffin² galle.

*[Fol. 214, col. 2.]*

Hwo mouthe agey[n]³ so mani stonde,
But als þis man of ferne londe
Haueth hem slawen with a tre ? 2032
Mikel ioie haue he !
God yeue him mikel god to welde,
Boþe in tun, and ek in felde !
We[l]⁴ is set he etes mete." 2036

*Ubbe sends for Havelok,*

Quoth ubbe, "doth him swiþe fete,

---

¹ MS. ine.   ² *Qu.* gritfin.   ³ MS. agey.
⁴ Cf. ll. 772, 907.

þat y mouthe his woundes se,
Yf that he mouthen heled¹ be.
For yf he mouthe couere yet,                           2040
And gangen wel up-on hise fet,
Mi-self shal dubbe him to knith,              *to dub him knight.*
For-þi þat he is so with.
And yif he liuede, þo foule theues,           2044
Þat weren of kaym kin and eues,
He sholden hange bi þe necke;
Of here ded daþeit wo recke,
Hwan he yeden þus on nithes                   2048
To binde boþe burgmen and knithes.
For bynderes loue ich neuere mo,
Of hem ne yeue ich nouht a slo."

Hauelok was bifore ubbe browth,               2052  *Havelok is brought before Ubbe.*
  Þat hauede for him ful mikel þouth,
And mikel sorwe in his herte
For hise wundes, þat we[r] so smerte.

But hwan his wundes weren shewed,             2056
  And a leche hauede knawed,                        *A leech says he can be healed.*
Þat he hem mouthe ful wel hele,
Wel make him gange, and ful wel mele,
And wel a palefrey bistride,                  2060
And wel up-on a stede ride,
Þo let ubbe al his care
And al his sorwe ouer-fare;
And seyde, "cum now forth with me,            2064  *Ubbe invites him and Goldborough to his own castle.*
And goldeboru, þi wif, with þe,
And þine seriaunz al þre,
For nou wile y youre warant be;
Wile y non of here frend                      2068
Þat þu slowe with þin hend
Moucte wayte þe [to] slo,

¹ MS. holed. See l. 2058.

[Fol. 214 b, col. 1.]

*He promises to protect Goldborough.*

Also þou gange to and fro.
I shal lene þe a bowr, 2072
þat is up in þe heye tour,
Til þou mowe ful wel go,
And wel ben hol of al þi wo.
It ne shal no þing ben bitwene 2076
þi bour and min, also y wene,
But a fayr firrene wowe ;—
Speke y loude, or spek y lowe,
þou shalt[1] ful wel heren me, 2080
And þan þu wilt, þou shalt me se.
A rof shal hile us boþe o-nith,
þat none of mine, clerk ne knith,
Ne sholen þi wif no shame bede, 2084
No more þan min, so god me rede !"

*The first night, about midnight,*

*Ubbe wakes and sees a great light.*

HE dide un-to þe borw bringe
Sone anon, al with ioynge,
His wif, and his serganz þre, 2088
þe beste men þat mouthe be.
þe firste nith he lay þer-inne,
Hise wif, and his serganz þrinne,
Aboute þe middel of þe nith 2092
Wok ubbe, and saw a mikel lith
In þe bour þat hauelok lay,
Also brith so it were day.

*Ubbe says he must go and see what it means.*

"Deus !" quoth ubbe, " hwat may þis be ? 2096
Betere is i go miself, and se :
Hweþer he sitten nou, and wesseylen,
Or of ani shotshipe to-deyle,
þis tid nithes, also foles ; 2100
þan birþe men casten hem in poles,
Or in a grip, or in þe fen :

---

[1] MS. sahalt; *and the second* a *is expuncted by mistake, instead of the first.*

Nou ne sitten none but wicke men,
Glotuns, reu[e]res, or wicke þeues,    2104
Bi crist, þat alle folk onne leues!"

He stod, and totede in at a bord,    *He peeps in, and sees them all asleep.*
Her he spak anilepi word,
And saw hem slepen faste ilkon,    2108
And lye stille so þe ston;
And saw al þat mikel lith
Fro hauelok cam, þat was so brith.
Of his mouth it com il del,    2112   *The light issues from Havelok's mouth.*
Þat was he war ful swiþe wel.
"Deus!" quoth he, "hwat may þis mene!"
He calde boþe arwe men and kene,
Knithes, and serganz swiþe sleie,    2116
Mo þan an hundred, with-uten leye,
And bad hem alle comen and se,
Hwat þat selcuth mithe be.

Als þe knithes were comen alle,    2120   [Fol. 214 b, col. 2.]
Þer hauelok lay, ut of þe halle,
So stod ut of his mouth a glem,
Rith al swilk so þe sunne-bem;
Þat al so lith wa[s] þare, bi heuene!    2124   *The light is like that of 107 candles.*
So þer brenden serges seuene,
And an hundred serges ok:
Þat durste hi sweren on a bok.
He slepen faste alle fiue,    2128
So he weren brouth of liue;
And hauelok lay on his lift side,    *Havelok and Goldborough are fast asleep.*
In his armes his brithe bride.
Bi þe pappes he leyen naked:    2132
So faire two weren neuere maked
In a bed to lyen samen:—
Þe knithes þouth of hem god gamen,
Hem forto shewe, and loken to.    2136

    Rith also he stoden alle so,
And his bac was toward hem wend,
So weren he war of a croiz ful gent,
On his rith shuldre sw[iþ]e¹ brith,     2140
Brithter þan gold ageyn þe lith.
So þat he wiste heye and lowe,
Þat it was kunrik þat he sawe.
It sparkede, and ful brith shon,     2144
So doth þe gode charbucle ston,
Þat men Mouthe se by þe lith,
A peni chesen, so was it brith.
Þanne bihelden he him faste,     2148
So þat he knewen at þe laste,
Þat he was birkabeynes sone,
Þat was here king, þat was hem wone
Wel to yeme, and wel were     2152
Ageynes uten-laddes here.
"For it was neuere yet a broþer
In al denemark so lich anoþer,
So þis man þat is so fayr     2156
Als birkabeyn, he is hise eyr."

He fellen sone at hise fet,
    Was non of hem þat he ne gret,
Of ioie he weren alle so fawen,     2160
So he him haueden of erþe drawen.
Hise fet he kisten an hundred syþes,
Þe tos, þe nayles, and þe lithes,
So þat he bigan to wakne,²     2164
And wit hem ful sore to blakne,
For he wende he wolden him slo,
Or elles binde him, and do wo.

Quoth ubbe, "louerd, ne dred þe nowth,     2168
    Me þinkes that I se þi þouth.

¹ MS. swe, *for* swiþe. Cf. l. 1252.
² Here follows the catchword—"And wit hem."

Dere sone, wel is me, — Ubbe offers homage to him,
þat y þe with eyn[e]¹ se.
Man-red, louerd, bede y þe, — 2172
þi man auht i ful wel to be,
For þu art comen of birkabeyn,
þat hauede mani knith and sweyn;
And so shalt þou, louerd, haue, — 2176
þou þu be yet a ful yung knaue.
þou shalt be king of al denemark, — and says he shall be king of Denmark.
Was þer-inne neuere non so stark.
To-morwen shaltu manrede take — 2180
Of þe brune and of þe blake;
Of alle þat aren in þis tun,
Boþe of erl, and of barun,
And of dreng, and of thayn, — 2184
And of knith, and of sweyn.
And so shaltu ben mad knith
Wit blisse, for þou art so with."

Þo was hauelok swiþe bliþe, — 2188 Havelok is blithe, and thanks God.
And þankede God ful fele siþe.
On þe morwen, wan it was lith,
And gon was þisternesse of þe nith,
Vbbe dide up-on a stede — 2192
A ladde lepe, and þider bede
Erles, barouns, drenges, theynes, — Ubbe summons all his lords.
Klerkes, knithes, bu[r]geys,² sweynes,
þat he sholden comen a-non, — 2196
Biforen him sone euerilkon,
Also he louen here liues,
And here children, and here wiues.

Hise bode ne durste he non at-sitte, — 2200 All come to receive his orders.
þat he ne neme³ for to wite

¹ We find *eyne* in ll. 680. 1273, &c.  ² MS. bugeyf.
³ MS. meme; *miswritten for* neme; *see* ll. 1207, 1931.

|   | UBBE RELATES HAVELOK'S HISTORY. |   |
|---|---|---|
|   | Sone, hwat wolde þe iustise: |   |
|   | And [he] bigan anon to rise, |   |
|   | And seyde sone, "liþes me, | 2204 |
|   | Alle samen, þeu and fre. |   |
|   | A þing ich wile you here shauwe, |   |
|   | Þat ye¹ alle ful wel knawe. |   |
| Ubbe tells them about Birkabeyn, | Ye witen wel, þat al þis lond | 2208 |
|   | Was in birkabeynes hond, |   |
| [Fol. 215, col. 2.] | Þe day þat he was quic and ded; |   |
|   | And how þat he, bi youre red, |   |
| who commended his children to Godard; | Bitauhte hise children þre | 2212 |
|   | Godard to yeme, and al his fe. |   |
|   | Hauelok his sone he him tauhte, |   |
|   | And hise two douhtres, and al his auhte, |   |
|   | Alle herden ye him swere | 2216 |
|   | On bok, and on messe-gere, |   |
|   | Þat he shulde yeme hem wel, |   |
|   | With-uten lac, with-uten tel. |   |

| and how Godard slew the two girls, | He let his oth al ouer-go, | 2220 |
|---|---|---|
|   | Euere wurþe him yuel and wo! |   |
|   | For² þe maydnes here lif |   |
|   | Refte he boþen, with a knif, |   |
|   | And him shulde ok haue slawen, | 2224 |
|   | Þe knif was at his herte drawen, |   |
| but had pity on the boy; | But god him wolde wel haue sauc, |   |
|   | He hauede reunesse of þe knaue, |   |
|   | So þat he with his hend | 2228 |
|   | Ne drop him nouth, þat sor[i] fend, |   |
| but afterwards ordered Grim to drown him. | But sone dide he a fishere |   |
|   | Swiþe grete oþes swere, |   |
|   | Þat he sholde drenchen him | 2232 |
|   | In þe se, þat was ful brim. |   |

| But Grim fled with him to England. | Hwan grim saw þat he was so fayr, |   |
|---|---|---|
|   | And wiste he was þe Rith eir, |   |

¹ MS. he.   ² Qu. Fro.

Fro denemark ful sone he fledde 2236
In-til englond, and þer him fedde
Mani winter, þat til þis day
Haues he ben fed and fostred ay.
Lokes, hware he stondes her: 2240 *Then Ubbe shows Havelok to them all,*
In al þis werd ne haues he per;
Non so fayr, ne non so long,
Ne non so mikel, ne non so strong.
In þis middelerd nis no knith 2244
Half so strong, ne half so with.
Bes of him ful glad and bliþe,
And cometh alle hider swiþe,
Manrede youre louerd forto make, 2248 *and bids them swear fealty to him.*
Boþe brune and þe blake.
I shal mi-self do first þe gamen,
And ye siþen alle samen."

Oknes ful fayre he him sette, 2252 *Ubbe swears fealty first.*
Mouthe noþing him þer-fro lette,
And bi-cam is man Rith þare,
þat alle sawen þat þere ware. [Fol. 215 *b*, col. 1.]

After him stirt up laddes ten, 2256 *All the rest do the same.*
And bi-comen hise men;[1]
And siþen euerilk a baroun,
þat euere weren in al that toun;
And siþen drenges, and siþen thaynes, 2260
And siþen knithes, and siþen sweynes;
So þat, or þat day was gon,
In al þe tun ne was nouth on
þat it ne was his man bicomen: 2264
Manrede of alle hauede he nomen.

Hwan he hauede of hem alle *Havelok makes them swear to be*
Manrede taken, in the halle,

---

[1] A word is added in the MS. after *men*, apparently *beye*. Perhaps we should read: *hise heye men.*

| | | |
|---|---|---|
| faithful to him always. | Grundlike dide he hem swere, | 2268 |
| | þat he sholden him god feyth bere | |
| | Ageynes alle þat woren on liue; | |
| | þer-yen ne wolde neuer on striue, | |
| | Þat he ne maden sone þat oth, | 2272 |
| | Riche and poure, lef and loth. | |
| | Hwan þat was maked, sone he sende, | |
| Ubbe sends for all the sheriffs and constables. | Vbbe, writes fer and hende, | |
| | After alle þat castel yemede, | 2276 |
| | Burwes, tunes, sibbe an fremde, | |
| | Þat þider sholden comen swiþe | |
| | Til him, and heren tiþandes bliþe, | |
| | Þat he hem alle shulde telle: | 2280 |
| | Of hem ne wolde neuere on dwelle, | |
| | Þat he ne come sone plattinde, | |
| | Hwo hors ne hauede, com gangande. | |
| | So þat with-inne a fourtenith, | 2284 |
| | In al denemark ne was no knith, | |
| | Ne conestable, ne shireue, | |
| | Þat com of adam and of eue, | |
| They all come. | Þat he ne com biforn sire ubbe: | 2288 |
| | He dredden him so þhes[1] doth clubbe. | |

Hwan he haueden alle þe king gret,
And he weren alle dun set,

Ubbe shows Havelok to them all.
Þo seyde ubbe, " lokes here,        2292
Vre louerd swiþe dere,
Þat shal ben king of al þe lond,
And haue us alle under hond.
For he is birkabeynes sone,          2296
Þe king þat was vmbe stonde wone
For to yeme, and wel were,
Wit sharp[e][2] swerd, and longe spere.

[1] Qu. þes, i. e. thighs; or the spelling þhes may be intentional; see l. 1984. But Sir F. Madden suggests þeues.
[2] See l. 2645 for the final e.

Lokes nou, hw he is fayr;　　2300
Sikerlike he is hise eyr.
Falles alle to hise fet,
Bicomes hise men ful sket."
He weren for ubbe swiþe adrad,　　2304   *All swear to obey Havelok.*
And dide sone al þat he bad,
And yet deden he sumdel more,
O bok ful grundlike he swore,
þat he sholde with him halde　　2308
Boþe ageynes stille and bolde,
þat euere wo[l]de his bodi dere :
þat dide [he] hem o boke swere.

Hwan he hauede manrede and oth　　2312
Taken of lef and of loth,
Vbbe dubbede him to knith,　　  *Ubbe dubs Havelok a knight,*
With a swerd ful swiþe brith,
And þe folk of al þe lond　　2316
Bitauhte him al in his hond,
þe cunnriche eueril del,
And made him king heylike and wel.　　  *and makes him king.*
Hwan he was king, þer mouthe men se　　2320
þe moste ioie þat mouhte be :
Buttinge with sharpe speres,　　  *Great joy and many sports.*
Skirming with taleuaces, þat men beres,
Wrastling with laddes, putting of ston,　　2324
Harping and piping, ful god won,
Leyk of mine, of hasard ok,
Romanz reding on þe bok ;
þer mouthe men here þe gestes singe,　　2328
þe gleymen on þe tabour dinge ;
þer mouhte men se þe boles beyte,　　  *There is baiting of bulls and boars,*
And þe bores, with hundes teyte ;
þo mouthe men se eueril gleu,　　2332
þer mouthe men se hw grim greu ;
Was neuere yete ioie more

## HAVELOK IS MADE KING OF DENMARK.

In al þis werd, þan þo was þore.
þer was so mike¹ yeft of cloþes,     2336
þat þou i swore you grete othes,
I ne wore nouth þer-offe croud :
þat may i ful wel swere, bi god !

*and plenty of meat and wine.*

þere was swiþe gode metes,     2340
And of wyn, þat men fer fetes,
Rith al so mik and gret plente,
So it were water of þe se.
þe feste fourti dawes sat,     2344

[Fol. 216, col. 1.] So riche was neuere non so þat.

*The king makes Robert, William, and Hugh all barons.*

þe king made Roberd þere knith,
þat was ful strong, and ful with,
And willam, wendut het, his broþer,     2348
And huwe rauen, þat was þat oþer,
And made hem barouns alle þr·
And yaf hem lond, and oþer fe,
So mikel, þat ilker twent[i] knihtes     2352
Hauede of genge, dayes and nithes.

Hwan þat feste was al don,

*A thousand knights accompany the king,*

A thusand knihtes ful wel o bon
With-held þe king, with him to lede ;     2356
þat ilkan hauede ful god stede,
Helm, and sheld, and brinie brith,
And al þe wepne þat fel to knith.

*and five thousand sergeants.*

With hem fiue thusand gode     2360
Sergaunz, þat weren to fyht wode,
With-held he al     genge :    *of his*
Wile I na more þe storie lenge.
Yet hwan he hauede of al þe lond     2364
þe casteles alle in his hond,
And conestables don þer-inne,

*He swears to be*    He swor, he ne sholde neuer blinne,

---

¹ See l. 2342.

Til þat he were of godard wreken, 2368 *avenged of Godard,*
þat ich haue of ofte speken.
Hal hundred knithes dede he calle,
And hise fif thusand sergaunz alle,
And dide sweren on the bok 2372
Sone, and on þe auter ok,
þat he ne sholde neuere blinne,
Ne for loue, ne for sinne,
Til þat he haueden godard funde, 2376 *and to find and bind him.*
And brouth biforn him faste bunde.

Þanne he haueden swor þis oþ,
Ne leten he nouth for lef ne loth,
þat he ne foren swiþe rathe, 2380
þer he was unto þe paþe, *He goes to meet Godard.*
þer he yet on huntin̄g for,
With mikel genge, and swiþe stor.
Robert, þat was of al þe ferd 2384
Mayster, was girt wit a swerd,
And sat up-on a ful god stede,
þat vnder him Rith wolde wede;
He was þe firste þat with godard 2388 *Robert accosts Godard,*
Spak, and seyde, "hede¹ cauenard!
Wat dos þu here at þis paþe? [Fol. 216, col. 2.]
Cum to þe king, swiþe and rape. *and tells him to come to the king,*
þat sendes he þe word, and bedes, 2392
þat þu þenke hwat þu him dedes,
Hwan þu reftes with a knif
Hise sistres here lif,
An siþen bede þu in þe se 2396
Drenchen him, þat herde he.
He is to þe swiþe grim:
Cum nu swiþe un-to him,
þat king is of þis kuneriche. 2400
þu fule man! þu wicke swike!

¹ Qu. helde, i. e. old. Unless it means "heed!"

| | | |
|---|---|---|
| *who will repay him.* | And he shal yelde þe þi mede, Bi crist þat wolde on rode blede!" | |
| *Godard and Robert strike each other.* | Hwan godard herde þat þer þrette, With þe neue he robert sette Biforn þe teth a dint ful strong. And robert kipt ut a knif long, And smot him þoru þe rith arum: Þer-of was ful litel harum. | 2404<br><br><br>2408 |
| | Hwan his folk þat sau and herde, Hwou robert with here louerd ferde, He haueden him wel ner browt of liue, Ne weren his two breþren and oþre fiue Slowen of here laddes ten, Of godardes alþer-beste men. | 2412 |
| *Godard's men flee,* | Hwan þe oþre sawen þat, he fledden, And godard swiþe loude gredde: "Mine knithes, hwat do ye? Sule ye þus-gate fro me fle? Ich haue you fed, and yet shal fede, Helpe me nu in þis nede, | 2416<br><br><br>2420 |
| *but Godard rallies them.* | And late ye nouth mi bodi spille, Ne hauelok don of me hise wille. Yif ye id¹ do, ye do you shame, And bringeth you-self in mikel blame." Hwan he þat herden, he wenten ageyn, And slowen a knit and² a sweyn Of þe kinges oune men, And woundeden abuten ten. | 2424<br><br><br>2428 |
| *The king's men kill all Godard's men.* | The kinges men hwan he þat sawe, Scuten on hem, heye and lowe, And euerilk fot of hem slowe, But godard one, þat he flowe, | 2432 |

¹ *Qu.* it.  ² MS. and and.

So þe þef men dos henge,
Or hund men shole in dike slenge. [Fol. 216 b, col. 1.]
He bunden him ful swiþe faste, 2436
Hwil þe bondes wolden laste,
þat he rorede als a bole,
þat he wore parred in an hole,
With dogges forto bite and beite : 2440
Were þe bondes nouth to leite.
He bounden him so ¹ fele sore, They bind Godard,
þat he gan crien godes ore,
þat he sholde of his hend plette, 2444
Wolden he nouht þer-fore lette,
þat he ne bounden hond and fet :
Daþeit þat on þat þer-fore let !
But dunten him so man doth bere, 2448
And keste him on a scabbed mere, and cast him on an old mare, to
Hise nese went un-to þe crice : take him to Havelok.
So ledden he þat fule swike,
Til he was biforn hauelok brouth, 2452
þat he haue[de] ful wo wrowht,
Boþe with hungre ² and with cold,
Or he were twel winter old,
And with mani heui swink, 2456
With poure mete, and feble drink,
And [with] swiþe wikke cloþes,
For al hise manie grete othes.
Nu beyes he his holde blame : 2460
'Old sinne makes newe shame :' "Old sin makes new shame."
Wan he was [brouht] so shamelike
Biforn ³ þe king, þe fule swike,
þe king dede ubbe swiþe calle 2464 The king summons Ubbe and the rest.
Hise erles, and hise barouns alle,
Dreng and thein, burgeis and knith,

¹ MS. fo.
² MS. hungred.
³ MS. Brouht biforn; *but the word* brouht *clearly belongs to the preceding line, in which, however, it is omitted.*

## HE IS CONDEMNED TO BE HUNG.

And bad he sholden demen him rith :
For he kneu, þe swike dam,     2468
Euerildel god was him gram.
He setten hem dun bi þe wawe,
Riche and pouere, heye and lowe,

*They sit in judgment.*

þe helde men, and ek þe grom,     2472
And made þer þe rithe dom,
And seyden unto þe king anon,
þat stille sat [al] so þe ston :

*"He is to be flayed, drawn, and hung."*

" We deme, þat he be al quic slawen,[1]     2476
And siþen to þe galwes drawe[n],
At þis foule mere tayl ;
þoru is fet a ful stronʒ nayl ;

*[Fol. 216 b, col. 2.]*

And þore ben henged wit two feteres,     2480
And þare be writen þise leteres :
' Þis is þe swike þat wende wel,
Þe king haue reft þe lond il del,
And hise sistres with a knif     2484
Boþe refte here lif.'
Þis writ shal henge bi him þare ;
Þe dom is demd, seye we na more."

*Godard is shriven.*

Hwan þe dom was demd and giue,     2488
  And he was wit þe prestes shriue,
And it ne mouhte ben non oþer,
Ne for fader, ne for broþer,
þat he sholde þarne lif ;     2492

*A lad flays him.*

Sket cam a ladde with a knif,
And bigan Rith at þe to
For to ritte, and for to flo,
And he bigan for to rore,     2496
So it were grim or gore,
þat men mithe þeþen a mile

*He roars.*

Here him rore, þat fule file.
Þe ladde ne let no with for-þi,     2500

[1] We should perhaps read *flawen*, as required by the sense. *See* ll. 2495, 2502.

þey he criede 'merci! merci!'
þat [he] ne flow [him] eueril del
With knif mad of grunden stel.
Þei garte bringe þe mere sone,   2504  He is bound on an old mare,
Skabbed [1] and ful iuele o bone,
And bunden him rith at hire tayl
With a rop of an old seyl,
And drowen him un-to þe galwes,  2508  drawn over rough ground,
Nouth bi þe gate, But ouer þe falwes;
And henge [him] þore Bi þe hals :   and hung.
Daþeit hwo recke! he was fals.

Þanne he was ded, þat sathanas,   2512
  Sket was seysed al þat his was
In þe kinges hand il del,
Lond and lith, and oþer catel,
And þe king ful sone it yaf    2516  Havelok makes Ubbe his steward.
Vbbe in þe hond, wit a fayr staf,
And seyde, "her ich sayse þe
In al þe lond, in al þe fe."
Þo swor hauelok he sholde make,   2520  He founds a priory of black monks for Grim's soul,
Al for grim, of monekes blake
A priorie to seruen inne ay
Ihesu crist, til domesday,
For þe god he haueden him don,   2524
Hwil he was pouere and iuel [2] o bon.   [Fol. 217, col. 1.]
And þer-of held he wel his oth,
For he it made, god it woth!
In þe tun þer grim was grauen,   2528  in the town of Grimsby.
Þat of grim yet haues þe name.
Of grim bidde ich na more spelle.[3]—
But wan godrich herde telle,   Godrich, earl of Cornwall,

[1] MS. Skabbeb.
[2] The MS. has "we," which the scribe several times writes instead of "wel." But "wel" is a manifest blunder, since "iuel" is meant. Cf. l. 2505.
[3] The author has here omitted to tell us that Havelok, at the desire of his wife, invades England. See the note.

## GODRICH RAISES AN ARMY AGAINST HAVELOK.

<table>
<tr><td></td><td>Of cornwayle þat was erl,</td><td>2532</td></tr>
<tr><td></td><td>(þat fule traytour, that mixed cherl!)</td><td></td></tr>
<tr><td></td><td>þat hauelok was king of denemark,</td><td></td></tr>
<tr><td></td><td>And ferde with him strong and stark,</td><td></td></tr>
<tr><td>hears that Havelok has invaded England.</td><td>Comen engelond with-inne,<br>Engelond al for to winne,</td><td>2536</td></tr>
<tr><td></td><td>And þat she, þat was so fayr,</td><td></td></tr>
<tr><td></td><td>Þat was of engelond rith eir,</td><td></td></tr>
<tr><td></td><td>Þat was comen up at grimesbi,</td><td>2540</td></tr>
<tr><td></td><td>He was ful sorful and sori,</td><td></td></tr>
<tr><td>He says he will slay Havelok and his wife.</td><td>And seyde, "Hwat shal me to raþe?<br>Goddoth! i shal do slou hem baþe.</td><td></td></tr>
<tr><td></td><td>I shal don hengen hem ful heye,</td><td>2544</td></tr>
<tr><td></td><td>So mote ich brouke mi Rith eie!</td><td></td></tr>
<tr><td></td><td>But yif he of mi lond[e][1] fle;</td><td></td></tr>
<tr><td></td><td>Hwat? wenden he to desherite me?"</td><td></td></tr>
<tr><td>He raises a great army.</td><td>He dide sone ferd ut bidde,</td><td>2548</td></tr>
<tr><td></td><td>Þat al þat euere mouhte o stede</td><td></td></tr>
<tr><td></td><td>Ride, or helm on heued bere,</td><td></td></tr>
<tr><td></td><td>Brini on bac, and sheld, and spere,</td><td></td></tr>
<tr><td></td><td>Or ani oþer wepne bere,</td><td>2552</td></tr>
<tr><td></td><td>Hand-ax, syþe, gisarm, or spere,</td><td></td></tr>
<tr><td></td><td>Or aunlaz,[2] and god long knif,</td><td></td></tr>
<tr><td></td><td>Þat als he louede leme or lif,</td><td></td></tr>
<tr><td></td><td>Þat þey sholden comen him to,</td><td>2556</td></tr>
<tr><td></td><td>With ful god wepne ye ber so,</td><td></td></tr>
<tr><td>The army is to meet at Lincoln on the 17th of March.</td><td>To lincolne, þer he lay,<br>Of marz þe seuentenþe day,</td><td></td></tr>
<tr><td></td><td>So þat he couþe hem god þank;</td><td>2560</td></tr>
<tr><td></td><td>And yif þat ani were so rang,</td><td></td></tr>
<tr><td></td><td>That he þanne ne come anon,</td><td></td></tr>
<tr><td></td><td>He swor bi crist, and [bi][3] seint Iohan,</td><td></td></tr>
</table>

[1] Cf. l. 2599.
[2] Printed "alinlaz" in the former edition. The first stroke of the *u* is longer than the second, and the tail of the *x* in the line above converts the second downstroke of the *u* into an apparent *i*.
[3] Cf. l. 1112.

That he sholde maken him þral, 2564
And al his of-spring forth with-al.

Þe englishe þat herde þat,
  Was non þat euere his bode sat,
For he him dredde swiþe sore, 2568
So Runci spore, and mikle more.
At þe day he come sone    [Fol. 217, col. 2.]
Þat he hem sette, ful wel o bone,
To lincolne, with gode stedes, 2572 *All come to Lincoln on that day.*
And al þe wepne þat knith ledes.
Hwan he wore come, sket was þe erl yare,[1]
Ageynes denshe men to fare,
And seyde, " lyþes me [2] alle samen, 2576
Haue ich gadred you for no gamen,
But ich wile seyen you forþi ;
Lokes hware here at grimesbi,   *Godrich tells them what*
Hise uten-laddes here comen, 2580 *Havelok is doing at Grimsby.*
And haues nu þe priorie numen ;
Al þat euere mithen he finde,
He brenne kirkes, and prestes binde ;
He strangleth monkes, and nunnes boþe : 2584
Wat wile ye, frend, her-offe Rede ?
Yif he regne þus-gate longe,
He Moun us alle ouer-gange,
He moun vs alle quic henge or slo, 2588
Or þral maken, and do ful wo,
Or elles reue us ure liues,
And ure children, and ure wiues.
But dos nu als ich wile you lere, 2592 *He excites them to attack Havelok.*
Als ye wile be with me dere ;
Nimes nu swiþe forth and raþe,
And helpes me and yu-self baþe,
And slos up-o[n] þe dogges swiþe : 2596
For shal [i] neuere more be bliþe,

---

[1] *Or* þare; but see l. 2954.   [2] MS. mi.  Cf. l. 2204.

|                          |                                                |      |
|--------------------------|------------------------------------------------|------|
|                          | Ne hoseled ben, ne of p*r*est shriuen,         |      |
|                          | Til þat he ben of londe driuen.                |      |
|                          | Nime we swiþe, and do hem fle,                 | 2600 |
|                          | And folwes alle faste me,                      |      |
| He will lead them himself. | For ich am he, of al þe ferd,                |      |
|                          | þat first shal slo with drawe*n* swerd.        |      |
|                          | Daþeyt hwo ne stonde faste                     | 2604 |
|                          | Bi me, hwil hise armes laste!"                 |      |
| Earl Gunter and Earl Reyner of Chester support him. | "Ye! lef, ye!"[1] couth þe erl gunter; |  |
|                          | "Ya!" quoth þe erl of cestre, reyner.          |      |
|                          | And so dide alle þat þer stode,                | 2608 |
|                          | And stirte forth so he were wode.              |      |
|                          | Þo mouthe me*n* se þe brinies brihte           |      |
|                          | On backes keste, and late rithe,               |      |
|                          | Þe helmes heye on heued sette;                 | 2612 |
|                          | To armes al so swiþe plette,                   |      |
|                          | Þat þei wore on a litel stunde                 |      |
| [Fol. 217 b, col. 1.]    | Grethet, als me*n* mithe telle a pund,         |      |
|                          | And lopen on stedes sone anon,                 | 2616 |
| They approach Grimsby.   | And toward g*r*imesbi, ful god won,            |      |
|                          | He foren softe bi þe sti,                      |      |
|                          | Til he come ney at grimesbi.                   |      |

| | | |
|--|--|--|
| Havelok meets them boldly, | Hauelok, þat hauede spired wel | 2620 |
| | Of here fare, eueril del, | |
| | With al his ferd cam hem a-geyn, | |
| | For-bar he noþer knith ne sweyn. | |
| and kills the foremost knight. | Þe firste knith þat he þer mette, | 2624 |
| | With þe swerd so he him grette, | |
| | For his heued of he plette, | |
| | Wolde he nouth for sinne lette. | |
| Robert kills a second. | Roberd saw þat dint so hende, | 2628 |
| | Wolde he neuere þeþe[n] wende, | |
| | Til þat he hauede anoþer slawen, | |
| | With þe swerd he held ut-drawen. | |

[1] MS. *has* þe, pe, *or* ye *in both places*. But see l. 1888.

| | | |
|---|---|---|
| Willam wendut his swerd vt-drow, | 2632 | William disables a third. |
| And þe þredde so sore he slow, | | |
| Þat he made up-on the feld | | |
| His lift arm fleye, with the swerd.[1] | | |

| | | |
|---|---|---|
| Huwe rauen ne forgat nouth | 2636 | Hugh Raven seizes his sword, |
|    Þe swerd he hauede þider brouth, | | |
| He kipte it up, and smot ful sore | | |
| An erl, þat he saw priken þore, | | |
| Ful noblelike upon a stede, | 2640 | |
| Þat with him wolde al quic wede. | | |
| He smot him on þe heued so, | | and cleaves an earl's head in two. |
| Þat he þe heued clef a-two, | | |
| And þat bi þe shu[l]dre-blade | 2644 | |
| Þe sharpe swerd let [he] wade, | | |
| Þorw the brest unto þe herte ; | | |
| Þe dint bigan ful sore to smerte, | | |
| Þat þe erl fel dun a-non, | 2648 | |
| Al so ded so ani ston. | | |
| Quoth ubbe, " nu dwelle ich to longe," | | Ubbe attacks Godrich. |
| And leth his stede sone gonge | | |
| To godrich, with a god spere, | 2652 | |
| Þat he saw a-noþer bere, | | |
| And smoth godrich, and Godrich him, | | |
| Hetelike with herte grim, | | |
| So þat he boþe felle dune, | 2656 | Both fall. |
| To þe erþe first þe croune. | | |
| Þanne he woren fallen dun boþen, | | |
| Grundlike here swerdes ut-drowen, | | |
| Þat weren swiþe sharp and gode, | 2660 | [Fol. 217 b, col. 2.] |
| And fouhten so þei woren wode, | | They fight on foot. |
| Þat þe swot ran fro þe crune | | |
| [To the fet rith þere adune.][2] | | |

---

[1] Cf. l. 1825. We should otherwise be tempted to read *sheld ;* especially as the *shield* is more appropriate to the *left* arm.
[2] Cf. l. 1904.

|  |  |  |
|---|---|---|
| | þer mouthe men se to knithes bete | 2664 |
| | Ayþer on oþer dintes grete, | |
| | So þat with alþer-lest[e] dint | |
| | Were al to-shiuered a flint. | |
| The fight lasts from morn to night. | So was bi-twenen hem a fiht, | 2668 |
| | Fro þe morwen ner to þe niht, | |
| | So þat þei nouth ne blinne, | |
| | Til þat to sette bigan þe sunne. | |
| Godrich wounds Ubbe sorely. | Þo yaf godrich þorw þe side | 2672 |
| | Vbbe a wunde ful un-ride, | |
| | So þat þorw þat ilke wounde | |
| | Hauede ben brouth to þe grunde, | |
| | And his heued al of-slawen, | 2676 |
| Hugh Raven rescues him. | Yif god ne were, and huwe rauen, | |
| | þat drow him fro godrich awey, | |
| | And barw him so þat ilke day. | |
| | But er he were fro godrich drawen, | 2680 |
| A thousand knights slain. | þer were a þousind knihtes slawen | |
| | Bi boþe halue, and mo y-nowe, | |
| | þer þe ferdes to-gidere slowe. | |
| | þer was swilk dreping of þe folk, | 2684 |
| The pools are full of blood. | þat on þe feld was neuere a polk | |
| | þat it ne stod of blod so ful, | |
| | þat þe strem ran intil þe hul. | |
| Godrich attacks the Danes like lightning. | Þo tarst¹ bigan godrich to go | 2688 |
| | Vp-on þe danshe, and faste to slo, | |
| | And forth rith also leuin fares, | |
| | þat neuere kines best ne spares, | |
| | þanne his [he] gon, for he garte alle | 2692 |
| | þe denshe men biforn him falle. | |
| | He felde browne, he felde blake, | |
| | þat he mouthe ouer-take. | |
| | Was neuere non þat mouhte þaue | 2696 |
| | Hise dintes, noyþer knith ne knaue, | |
| He mows them down like grass. | þat he felden so dos þe gres | |

¹ So in MS.  *Qu.* faste, as in next line.

## COMBAT BETWEEN GODRICH AND HAVELOK.

Bi-forn þe syþe þat ful sharp is.
Hwan hauelok saw his folk so brittene, 2700
And his ferd so swiþe littene,
He cam driuende up-on a stede,
And bigan til him to grede,
And seyde, " godrich, wat is þe 2704
þat þou fare þus with me?
And mine gode knihtes slos, [Fol. 21S, col. 1.]
Siker-like þou mis-gos.
þou wost ful wel, yif þu wilt wite, 2708 Havelok reproves Godrich,
þat aþelwold þe dide site
On knes, and sweren on messe-bok,
On caliz, and on [pateyn]¹ hok
þat þou hise douhter sholdest yelde, 2712
þan she were winnan² of elde,
Engelond eueril del:
Godrich þe erl, þou wost it wel.
Do nu wel with-uten fiht, 2716 and bids him perform his oaths.
Yeld hire þe lond, for þat is rith.
Wile ich forgiue þe þe lathe,
Al mi dede and al mi wrathe,
For y se þu art so with, 2720
And of þi bodi so god knith."
"þat ne wile ich neuere mo," Godrich refuses.
Quoth erl godrich, " for ich shal slo
þe, and hire for-henge heye. 2724
I shal þrist ut þi rith eye
þat þou lokes with on me,
But þu swiþe heþen fle."
He grop þe swerd ut sone anon, 2728
And hew on hauelok, ful god won,
So þat he clef his sheld on two: He cleaves Havelok's shield in two.
Hwan hauelok saw þat shame do

---

¹ MS. *here repeats* messe, *by mistake. Read* pateyn. Cf. l. 187.
² MS. wīman, *i.e.* winnan *or* wimman; *but we are sure, from* l. 174, *that* winnan *is meant.*

|   |   |   |
|---|---|---|
| | His bodi þer bi-forn his ferd, | 2732 |
| | He drow ut sone his gode swerd, | |
| Havelok smites him down. | And smot him so up-on þe crune, | |
| | þat godrich fel to þe erþe adune. | |
| | But godrich stirt up swiþe sket, | 2736 |
| | Lay he nowth longe at hise fet, | |
| Godrich rises, and wounds Havelok in the shoulder. | And smot him on þe sholdre so, | |
| | þat he dide þare undo | |
| | Of his brinie ringes mo, | 2740 |
| | þan þat ich kan tellen fro; | |
| | And woundede him rith in þe flesh, | |
| | þat tendre was, and swiþe nesh, | |
| | So þat þe blod ran til his to: | 2744 |
| Havelok is enraged, | þo was hauelok swiþe wo, | |
| | þat he hauede of him drawen | |
| | Blod, and so sore him slawen. | |
| | Hertelike til him he wente, | 2748 |
| and cuts off his foe's hand. | And godrich þer fulike shente; | |
| | For his swerd he hof up heye, | |
| [Fol. 218, col. 2.] | And þe hand he dide of fleye, | |
| | þat he smot him with so sore: | 2752 |
| | Hw mithe he don him shame more? | |
| | Hwan he hauede him so shamed, | |
| | His hand of plat, and yuele lamed, | |
| | He tok him sone bi þe necke | 2756 |
| | Als a traytour, daþeyt wo recke! | |
| He has him bound and fettered, | And dide him binde and fetere wel | |
| | With gode feteres al of stel, | |
| and sends him to the queen. | And to þe quen he sende him, | 2760 |
| | þat birde wel to him ben grim; | |
| | And Bad she sholde don him gete, | |
| | And þat non ne sholde him bete, | |
| | Ne shame do, for he was knith, | 2764 |
| | Til knithes haueden demd him Rith. | |
| When the English find out | þan þe englishe men þat sawe, | |

Þat þei wisten, heye and lawe,
Þat Goldeboru, þat was so fayr, 2768 that Goldborough is the heiress,
Was of engeland rith eyr,
And þat þe king hire hauede wedded,
And haueden ben samen bedded,
He comen alle to crie merci, 2772 they submit to Havelok.
Vnto þe king, at one cri,
And beden him sone manrede and oth,
Þat he ne sholden, for lef ne loth,
Neuere more ageyn him go, 2776
Ne ride, for wel ne for wo.

Þe king ne wolde nouth for-sake,
  Þat he ne shulde of hem take
Manrede þat he beden, and ok 2780
Hold oþes sweren on þe bok;
But or bad he, þat þider were brouth     Havelok wishes to show Gold-
Þe quen, for hem, swilk was his þouth,   borough to the
For to se, and forto shawe, 2784         English.
Yif þat he hire wolde knawe.
Þoruth hem witen wolde he,
Yif þat she aucte quen to be.

Sixe erles weren sone yare, 2788 Six earls fetch her in.
  After hire for to fare.
He nomen on-on, and comen sone,
And brouthen hire, þat under mone
In al þe werd ne hauede per, 2792
Of hende-leik, fer ne ner.
Hwan she was come þider, alle
Þe englishe men bi-gunne to falle
O knes, and greten swiþe sore, 2796 [Fol. 218 b, col. 1.]
And seyden, "leuedi, k[r]istes ore,
And youres! we hauen misdo mikel,       The English ask her pardon.
Þat we ayen you haue be fikel,
For englond auhte forto ben youres, 2800

## GODRICH IS CONDEMNED TO BE BURNT.

  And we youre men and youres.
  Is non of us, yung ne old,
  þat we ne wot, þat aþelwold
  Was king of þis kunerike,      2804

*They admit she is heiress.*
  And ye his eyr, and þat þe swike
  Haues it halden with mikel wronge :
  God leue him sone to honge !"

  Quot¹ hauelok, "hwan þat ye it wite.   2808

*Havelok says they must pass judgment on Godrich.*
  Nu wile ich þat ye doun site,
  And after godrich haues wrouht,
  þat haues in sorwe him-self brouth,
  Lokes þat ye demen him rith,      2812
  For dom ne spared ² clerk ne knith,
  And siþen shal ich under-stonde
  Of you, after lawe of londe,
  Manrede, and holde oþes boþe,     2816
  Yif ye it wilen, and ek rothe."
  Anon þer dune he hem sette,
  For non þe dom ne durste lette,

*They say he is to be bound on an ass's back,*
  And demden him to binden faste     2820
  Vp-on an asse swiþe un-wraste,
  Andelong, nouht ouer-þwert,
  His nose went unto þe stert ;

*taken to Lincoln,*
  And so to lincolne lede,       2824
  Shamelike in wicke wede,
  And hwan he cam un-to þe borw,
  Shamelike ben led þer-þoru,
  Bisouþe þe borw, un-to a grene,     2828
  þat þare is yet, als[o] y wene,

*bound to a stake, and burnt.*
  And þere be bunden til a stake,
  Abouten him ful gret fir make,
  And al to dust be brend Rith þere ;    2832
  And yet demden he þer more,
  Oþer swikes for to warne,

¹ MS. Guot. Cf. l. 1954.      ² *Qu.* spares.

## THE EARL OF CHESTER MARRIES GUNILD.

Þat hise children sulde þarne
Euere more þat eritage, 2836
Þat his was, for hise utrage.

Hwan þe dom was demd and seyd,
Sket was þe swike on þe asse leyd, *So he is laid on the ass,*
And [led vn-]til¹ þat ilke grene, 2840 *and burnt.*
And brend til asken al bidene. [Fol. 218 b, col. 2.]
Þo was Goldeboru ful bliþe,
She þanked god fele syþe,
Þat þe fule swike was brend, 2844
Þat wende wel hire bodi haue shend,
And seyde, "nu is time to take *Goldborough rejoices.*
Manrede of brune and of blake,
Þat ich se ride[n] and go: 2848
Nu ich am wreke[n]² of mi fo."

Hauelok anon manrede tok *Havelok makes the English swear fealty.*
Of alle englishe, on þe bok,
And dide hem grete oþes swere, 2852
Þat he sholden him god feyth bere
Ageyn alle þat woren liues,
And þat sholde ben born of wiues.

Þanne he hauede³ sikernesse 2856
Taken of more and of lesse,
Al at hise wille, so dide he calle
Þe erl of cestre, and hise men alle, *He proposes that Earl Reyner*
Þat was yung knith wit-uten wif, 2860 *of Chester*
And seyde, "sire erl, bi mi lif,
And þou wile mi conseyl tro,
Ful wel shal ich with þe do,
For ich shal yeue þe to wiue 2864
Þe fairest þing that is oliue.

---

¹ MS. "And him til," which is nonsense. See l. 2827.
² See l. 2992.    ³ MS. haueden.

| | | |
|---|---|---|
| shall marry Gunild, Grim's daughter; | Þat is gunnild of grimesby, | |
| | Grimes douther, bi seint dauy! | |
| | Þat me forth broute, and wel fedde, | 2868 |
| | And ut of denemark with me fledde, | |
| | Me for to burwe fro mi ded: | |
| | Sikerlike, þoru his red | |
| | Haue ich liued in-to þis day, | 2872 |
| | Blissed worþe his soule ay! | |
| | I rede þat þu hire take, | |
| | And spuse, and curteyse make, | |
| | For she is fayr, and she is fre, | 2876 |
| | And al so hende so she may be. | |
| | Þertekene she is wel with me, | |
| and he will then always be his friend. | Þat shal ich ful wel shewe þe, | |
| | For ich giue þe a giue, | 2880 |
| | Þat euere more hwil ich liue, | |
| | For hire shal-tu be with me dere, | |
| | Þat wile ich þat þis folc al here." | |
| | Þe erl ne wolde nouth ageyn | 2884 |
| | Þe king[e] be, for knith ne sweyn, | |
| [Fol. 219, col. 1.] | Ne of þe spusing seyen nay, | |
| | But spusede [hire] þat ilke day. | |
| | Þat spusinge was god time maked, | 2888 |
| They are married, | For it ne were neuere clad ne naked, | |
| | In a þede samened two | |
| | Þat cam to-gidere, liuede so, | |
| | So þey dide[n] al here liue: | 2892 |
| and have five sons. | He geten samen sones fiue, | |
| | Þat were þe beste men at nede, | |
| | Þat mouthe riden on ani stede. | |
| | Hwan gunnild was to cestre brouth, | 2896 |
| Havelok remembers Bertram, the earl's cook | Hauelok þe gode ne for-gat nouth | |
| | Bertram, þat was the erles kok, | |
| | Þat he ne dide callen ok, | |
| | And seyde, "frend, so god me rede! | 2900 |
| | Nu shaltu haue riche mede, | |

For wissing, and þi gode dede,
þat tu me dides in ful gret nede.
For þanne y yede in mi cuuel, 2904
And ich ne haue[de] bred, ne sowel,
Ne y ne hauede no catel,
þou feddes and claddes me ful wel.
Haue nu for-þi of cornwayle 2908 *and makes him Earl of Cornwall.*
þe erldom ildel, with-uten fayle,
And al þe lond þat godrich held,
Boþe in towne, and ek in feld ;
And þerto wile ich, þat þu spus , 2912
And fayre bring hire un-til hu ,
Grimes douther, leuiue þe hende, *He is to marry Levive, Grim's daughter,*
For þider shal she with þe wende.
Hire semes curteys forto be, 2916
For she is fayr so flour on tre ;
þe heu is swilk in hire ler
So [is] þe rose in roser, *who is as fair as a rose.*
Hwan it is fayr sprad ut newe 2920
Ageyn þe sunne, brith and lewe."
And girde him sone with þe swerd
Of þe erldom, bi-forn his ferd,
And with his hond he made him knith, 2924
And yaf him armes, for þat was rith,
And dide him þere sone wedde *They are married.*
Hire þat was ful swete in bedde.

After þat he spused wore, 2928
Wolde þe erl nouth dwelle þore,
But sone nam until his lond, *Havelok and Goldborough*
And seysed it al in his hond, *[Fol. 219, col. 2.]*
And liuede þer-inne, he and his wif, 2932 *lived 100 years, and had many children.*
An hundred winter in god lif,[1]

[1] Between this line and the next are inserted in the MS. the words : *For he saw þat he*, which have been subsequently struck out by the same hand, and the word *vacat* affixed.

And gaten mani children samen,
And lieueden ay in blisse and gamen.
Hwan þe maydens were spused boþe, 2936
Hauelok anon bigan ful rathe
His denshe men to feste wel
Wit riche landes and catel,
So þat he weren alle riche: 2940
For he was large and nouth chinche.

Þer-after sone, with his here,
  For he to lundone, forto bere
Corune, so þat [alle] it sawe, 2944
Henglishe ant denshe, heye and lowe,
Hwou he it bar with mikel pride,
For his barnage þat was un-ride.

Þe feste of his coruni[n]g[1] 2948
  Laste[de] with gret ioying
Fourti dawes, and sumdel mo;
Þo bigunnen þe denshe to go
Vn-to þe king, to aske leue, 2952
And he ne wolde hem nouth greue.
For he saw þat he woren yare
In-to denemark for to fare,
But gaf hem leue sone anon, 2956
And bitauhte hem seint Johan;
And bad ubbe, his iustise,
Þat he sholde on ilke wise
Denemark yeme and gete so, 2960
Þat no pleynte come him to.

Hwan he wore parted alle samen,
  Hauelok bi-lefte wit ioie and gamen

[1] MS. corunig.

In engelond, and was þer-inne | 2964 | England for sixty years.
Sixti winter king with winne,
And Goldeboru quen, þat I wene :
So mikel loue was hem bitwene,
Þat al þe werd spak of hem two : | 2968
He louede hire, and she him so,
Þat neyþer oþe[r] mithe be | | He and Gold-borough were never apart.
For [1] oþer, ne no ioie se,
But yf he were to-gidere [2] boþe ; | 2972
Neuere yete ne weren he wroþe,
For here loue was ay newe,
Neuere yete wordes ne grewe | | [Fol. 219 t, col. 1.]
Bitwene hem, hwar-of ne lathe | 2976
Mithe rise, ne no wrathe.

He geten children hem bi-twene | | They had 15 children, all kings and queens.
Sones and douthres rith fiuetene,
Hwar-of þe sones were kinges alle, | 2980
So wolde god it sholde bifalle ;
And þe douhtres alle quenes :
Him stondes wel þat god child strenes.
Nu haue ye herd þe gest al þoru | 2984 | Such is the *geste* of Havelok and Goldborough.
Of hauelok and of goldeborw.
Hw he weren born, and hw fedde,
And hwou he woren with wronge ledde
In here youþe, with trecherie, | 2988
With tresoun, and with felounye,
And hwou þe swikes haueden thit
Reuen hem þat was here rith,
And hwou he weren wreken wel, | 2992
Haue ich sey you euerildel ;
And forþi ich wolde biseken you,
Þat hauen herd þe rim[e] nu,
Þat ilke of you, with gode wille, | 2996 | Each of you say a

[1] *Qu.* Fro.  [2] MS. togidede.

## SAY A PATERNOSTER FOR THE AUTHOR.

*pater-noster for the author.*

Seye a pater-noster stille,
For him þat haueth þe rym[e] maked,
And þer-fore fele nihtes waked ;
Þat ihesu crist his soule bringe       3000
Bi-forn his fader at his endinge.

**Amen.**

# NOTES.

[The following notes are abridge ,rom the notes in Sir F. Madden's excellent edition, the abridgement being effected almost entirely by occasional omissions, and with but very slight unimportant changes of a few words, chiefly in the case of references to later editions of various works than were existing in 1828. I have added one or two short notes upon difficult constructions, but these are distinguished by being enclosed within square brackets.—W. W. S.]

9. *He was the wicteste man at nede*
*That thurte riden on ani stede.*

This appears to have been a favourite expression of the poet, and to have comprehended, in his idea, the perfection of those qualifications required in a knight and hero. He repeats it, with some slight variation, no less than five times, viz. in ll. 25, 87, 345, 1757, and 1970. The lines, however, are by no means original, but the common property of all our early poetical writers. We find them in Laȝamon :

> þis wes þe feiruste mon
> þe æuere æhte ær þusne kinedom,
> þa he mihte beren wepnen,
> & his hors wel awilden.
> *Laȝamon,* vol. i. p. 174.

So also in the Romance of *Guy of Warwick :*

> He was the best knight at neede
> That euer bestrode any stede.
> Coll. Garrick, K. 9. sign. Ll. ii.

Again, in the *Continuation of Sir Gy,* in the Auchinleck MS., (ed. for the Abbotsford Club, 1840, 4to ; p. 266),

> The best bodi he was at nede
> That ever might bistriden stede,
> And freest founde in fight.

And again, in the *Chronicle of England,* published by Ritson from a copy in the British Museum, MS. Reg. 12. C. xii.

After him his sone Arthur
Hevede this lond thourh and thourh.
He was the beste kyng at nede
That ever mihte ride on stede,
Other wepne welde, other folk out-lede,
Of mon ne hede he never drede.—l. 261.

The very close resemblance of these lines to those in Havelok, ll. 87—90, would induce a belief that the writer of the *Chronicle* had certainly read, and perhaps copied from, the Romance. The MS. followed by Ritson was undoubtedly written soon after the death of Piers Gaveston, in 1313, with the mention of which event it concludes; but in the Auchinleck copy it is continued, by a later hand, to the minority of Edward III. It only remains to be observed, that the poem in MS. Reg. 12. C. xii. is written by the same identical hand as the MS. Harl. 2253 (containing *Kyng Horn*, &c.), whence some additional light is thrown on the real age of the latter, respecting which our antiquaries so long differed.

[15. "And I will drink ere I tell my tale." *Her* = ere.

19. *And wite, &c.*, i.e. And ordain that it may be so; cf. ll. 517, 1316. Both metre and grammar require the final *e.*]

31. *Erl and barun*, dreng *and kayn*. The appellation of *Dreng*, and, in the plural, *Drenges*, which repeatedly occurs in the course of this poem, is uniformly bestowed on a class of men who hold a situation between the rank of *Baron* and *Thayn*. We meet with the term more than once in Doomsday Book, as, for instance, in Tit. Cestresc: "Hujus manerii [Neuton] aliam terram xv. hom. quos *Drenches* vocabant, pro xv. maneriis tenebant." And in a Charter of that period we read: "Alger Prior, et totus Conventus Ecclesiæ S. Cuthberti, Edwino, et omnibus Teignis et *Drengis*, &c." Hence Spelman infers, that the Drengs were military vassals, and held land by knight's service, which was called *Drengagium*. This is confirmed by a document from the Chartulary of Welbeck, printed in Dugdale, *Mon. Angl.* V. ii. p. 598, and in Blount, *Jocular Tenures*, p. 177, where it is stated, "In eadem villa [Cukeney, co. Nottingh.] manebat quidam homo qui vocabatur Gamelbere, et fuit vetus *Dreyinghe* ante Conquestum." It appears from the same document, that this person held two carucates of land of the King *in capite*, and was bound to perform military service for the same, whenever the army went into Wales. In the Epistle also from the Monks of Canterbury to Henry II. printed by Somner, in his Treatise on Gavelkind, p. 123, we find: "Quia vero non erant adhuc tempore Regis Willelmi Milites in Anglia, sed *Threnges*, præcepit Rex, ut de eis Milites fierent, ad terram defendendam." In Laȝamon's translation of Wace the term is frequently used in the acceptation of thayn, and spelt either *dringches, drenches, dranches,* or *dringes*. [Cf. Sw. *dräng*, a man, servant; Dan. *dreng*, a boy.] In the Isl. and Su. Goth. *Dreng* originally signified *vir fortis, miles strenuus*, and hence Olaf, King of Norway, received the epithet of *Goddreng*. See Wormii Lex. Run. p. 26. Ihre, Vet. Cat. Reg.

p. 109. Langebek, Script. Rer. Danic. V. I. p. 156. The term subsequently was applied to persons in a servile condition, and is so instanced by Spelman, as used in Denmark. In this latter sense it may be found in Hickes, Diction. Isl., and in Sir David Lyndsay's Poems,

> Quhilk is not ordanit for *dringis*
> But for Duikis, Empriouris, and Kingis.
> V. Pinkerton's Scotish Poems Reprinted, ii. 97.

V. Jamieson, Dict. *in voce.*

45. *In that time a man that bore*
*(Wel fyfty pund, y woth, or more.)*

This insertion receives additional authority from a similar passage in the Romance of *Guy of Warwick,* where it is mentioned as a proof of the rigorous system of justice pursued by Earl Sigard,

> Though a man bore an hundred pound,
> Upon him of gold so round,
> There n'as man in all this land
> That durst him do shame no schonde.
> Ellis, *Metr. Rom.* V. II. p. 9. Ed. 1811.

Many of the traits here attributed to Athelwold appear to be borrowed from the praises so universally bestowed by our ancient historians on the character of King Alfred, in whose time, as Otterbourne writes, p. 52, " armillas aureas in bivio stratas vel suspensas, nemo abripere est ausus." Cf. *Annal. Eccl. Roffens.* MS. Cott. Nero, D. II. The same anecdote is related of Rollo, Duke of Normandy, by Guillaume de Jumieges, and Dudon de Saint Quentin.

91. *Sprong forth so sparke of glede.* Cf. l. 870. It is a very common metaphor in early English poetry.

> He sprong forð an stede,
> swa sparc ded of fure.
> *Laʒamon,* v. ii. p. 565.

> He sprange als any sparke one glede.
> *Sir Isumbras,* st. 39 (Camd. Soc. 1844)

> He spronge as sparkle doth of glede.
> *K. of Tars,* l. 194.

> And lepte out of the arsoun,
> As sperk thogh out of glede.
> *Ly Beaus Desconus,* l. 623.

Cf. Chaucer, Cant. Tales, l. 13833, and Tyrwhitt's note.

110. *Of his bodi,* &c. Compare the French text, l. 208.

> Mes entre eus n'eurent enfant
> Mes qe vne fille bele ;
> Argentille out non la pucele.
> Rois Ekenbright fut enfermez,
> Et de grant mal forment greucz ;
> Bien siet n'en poet garrir.

[Here *Argentille* is *Goldborough*, and *Ekenbright* answers to *Athelwold*. This quotation, and others below, shewing the passages of the French text which most nearly resemble the English poem, are from a MS. in the Herald's College, marked E. D. N. No. 14. See the Preface.]

[118. *Wat shal me to rede*, lit. what shall be for a counsel to me. See *Rede* in the Glossary to *William of Palerne*.

130. *And don hem of þar hire were queme*, lit. and do them off where it should be agreeable to her; i. e. and keep men at a distance as she pleased. Such seems to me the meaning of this hitherto unexplained line.

132. For *me* we ought probably to read *hit*.]

136. *He sende* writes *sone onon*. We must here, and in l. 2275, simply understand *letters*, without any reference to the official summonses of parliament, which subsequently were so termed, κατ' εξοχην. The word *briefs* is used in the same sense by the old French writers, and in Laȝamon we meet with some lines nearly corresponding with the present; see ll. 6669—6678.

[175. þa. Frequently written for þat. See *William of Palerne*.]

189—203. *Ther-on he garte*, &c. Compare the French Romance, ll. 215—228.

> Sa fille li ad comandée,
> Et sa terre tote liuerée.
> Primerement li fet iurer,
> Veiant sa gent & affier,
> Qe leaument la nurrireit,
> Et sa terre lui gardereit,
> Tant q'ele fust de tiel age
> Qe suffrir porroit mariage.
> Quant la pucele seit granz,
> Par le consail de ses tenanz,
> Au plus fort home la dorroit
> Qe el reaume troueroit;
> Qu'il li baillast ses citez,
> Ses chasteus & ses fermetez.

263. *Justises dede he maken newe,*
    *Al Engelond to faren thorw.*

The earliest instance produced by Dugdale of the Justices Itinerant, is in 23 Hen. II. 1176, when by the advice of the Council held at Northampton, the realm was divided into six parts, and into each were sent three Justices. *Orig. Judic.* p. 51. This is stated on the authority of Hoveden. Dugdale admits however the custom to have been older, and in Gervasius Dorobernensis, we find, in 1170, certain persons, called *inquisitores*, appointed to perambulate England. Gervase of Tilbury, or whoever was the author of the *Dialogus de Scaccario*, calls them *deambulantes, vel perlustrantes judices*. See Spelman, *in voc.* The office continued to the time of Edward III., when it was superseded by that of the Justices of Assize.

280. *The kinges douther*, &c. Comp. the Fr. l. 283.

> Argentille,
> La meschine qu'ert sa fille,
> Que ia estoit creue & grant,
> Et bien poeit auoir enfant.

[338. *Sawe*, put for "Say we." Cf. *biddi* for "bidde i," l. 484; *hauedet* for "hauede it," 714; &c.

365. *His quiste*, &c. "His bequest made, and (things) distributed for him."]

433. *Crist warie him with his mouth!*
*Waried wrthe he of north and suth!*

So, in the Romance of Merlin, Bishop Brice curses the enemies of Arthur,

> Ac, for he is king, and king's son,
> Y curse alle, and y dom
> His enemies with Christes mouth,
> By East, by West, by North, and South!
>    Ellis, *Metr. Rom.* V. I. p. 260.

[506. For *nouth* we must read *mouth* or *wolde*. The sense is—"He thought that he would he were dead, except that he might not (*or* would not) slay him with his (own) hand."

550. The sense is—"When he had done that deed (i. e. gagged the child), *then* the deceiver had commanded him," &c.

560. *with* may mean *knowest*, but this hardly gives sense. Perhaps we should read *wilt*, i. e. "As thou wilt have (preserve) my life."

567. Mr Morris suggests that the riming words are *adoun* and *croune*. We might then read—

> "And caste þe knaue so harde adoun,
>  þat he crakede þer hise croune."]

591. *Of hise mouth*, &c. Comp. the Fr. l. 71. sq.

> Totes les houres q'il dormoit,
> Vne flambe de lui issoit.
> Par la bouche li venoit fors,
> Si grant chalur auoit el cors.
> La flambe rendoit tiel odour,
> Onc ne sentit nul home meillour.

676. *And with thi chartre make (me) fre.* Instances of the manumission of villains or slaves by charter may be found in Hickes, *Diss. Epistol.* p. 12, Lye's Dict. *ad calc.*, and Madox's *Formulare Anglicanum*, p. 750. The practice was common in the Saxon times, and existed so late as the reign of Henry VIII.

[694. *Wite he him onliue*, if he knows him (to be) alive.

701. It is evident that the words *and gate* = and goats, must be supplied. For the spelling *gate*, cf. *Pricke of Conscience*, ed. Morris, l. 6134, where *gayte* is used collectively as a plural.]

706. *Hise ship,* &c. Comp. the Fr. l. 89.

   Grim fet niefs apparailler,
   Et de viande bien charger.

715—720. *Hauelok the yunge,* &c. Comp. the Fr. ll. 97—105.

   Quant sa nief fut apparaillée,
   Dedenz fist entrer sa meisnée,
   Ses cheualers & ses serganz,
   Sa femme demeine & ses enfanz :
   La reyne mist el batel,
   Haueloc tint souz son mantel.
   Il meismes apres entra,
   A Dieu del ciel se comanda,
   Del hauene sont desancré,
   Car il eurent bon orré.

Instead of the storm, in the French text Grim's ship is attacked by pirates, who kill the whole of the crew, with the exception of himself and family, whom they spare on the score of his being an old acquaintance.

733—749. *In Humber,* &c. So in the Fr. *Ceo fut el north,* &c. Cf. ll. 122—135.

   Tant ont nagé & tant siglé,
   Q'en vne hauene ont parvenu,
   Et de la nief a terre issu.
   Ceo fut el North, a Grimesbi ;
   A icel tens qe ieo vus di,
   Ni out onques home habité,
   Ne cele hauene n'ert pas haunté.
   Il i adresca primes maison,
   De lui ad Grimesbi a non.
   Quant Grim primes i ariua,
   En .ii. moitez sa nief trencha,
   Les chiefs en ad amont drescé,
   Iloec dedenz s'est herbergé.
   Pescher aloit sicome il soloit,
   Siel vendoit & achatoit.

753. *He took the sturgiun and the qual,*
   *And the turbut, and lax withal,*
   *He tok the sele, and the hwel,* &c.

The list of fish here enumerated may be increased from l. 896, and presents us with a sufficiently accurate notion of the different species eaten in the 13th century. Each of the names will be considered separately in the Glossary, and it is only intended here to make a few remarks on those, which in the present day appear rather strangely to have found a place on the tables of our ancestors. The sturgeon is well known to have been esteemed a dainty, both in England and France, and specially appropriated to the King's service, but that the whale, the seal, and the porpoise should have been rendered palatable, excites our astonishment. Yet that the whale was caught for that purpose, appears not only from the present passage, but also from the Fabliau intitled *Bataille de Charnage et de Caresme*, written probably about the same period, and printed by Barbazan. It is confirmed, as we learn from Le Grand, by the French writers; and even Rabelais, near three centuries later, enumerates the whale among the dishes eaten by the Gastrolatres. In the list of fish also published by Le Grand from a MS. of the 13th century, and which corresponds remarkably with the names in the Romance, we meet with the *Baleigne*. See *Vie Privée des François*, T. II. sect. 8.

Among the articles at Archbishop Nevil's Feast, 6 Edw. IV., we find, *Porposes and Seales* XII. and at that of Archbishop Warham, held in 1504, is an item: *De Seales & Porposs. prec. in gross* XXVI. *s.* VIII. *d.* Champier asserts that the Seal was eaten at the Court of Francis I., so that the taste of the two nations seems at this period to have been nearly the same. For the courses of fish in England during the 14th and 15th centuries, see Pegge's *Form of Cury*, and Warner's *Antiquitates Culinariæ*, to which we may add MS. Sloane, 1986. [*Cf. Babees Book, &c.*, ed. Furnivall, 1868, p. 153.]

[784. For *setes* we should probably read *seten* or *sette*, which would be as good a rime as many others. The scribe has probably made the rime more perfect than the sense. It must mean, "In the sea were they oft set." We cannot here suppose *setes* = *set es* = set them.]

839. *And seyde, Hauelok, dere sone.* In the French, Grim sends Havelok away for quite a different reason, viz. because he does not understand fishing.

903. *The kok stod*, &c. Comp. the Fr. l. 242.

> Et vn keu le roi le retint,
> Purceo qe fort le vist & grant,
> Et mult le vist de bon semblant.
> Merueillous fes poeit leuer,
> Busche tailler, ewe porter.

The last line answers to l. 942 of the English version.

939. *He bar the turues, he bar the star.* The meaning of the latter term will be best illustrated by a passage in Moor's *Suffolk Words*, where, under the word *Bent*, he writes, "*Bent* or *Starr*, on the N.W. coast of England, and especially in Lancashire, is a coarse reedy shrub—like ours perhaps—of some importance formerly, if not now, on the sandy blowing lands of those counties. Its fibrous roots give some cohesion to the silicious soil. By the 15 and 16 G. II. c. 33, plucking up and carrying away *Starr* or Bent, or having it in possession within five miles of the sand hills, was punishable by fine, imprisonment, and whipping." The use stated in the Act to which the *Starr* was applied, is, "making of Mats, Brushes, and Brooms or Besoms," therefore it might very well be adapted to the purposes of a kitchen, and from its being coupled with *turves* in the poem, was perhaps sometimes burnt for fuel. The origin of the word is Danish, and still exists in the Dan. *Stær*, Swed. *Starr*, Isl.

*staer*, a species of sedge, or broom, called by Lightfoot, p. 560, *carex cespitosa*. Perhaps it is this shrub alluded to in the Romance of *Kyng Alisaunder*, and this circumstance will induce us to assign its author to the district in which the Starr is found.

> The speris craketh swithe thikke,
> So doth on hegge *sterre-stike*.—l. 4438.

945. *of alle men*, &c. Comp. the Fr. l. 254.

> Tant estoit franc & deboneire,
> Que tuz voloit lur pleisir fere,
> Pur la franchise q'il out.

959. *Of him ful wide the word sprong*. A phrase which from the Saxon times occurs repeatedly in all our old writers. A few examples may suffice.

> Beowulf wæs breme,
> Blæd wíde sprang.
> > *Beowulf*, ed. Thorpe, p. 2.

> Welle wide sprong þas eorles word.
> > *Laʒamon*, l. 26242.

> Of a knight is that y mene,
> His name is sprong wel wide.
> > *Sir Tristrem*, st. 2, p. 12.

> The word of Horn wide sprong,
> How he was bothe michel and long.
> > *Horn Childe*, ap. Rits. *Metr. Rom.* V. iii. p. 291.

See also the *Kyng of Tars*, ll. 19, 1007, *Emare*, l. 256, *Roland and Ferragus*, as quoted by Ellis, *Ly beaus Desconus*, l. 172, and *Chronicle of England*, l. 71.

984. *In armes him noman (ne) nam*
> *þat he doune sone ne caste.*

The same praise is bestowed on Havelok in the French text, l. 265,—

> Deuant eus liuter le fesoient
> As plus forz homes q'il sauoient,
> Et il trestouz les abatit—

and it was doubtless in imitation or ridicule of the qualities attributed to similar heroes, that Chaucer writes of Sir Thopas, "Of wrastling was ther non his per." Cant. Tales, l. 13670.

1006. *To ben þer at þe parlement*. Cf. l. 1178. If we examine our historical records, we shall find that the only parliament held at Lincoln was in the year 1300, 28 Edw. I., and the writs to the *Archbishop of York*, and other Nobles, both ecclesiastical and secular, are still extant. The proceedings are detailed at some length by Robert of Brunne, Vol. II. p. 312, who might have been in Lincoln at the time, or, at all events, was sufficiently informed of all that took place, from his residence in the county. If we could suppose that the author of the Romance alluded to this very parliament, it would reduce the period of the poem's composition to a later date, than either the style or the writing of the MS. will possibly admit of. It is therefore far more probable the writer here makes use of a poetical, and very pardonable licence, in transferring the parliament to the chief city of the county in which he was evidently born, or brought up, without any reference whatever to historical data.

1022.  *Biforn here fet þanne lay a tre,*
*And putten with a mikel ston,* &c.

This game of *putting the stone,* is of the highest antiquity, and seems to have been common at one period to the whole of England, although subsequently confined to the Northern counties, and to Scotland. Fitzstephen enumerates casting of stones among the amusements of the Londoners in the 12th century, and Dr Pegge, in a note on the passage, calls it "a Welch custom." The same sport is mentioned by Geoffrey of Monmouth, among the diversions pursued at King Arthur's feast, as will appear in a subsequent note (l. 2320). By an edict of Edward III. the practice of casting stones, wood, and iron, was forbidden, and the use of the bow substituted, yet this by no means superseded the former amusement, which was still in common use in the 16th century, as appears from Strutt's *Popular Pastimes,* Introd. pp. xvii, xxxix, and p. 56, sq. In the Highlands this sport appears to have been longer kept up than in any other part of Britain, and Pennant, describing their games, writes, " Those retained are, throwing the *putting-stone,* or stone of strength *(Cloch neart)* as they call it, which occasions an emulation who can throw a weighty one the farthest." *Tour in Scotl.* p. 214. 4to. 1769. See also *Statist. Account of Argyleshire,* xi. 287. In the French Romance of Horn, preserved in MS. Harl. 527, is almost a similar incident to the one in Havelok, and would nearly amount to a proof, that Tomas, the writer of the French text of Horn, was an Englishman.

In the Romance of *Octovian Imperator* it is said of Florent,

> At *wrestelyng,* and at *ston castynge*
> He wan the prys, without lesynge ;
> Ther n'as nother old ne yynge
>     So mochell of strength,
> That myght the ston to hys *but* bryng,
>     Bi fedeme lengthe.—l. 895.

It is singular enough, that the circumstance of Havelok's throwing the stone, mentioned in the Romance, should have been founded on, or preserved in, a local tradition, as attested by Robert of Brunne, p. 26.

> Men sais in Lyncoln castelle ligges ȝit a stone,
> That Hauelok kast wele forbi euerilkone.

1077—1088. *The king Athelwald,* &c. Comp. the Fr. text, ll. 354—370.

> Quart Ekenbright le roi fini,
> En ma garde sa fille mist ;
> Vn serement iurer me fist,
> Q'au plus fort home le dorroie,
> Qe el reaume trouer porroie.
> Assez ai quis & demandé,
> Tant q'en ai vn fort troué ;
> Vn valet ai en ma quisine,
> A qui ieo dorrai la meschine ; &c.

1103. *After Goldeborw*, &c. Comp. the Fr. l. 377.

> Sa niece lur fet amener,
> Et a Cuaran esposer ;
> Pur lui auiler & honir,
> La fist la nuit lez lui gesir.

The French Romance differs here very considerably from the English, and in the latter, the dream of Argentille, her visit to the hermit, and the conversation relative to Havelok's parents, is entirely omitted.

[1174. This may mean—" He (Havelok) is given to her, and she has taken (him) "—but this makes *yaf* and *tok* past participles, which they properly are not ; or else we must translate it—" He (Godard) gave them to her, and she took them," i. e. the pence. This alone is the grammatical construction, and it suits the context best; observe, that the words *ys* and *as* are equivalent to *es* = them. Cf. l. 970. See Morris ; *Gen. & Exod.*, Pref. p. xviii.]

1203. *Thanne he komen there*, &c. Comp. the Fr. l. 556.

> A Grimesby s'en alerent ;
> Mes li prodoms estoit finiz,
> Et la Dame q'is out nurriz.
> Kelloc sa fille i ont trouée,
> Vn marchant l'out esposée.

The marriage of Kelloc, Grim's daughter, with a merchant is skilfully introduced in the French, and naturally leads to the mention of Denmark. The plot of the English story is wholly dissimilar in this respect.

1247. *On the nith*, &c. Comp. the Fr. l. 381.

> Quant couché furent ambedui,
> Cele out grant honte de lui,
> Et il assez greindre de li.
> As deuz se geut, si se dormi.
> Ne voloit pas q'ele veist
> La flambe qe de lui issist.

The voice of the angel is completely an invention of the English author, and the dream (which is transferred from Argentille to Havelok) is altogether different in its detail.

1260. *He beth heyman*, &c. Comp. the Fr. l. 521.

> Il est né de real lignage,
> Oncore auera grant heritage.
> Grant gent fra vers li encline,
> Il serra roi & tu reyne.

[1334. The words *euere-il del* are corruptly repeated from line 1330 above. Perhaps we should read *wit-uten were*, i. e. without doubt.]

1430. *Hauede go for him gold ne fe.* Cf. 1. 44. So in Laȝamon :

> Ne sculde him neoðer gon fore
> Gold ne na gærsume, &c. ; vol. ii. p. 537.

[1444. The French text helps but little to supply the blank. It shows that Havelok and his wife sailed to Denmark, and, on their arrival, sought out the castle belonging to Sigar, who answers to the Ubbe of the English version.]

1632. *A gold ring drow he f. h anon*, &c. A similar incident, and in nearly the same words, occurs in Sir Tristrem.

> A ring he raught him tite,
> The porter seyd nought nay,
>    In hand :
> He was ful wis, y say,
> That first yave yift in land.—fytte i. st. 57, p. 39.

So also Wyntoun, who relates the subsidy of 40,000 moutons sent from France to Scotland in 1353, and adds,

> Qwha gyvis swilk gyftyis he is wyse.

[See also *Piers Plowman*, Text A. iii. 202.]

1646. *Hw he was wel of bones*, &c. Comp. the Fr. 1. 743.

> Gent cors & bele feture,
> Lungs braz & grant furcheure
> Ententiuement l'esgarda.

[1678. This line has two syllables too little.]

1722. *Thanne he were set*, &c. This is an amplification of the Fr. l. 677, sq.

> Quant fut houre del manger,
> Et qe tuz alerent lauer,
> Li prodoms a manger s'assist,
> Les .iii. valez seeir i fist,
> Argentille lez son seignur ;
> Serui furent a grant honur.

1726. *Kranes, swannes, veneysun*, &c. We have here the principal constituents of what formed the banquets of our ancestors. The old Romances abound with descriptions of this nature, which coincide exactly with the present. See *Richard Cœur de Lion*, l. 4221 ; *Guy of Warwick; The Squyr of Lowe Degre*, l. 317 ; and *Morte Arthure*, ed. Perry, p. 7.

"Wine is common," says Dr Pegge, speaking of the entertainments of the 14th century, "both red and white. This article they partly had of their own growth, and partly by importation from France and Greece." A few examples will illustrate this:

> He laid the cloth, and set forth bread,
> And also wine, both *white and red*.
> *Sir Degore*, ap. Ellis, *Metr. Rom.* V. 3, p. 375.

> And dronke wyn, and eke pyment,
> *Whyt and red*, al to talent.
> *Kyng Alisaunder*, 1. 4178.

[Cf. *Piers Plowman*, Text B, at the end of the *Prologue*.]
In the *Squyr of Lowe Degre* is a long list of these wines, which has received considerable illustration in the curious work of Dr Henderson.

[1736. I print *kiwing*, as in Sir F. Madden's edition; but I quite give up the meaning of it, and doubt if it is put for *kirving*. The word is obscurely written, and looks like *kilþing*, and my impression is that it is miswritten for *ilk þing*, the word þe being put for þer, as frequently elsewhere. We should thus get *hwan he haueden þer ilk þing deled*, when they had there distributed every thing. This is, at any rate, the sense of the passage.]

1749. *And sende him unto the greyues.* In the French, Havelok is simply sent to an *ostel*, and the *greyve* does not appear in the story.

1806. *Hauelok lifte up*, &c. In the French, all the amusing details relative to Robert and Huwe Raven are omitted, and Havelok is made to retire to a monastery, where he defends himself by throwing down the stones on his assailants.

[1826. *wolde*, offered at, intended to hit, *would* have hit.]

1838. *And shoten on him, so don on bere*
*Dogges, that wolden him to-tere.*]

The same comparison is made use of in the Romance of Horn Childe:

> The Yrise folk about him yode,
> As hondes do to bare.
> Rits. *Metr. Rom.* V. III. p. 289.

See Note on l. 2320.

[1914. "Cursed be he who cares! for they deserved it! What did they? There were they worried." A mark of interrogation seems required after *dide he.*]

1926—1930. *Sket cam tiding*, &c. Comp. the Fr. l. 719.

> La nouele vint a chastel,
> Au seneschal, qui n'est pas bel,
> Qe cil qu'il auoit herbergé
> Cinc de ses homes ont tué.

[1932. Apparently corrupt. Perhaps *is* should be *it*. "That this strife—as to what it meant."]

2045. *That weren of Kaym kin and Eues.* The odium affixed to the supposed progeny of Cain, and the fables engrafted on it, owe their origin to the theological opinions of the Middle Ages, which it is not worth while to trace to their authors. See *Beowulf*, ed. Thorpe, p. 8 ; and *Piers Plowman*, A. x. 135—156 ; answering to p. 177 of Whitaker's edition. See also the Romance of *Kyng Alisaunder:*

> And of Sab the duk Mauryn,
> He was of *Kaymes kunrede.*—l. 1932.

In *Ywaine and Gawaine*, l. 559, the Giant is called " the karl of *Kaymes kyn*," and so also in a poem printed by Percy, intitled *Little John Nobody*, written about the year 1550.

> Such caitives count to be come of *Cain's kind*.
> *Anc. Reliq.* V. II. p. 130. Ed. 1765.

2076. *It ne shal no thing ben b'·wene*
*Thi bour and min, also   wene,*
*But a fayr firrene wowe.*

These lines will receive some illustration from a passage in Sir Tristrem, where it is said,

> A borde he tok oway
> Of her bour.—p. 114.

On which Sir W. Scott remarks, "The bed-chamber of the queen was constructed of wooden boards or shingles, of which one could easily be removed." This will explain the line which occurs below, 2106, " He stod, and totede in at a bord."

2092. *Aboute the middel*, &c. In the French, a person is placed by the Seneschal to watch, who first discovers the light.

2132. *Bi the pappes he leyen naked.* "From the latter end of the 13th to near the 16th century, all ranks, and both sexes, were universally in the habit of sleeping quite naked. This custom is often alluded to by Chaucer, Gower, Lydgate, and all our ancient writers." Ellis, *Spec. Metr. Rom.* V. I. p. 324, 4th Ed. In the *Squyr of Lowe Degre* is a remarkable instance of this fact :

> How she rose, that lady dere,
> To take her leue of that squyer ;
> Al so naked as she was borne
> She stod her chambre-dore beforne.—l. 671.

The custom subsisted both in England and France to a very recent period, and hence probably was derived the phrase *naked-bed,* illustrated so copiously by Archdeacon Nares in his Glossary.

2192. Cf. the French, l. 843.

> Ses chapeleins fet demander,
> Ses briefs escriure & enseeler ;
> Par ses messages les manda,
> Et pur ses amis enuoia ;
> Pur ses homes, pur ses parenz ;
> Mult i assembla granz genz.

[2201. Read *ne neme* = took not, sc. their way, just as in l. 1207.]
2240—2265. *Lokes, hware he stondes her,* &c. Comp. the Fr. ll. 913—921.

"Veez ci nostre dreit heir,
Bien en deuom grant ioie aueir."
Tut primerain se desafubla,
Par deuant lui s'agenuilla ;
Sis homs deuint, si li iura
Qe leaument le seruira.
Li autre sont apres alé,
Chescuns de bone volenté ;
Tuit si home sont deuenu.

2314. *Vbbe dubbede him to knith,*
*With a swerd ful swithe brith.*

So likewise in the Fr. l. 928, *A cheualier l'out adubbé.* The ceremony of knighthood is described with greater minuteness in the Romance of *Ly beaus Desconus,* l. 73 ; and see *Kyng Horn,* ed. Lumby, ll. 495—504.

2320. *Hwan he was king, ther mouthe men se,* &c. Ritson has justly remarked, Notes to *Ywaine and Gawaine,* l. 15, that the elaborate description of Arthur's feast at Carlisle, given by Geoffrey of Monmouth, l. ix. c. 12, has served as a model to all his successors. The original passage stands thus in a fine MS. of the 13th century, MS. Harl. 3773. fol. 33 *b.* "Refecti autem epulis diversos ludos acturi campos extra civitatem adeunt. Tunc milites simulachra belli scientes *equestrem ludum* componunt, mulieribus ab edito murorum aspicientibus. Alii *cum cestibus,* alii *cum hastis,* alii *gravium lapidum jactu,* alii *cum facis,* [*saxis,* Edd.] alii *cum aleis,* diversisque alii alteriusmodi jocis contendentes." In the translation of this description by Wace we approach still nearer to the imitation of the Romance before us.

A plusurs iuis se departirent,
Li vns alerent *buhurder,*
E lur ignels cheuals mustrer,
Li altre alerent *eskermir,*
V *pere geter,* v *saillir ;*
Tels i-aueit ki *darz lanconent,*
E tels i-aueit ki *lutouent :*
Chescon del gru [geu ?] s'entremetait
Dunt entremettre se saueit.—MS. Reg. 13. A. xxi.

The parallel versions, from the French, of Laȝamon, Robert of Gloucester, and Robert of Brunne, may be read in Mr Ellis's *Specimens of Early English Poets.* At the feast of Olimpias, described in the Romance of *Kyng Alisaunder,* we obtain an additional imitation.

Withoute theo toun was mury,
Was reised ther al maner pley ;

There was knyghtis *turnyng*,
There was maidenes carolyng,
There was champions *skyrmyng*,
Of heom and of other *wrastlyng*,
Of liouns chas, of *beore baityng*,
And *bay of bor*, of *bole slatyng*.—l. 193. Cf. l. 1045.

Some additional illustrations on each of the amusements named in our text may not be unacceptable:

1. *Buttinge with sharpe speres.* This is tilting, or justing, expressed in Wace by *buhurder.* See Strutt's *Sports and Pastimes*, p. 96, sq. 108.

2. *Skirming with taleuaces.* This is described more at large by Wace, in his account of the feast of Cassibelaunus. Cf. *Laȝamon*, v. i. p. 347; l. 8144. In Strutt's *Sports and Pastimes* is a representation of this game, taken from MS. Bodl. 264, illuminated between 1338 and 1344, in which the form of the *talevas* is accurately defined. It appears to have been pursued to such an excess, as to require the interference of the crown, for in 1286 an edict was issued by Edward I. prohibiting all persons *Eskirmer au bokeler.* This, however, had only a temporary effect in restraining it, and in later times, under the appellation of *sword and buckler play*, it again became universally popular.

3. *Wrastling with laddes, puttinge of ston.* See the notes on ll. 984 and 1022.

4. *Harping and piping.* This requires no illustration.

5. *Leyk of mine, of hasard ok.* Among the games mentioned at the marriage of Gawain, in the Fabliau of *Le Chevalier à l'Epée*, we have:

Cil Chevalier jeuent as tables,
Et as eschés de l'autre part,
O à la *mine*, o à *hazart*.

Le Grand, in his note on this passage, T. i. p. 57, Ed. 1779, writes: " Le Hasard était une sorte de jeu de dez. Je ne connais point la *Mine*; j'ai trouvé seulement ailleurs un passage qui prouve que ce jeu était très-dangereux, et qu'on pouvait s'y ruiner en peu de tems." It appears however from the Fabliau of *Du Prestre et des deuz Ribaus*, to have been certainly a species of *Tables*, or *Backgammon*, and to have been played with dice, on a board called *Minete*. The only passage we recollect in which any further detail of this game is given, is that of Wace, in the account of Arthur's feast, Harl. MS. 6508, and MS. Cott. Vit. A. x., but it must be remarked, that the older copy 13 A. xxi. does not contain it, nor is it found in the translations of Laȝamon, or Robert of Gloucester.

6. *Romanz reding.* See Sir W. Scott's note on Sir Tristrem, p. 290, [p. 306, ed. 1811]; and the Dissertations of Percy, Ritson, and Ellis.

7. *Ther mouthe men se the boles beyte,*
*And the bores, with hundes teyte.*

Cf. ll. 1838, 2438. Both these diversions are mentioned by Lucianus, in his inedited tract *De laude Cestriæ*, MS. Bodl. 672, who is supposed by

Tanner to have written about A.D. 1100, but who must probably be placed near half a century later. They formed also part of the amusements of the Londoners in the 12th century, as we learn from Fitzstephen, p. 77, and are noticed in the passage above quoted from the Romance of *Kyng Alisaunder*. In later times, particularly during the 16th century, these cruel practices were in the highest estimation, as we learn from Holinshed, Stowe, Laneham, &c. See Strutt's *Sports and Pastimes*, p. 192, and the plate from MS. Reg. 2. B. vii. Also Pegge's Dissertation on Bull-baiting, inserted in Vol. ii. of Archæologia.

8. *Ther mouthe men se hw Grim greu.* If this is to be understood of scenic representation (and we can scarcely view it in any other light), it will present one of the earliest instances on record of any attempt to represent an historical event, or to depart from the religious performances, which until a much later period were the chief, and almost only, efforts towards the formation of the drama. Of course, the words of the writer must be understood to refer to the period in which he lived, i. e. according to our supposition, about the end of Hen. III's reign, or beginning of Edw. I. See Le Grand's notes to the *Lai de Courtois*, V. i. p. 329, and Strutt's *Sports and Pastimes*, B. 3, ch. 2.

2344. *The feste fourti dawes sat.* Cf. l. 2950. This is borrowed also from Geoffrey, and is the usual term of duration fixed in the Romances.

> Fourty dayes hy helden feste,
> Ryche, ryall, and oneste.—*Octouian Imperator*, l. 73.

> Fourty dayes leste the feste.—*Launfal*, l. 631.

> And certaynly, as the story sayes,
> The revell lasted forty dayes.
> *Squyr of Lowe Degre*, l. 1113.

2384. The French story here differs wholly from the English. Instead of the encounter of Robert and Godard, and the cruel punishment inflicted on the latter, in the French is a regular battle between the forces of Havelok and Hodulf (Godard). A single combat takes place between the two leaders, in which Hodulf is slain.

2450. Cf. ll. 2505 and 2822. This appears to have been a common, but barbarous, method in former times of leading traitors or malefactors to execution. Thus in the Romance of *Kyng Alisaunder*, the treatment of the murderers of Darius is described:

> He dude quyk harnesche hors,
> And sette theron heore cors,
> Hyndeforth they seten, saun faile;
> In heore hand they hulden theo tailes.—l. 4708.

2461. We find a similar proverb in the *Historie de Melusine, tirée des Chroniques de Poitou*, &c. 12mo. Par. 1698, in which (at p. 72) Thierry, Duke of Bretagne, says to Raimondin;—" Vous autorisez par votre silence *notre Proverbe*, qui dit, *Qu'un vieux peché fait nouvelle vergogne.*"

2513. *Sket was seysed*, &c. Comp. the Fr. l. 971.

Apres cest fet, ad receu
Le regne q'a son piere fu.

2516. *And the king ful sone it yaf*
*Vbbe in the hond, wit a fayr staf.*

So in *Sir Tristrem* :

Rohant he yaf *the wand*,
And bad him sitte him bi,
That fre ;
'Rohant lord mak y
To held this lond of me.'—fytte i. st. 83 ; p. 52.

The editor is clearly mistaken in explaining the *wand* to be a *truncheon*, or *symbol of power*. For the custom of giving seisin or investiture *per fustim*, and *per baculum*, see Mad_x's *Formul. Anglican.* pref. p. ix. and Spelman, Gloss. in v. *Investire*, d *Traditio*. The same usage existed in France, *par rain et par baton*.

2521. ——*of monekes blake*
*A priorie to seruen inne ay.*

The allusion here may be made either to the Abbey of Wellow, in Grimsby, which was a monastery of *Black Canons*, said to have been built about A.D. 1110, or (what is more probable) to the Augustine Friary of Black Monks, which is stated in the *Monumental Antiquities of Grimsby*, by the Rev. G. Oliver, to have been "founded *about* the year 1280," p. 110. No notice of it occurs in Tanner till the year 1304. Pat. 33 Edw. I. Some old walls of this edifice, which was dissolved in 1543, still remain, and the site is still called "The Friars." If the connection between this foundation and the one recorded in the poem be considered valid, the date of the composition must be referred to *rather* a later period than we wish to admit.

2530. The French supplies what is here omitted, viz. that Havelok sails to England by the persuasion of his wife.

[Indeed, ll. 979—1006 of the French text may serve to fill up the evident gap in the story ; a translation of the passage is added, to shew this more clearly.

| | |
|---|---|
| Quant Haueloc est rois pussanz, | When Havelok is a mighty king, |
| Le regne tint plus de .iiii. anz ; | He reigned more than 4 years, |
| Merueillos tresor i auna. | Marvellous treasure he amassed. |
| Argentille li commanda | Argentille (Goldborough) bade him |
| Qu'il passast en Engleterre | Pass into England |
| Pur son heritage conquerre, | To conquer her heritage, |
| Dont son oncle l'out engettée, | Whence her uncle had cast her out, |
| [Et] A grant tort desheritée. | And very wrongly disinherited her. |
| Li rois li dist qu'il fera | The king told her that he would do |
| Ceo qu'ele li comandera. | That which she should command him. |
| Sa nauie fet a-turner, | He got ready his fleet, |

| | |
|---|---|
| Ses genz & ses ostz mander. | And sent for his men and his hosts. |
| En mier se met quant orré a, | He puts to sea when he has prayed, |
| Et la reyne od lui mena. | And took the queen with him. |
| Quatre vinz & quatre cenz | Four score and four hundred (ships) |
| Out Haueloc, pleines de genz. | Had Havelok, full of men. |
| Tant out nagé & siglé, | So far has he steered and sailed |
| Q'en Carleflure est ariué. | That he has arrived at Carleflure. |
| Sur le hauene se herbergerent, | Hard by the haven they abode, |
| Par le pais viande quierent. | And sought food in the country round. |
| | |
| Puis enuoia li noble rois, | Then sent the noble king, |
| Par le consail de ses Danois, | By the advice of his Danes, |
| A Alsi qu'il li rendist | To Alsi (Godrich)—that he should restore to him |
| La terre qe tint Ekenbright, | The land that Ekenbright (Athelwold) held, |
| Q'a sa niece fut donée, | Which was given to his niece, |
| Dont il l'out desheritée ; | And of which he had deprived her. |
| Et, si rendre n'el voleit, | And, if he would not give it up, |
| Mande qu'il le purchaceroit. | He sends word that he will take it. |
| Av roi uindrent li messager— | To the king came the messengers.] |

The remainder of the French poem altogether differs in its detail from the English.

2927. *Hire that was ful swete in bedde.*] Among Kelly's Scotch Proverbs, p. 290, we find : "*Sweet in the bed*, and sweir up in the morning, was never a good housewife ; " and in a ballad of the last century quoted by Laing, the editor of that highly curious collection, the *Select pieces of Ancient Popular Poetry of Scotland*, we meet with the same expression :

A Clown is a Clown both at home and abroad,
When a Rake he is comely, and *sweet in his bed*.

[2990. The last word is written *thit* in the MS., but, as it rimes to *rith*, we should suppose *tiht* to be the word meant. *Thit* cannot be explained, but *tiht* (or perhaps *tith*, according to our scribe's spelling) is the pp. of a verb signifying *to purpose*, which is the exact meaning required. Cf.

" And y to turne to þee have tiȝt ; "
i. e. " I have resolved to turn to thee."

*Political, Religious, and Love Poems ;* ed. Furnivall, 1866 ; p. 177.]

# GLOSSARIAL INDEX.

### ABBREVIATIONS.

Barb. Barbour's Bruce.—Chauc. Chaucer.—Doug. Gawin Douglas's Transl. of the Æneid.—Ellis, M. R. Ellis's Specimens of Metrical Romances.—Gl. Glossary.—Jam. Jamieson's Dictionary.—Laȝam. Laȝamon's Transl. of Wace (ed. Madden).—Lynds. Sir D. Lyndsay's Works.—N.E. Northern English.—Percy, A. R. Percy's Reliques of Ancient English Poetry.—P. Plowm. Piers Plowman.—R. Br. Robert of Brunne.—R. Gl. Robert of Gloucester, ed. Hearne (2nd ed. 1810).—Rits. A. S. Ritson's Ancient Songs.—Rits. M. R. Ritson's Metrical Romances.—Sc. Scotch, Scotland.—Sir Tr. Sir Tristrem.—Wall. Wallace.—Web. Weber's Metrical Romances.—Wilb. Wilbraham's Cheshire Glossary.—Wynt. Wyntoun's Chronicle.—B. Lat. Barbarous Latin.—Belg. Belgic.—Fr. French.—Isl. Islandic.—Lat. Latin.—S. Saxon.—Sibb. Sibbald's Chronicle of Scottish Poetry.—Su. G. Suio-Gothic.—Teut. Teutonic.—*q. v.* Quod vide.—The Romances separately cited are sufficiently indicated by the Titles. The numbers refer to the line of the Poem.

It may be useful to add that the names of the Romances edited by Ritson are—vol. i. Ywaine and Gawin; Launfal.—vol. ii. Lybeaus Disconus; King Horn; King of Tars; Emare; Sir Orpheo; Chronicle of England.—vol. iii. Le bone Florence; Erle of Tolous; Squyr of Lowe Degre; Knight of Curtesy. Those edited by Weber are—vol. i. Kyng Alisaunder; Sir Cleges; Lai-le-freine.—vol. ii. Richard Cœur de Lion; Ipomydon; Amis and Amiloun.—vol. iii. Seuyn Sages; Octouian; Sir Amadas; Hunting of the Hare. Beowulf and the Codex Exoniensis are quoted from Thorpe's editions.

A, 610, 936. Apparently an error of the scribe for *Al*, but perhaps written as pronounced. N.E. and Sc. *aw*. V. Jam.

A before a *noun* is commonly a corruption of the S. *on*, as proved clearly by the examples in Tyrwhitt's Gl., Jam., and Gl. Lynds. *Adoun*, q. v. is an exception. *A-two*, 1413, 2643. *See* On.

Aboven, *prep.* S. above, 1700.

Abouten, *prep.* S. [*on-bútan*] about, 521, 670, 1010, &c. *Abuten*, 2429.

Adoun, *adv.* S. down, 567. *Adune*, 2735. *Doun*, 901, 925, &c. *Dun*, 888, 927. *Dune*, 1815, 2656. A.S. *of-dúne*.

Adrad, *part. pa.* S. afraid, 278, 1048, 1163, 1682, 2304. *Adradde*, 1787. *Adred*, 1258. *Odrat*, 1153. Sir Tr. p. 174; K. Horn, 124. *See* Dred.

Agen, *prep.* S. [*on-gean*] against, 1792. *Ageyn*, 493, 569, 2024, &c. *Ageynes*, 2153, 2270, &c. *Ayen*, 489, 1210, 2799. *Yen*, 2271. *Ageyn*, toward, 451, 1696, 1947;

opposite to, 1809; upon, on, 1828. *Ayen*, towards, 1207. *Ageyn him go*, 934, opposite him, so as to bear an equal weight. *Ageyn hire*, 1106, at her approach. *Ageyn þe lith*, 2141, opposed to the light, on which the light shines. V. R. Gl., R. Br., Chauc., &c.

Ageyn, *adv.* S. again, 2426.

Al, *adv.* S. wholly, entirely, 34, 70, 139, 203, &c.

Al, *adj.* S. all, 203, 264, &c.; every one, 104; every part, 224; *plu.* alle, 2, 150, &c.

Albidene, *adv. See* Bidene.

Als, Also, Also, *conj.* S. [*eal-swá*] as, like, so, 306, 319, &c. *Als*, 1912, as if. *Al so foles*, like fools, 2100. *Als* is merely the abbreviation of *Al so;* and the modern *as* is again shortened from *als*. In Laȝamon it is often written *alse*, as in l. 4953.

And he hæfde a swithe god wif
& he heo leouede *alse* his lif.

Cf. Havelok, l. 1663. *Als* and *Also* are used indifferently, and universally by the old English and Scotch poets.

Alþer-beste, *adj.* S. best of all, 182, 720, 1040, 1197, 2415. *Alþer-lest*, *Alþer-leste*, 1978, 2666, least of all. It is the gen. c. pl. of *Alle*, joined to an adj. in the superl. degree, and is extensively employed. *Alre-leofust, Alre-hendest, Alre-kenest*, Laȝamon, *Althe-werste*, K. Horn, MS. *Alder-best, Aldermost*, R. Br. *Alther-best, Altherformest*, &c. Web. *Alther-furste, Alther-next, Alther-last*, Rits. M. R. *Alder-first, Alder-last, Alderlevest*, Chauc. *Alder - liefest*, Shakesp.

Amideward, *prep.* S. in the midst, 872. *Amiddewart*, K. Horn, 556. *Amydward*, K. Alisaund. 690. *A mydward*, Ly Beaus Desc. 852. *Amydwart*, Doug. Virg. 137, 35.

An. *conj.* S. and, 29, 359, &c. So used by Laȝamon, and still in Somersetsh. V. Jennings. *Ant*, 36, 557, K. Horn, 9, &c.

And, *conj. if*, 2862.

Andelong, *adv.* S. lengthways, i. e. from the head to the tail, 2822.

Ovyrtwart and *endelang*
With strenges of wyr the stones hang.—*R. Cœur de Lion*, 2649.
Chauc. *endelong*, C. T. 1993.

Anilepi, *adj.* S. [*ánlepig*] one, a single, 2107. *Onlepi*, 1094. In the very curious collection of poems in MS. Digb. 86 (written in the Lincolnshire dialect, temp. Edw. I.) we meet with this somewhat rare word:

A ! quod the vox, ich wille the telle,
On *alpi* word ich lie nelle.
*Of the vox and of the wolf* (Rel. Ant. ii. 275).

It occurs also in the *Ormulum*.

Anoþer, *adj.* S. *Al another*, 1395, in a different way, on another project.

Ah al hit iwrath *on other*
Sone ther after.
Laȝamon, l. 21005.

Ac Florice thought al *another*.
*Flor. and Blaunchefl.* ap. Ellis, M. R. V. 3, p. 125, ed. 1803. (Cf. *Horn*, ed. Lumby, p. 52, l. 32.)

Anuye, *v.* Fr. to trouble, weary, 1735 ; R. Gl., K. Alisaund. 876 ; Chauc. Melibeus. *Noye*, Lynds. Gl. q. v.

Are, *adj.* S. former, 27. Cf. are, *adv.*, Sir Tr. p. 32; Rits. M. R., Web., R. Gl., R. Br., Minot. p. 31. *Air, Ayr*, Sc. V. Jam. *See* Er, Or.

Aren, 1 *and* 3 *p. pl.* S. are, 619, 1321, &c. *Arn*, Chauc.

Arke, *n.* S. Lat. a chest *or* coffer, 2018. R. Br., Jam.

Armes, *n. pl.* Lat. arms, armor, 2605, 2613, 2925.

Arum for Arm, 1982, 2408.

Arwe, S. [*earg*] timid, 2115.
Alter the punctuation, and read—
He calde boþe arwe meɴ and kene,
Knithes and serganz swiþe sleie.
"Arwe or ferefulle. *Timidus*."
Prompt. Parv. Cf. Stille, q. v.
As for Has, 1174.

Asayleden, *pa. t. pl.* Fr. assailed, 1862.

Asken, *n. pl.* S. ashes, 2841.
*Aske*, R. Gl. *Askes*, R. Br. *Ashen*, Chauc. *Assis*, Doug.

Astirte, *pa. t.* leaped, 893. *Astert*, King's Quair, ap. Jam. *See* Stirt.

At, *prep.* S. of *or* to, 1387. Yw. and Gaw. (Rits.) 963. Still existing in Scotland.

At-sitte, *v.* S. contradict, oppose, 2200. It corresponds with the term *with-sitten*, 1683. In R. Gl. it is used synonymously with *at-stonde*.

> For ther nas so god knygt non no
> -wer a-boute France,
> That in joustes scholde *at-sitte* the
> dynt of ys lance.—p. 137.

*See* Sat.

Aucte, Auchte, Auhte, Authe, *n.* S. possessions, 531, 1223, 1410, 2215.

> And alle the *æhten* of mine londe.
> *Laʒamon*, l. 25173.

*Aughtte*, K. Alisaund. 6884. *Aucht*, Doug. Virg. 72, 4; Lynds. Gl.

Aucte, Auht, Auhte, *v. imp.* (originally *pa. t.* of Aw, or Owe) S. [*ágan, áhte*] ought, 2173, 2787, 2800. *Aught*, Sir Tr. p. 44. *Ohte*, K. Horn, 418. *Aght*, Yw. and Gaw. 3229. *Aute*, R. Gl. *Aught*, Chauc. Troil. 3, 1801. *Aucht*, Doug. Virg. 110, 33.

Aute, Awcte, (*pa. t.* of the same verb), possessed, 207, 743. *Aught*, Sir Tr. p. 182. Ly Beaus Desc. 1027. *Oght*, Le bone Flor. 650. *Auht*, R. Br. p. 126; Wynt., Lynds. Gl.

Aueden. *See* Haueden.

Aunlaz, *n.* Anelace, 2554. "A kind of knife or dagger, usually worn at the girdle." Tyrw. note on Chauc. l. 359. So in Matth. Paris, "Genus cultelli, quod vulgariter *Anelacius* dicitur." V. Gl. in voc. and Todd's Gl. to Illustr. of Chauc. In *Sir Gawan and Sir Galoran*, ii. 4, an *anlas* signifies a sharp spike fixed in the chaufron of a horse. Probably from the Francic *Anelaz, Analeze*. V. Jam.

Auter, *n.* Fr. Lat. altar, 389, 1386, 2373. Sir Tr. p. 61, Octovian, 1312. R. Br., Chauc. *Awter*, Barb.

Ax, *n.* S. axe, 1776, 1894.

Ay, *adv.* S. ever, aye, always, 159, 946, 1201, &c. *Ae*, Sc. V. Jam.

Ayen. *See* Agen.

Ayþer, *pron.* S. [*Ægþer*] either, each, 2665. *Eþer*, 1882. *Athir*, Sc. V. Jam. *See* Other.

Awe, *v.* S. to owe, own, possess, 1292. It may also very possibly be a corruption of *Have*. Cf. ll. 1188, 1298.

Bac, *n.* S. back, 1844, 1950, &c.; *backes, pl.* 2611.

Baldelike, *adv.* S. boldly, 53. *Baldeliche*, R. Glouc. *Baldely*, R. Br., Minot, p. 20.

Bale, *n.* S. sorrow, misery, 327.

Bar. *See* Beren.

Baret, *n.* (O. Fr. *barat*, Isl. *baratta*) contest, hostile contention, 1932.

> Ther nis *baret*, nothir strif,
> Nis ther no deth, ac euer lif.
> *Land of Cokaygne*, ap. Hickes, Thes. 1, p. 231.

In alle this *barette* the kynge and Sir Symon Tille a lokyng thaun sette, of the prince suld it be don. R. *Brunne*, p. 216. Cf. p. 274.

That mekill bale and *barete* till Ynglande sall brynge. *Awntyrs of Arthure*, st. 23.

Barfot, *adj.* S. barefoot, 862.

Barnage, *n.* Fr. barons or noblemen collectively, baronage, 2947. Yw. and Gaw. 1258. Web. Doug. Virg. 314, 48.

Barre, *n.* Fr. bar of a door, 1794, 1811, 1827. Synonymous with Dore-tre, q. v. Chauc. C. T. 552.

Barw. *See* Berwen.

Baþe, *adj.* S. both, 1336, 2543. *Bethe*, 694, 1680.

Be. *See* Ben.

Be-bedde, *v.* S. to provide with a bed, 421.

Bede, *n.* S. prayer, 1385.

Bede, *v.* S. to order, to bid, 668, 2193, 2396; to offer, 1665, 2084, 2172. *Beden, pa. t. pl.* offered, 2774, 2780. *Bedes,* bids, 2392. Of common occurrence in both senses. *See* Bidd.

Bedden, *v.* S. to bed, put to bed, 1235. *Bedded, Beddeth, part. pa.* put to bed, 1128, 2771.

Bedels, *n. pl.* S. beadles, 266. V. Spelm. in v. *Bedellus,* and Blount, *Joc. Ten.* p. 120, ed. 1784.

Beite, Beyte, *v.* to bait, to set dogs on, 1840, 2330, 2440. *Bayte,* R. Br. From the Isl. *Beita,* incitare; Su. Goth. *Beita biorn,* to bait the bear. V. Jam. and Thomson's Etymons.

Bem. *See* Sunne-bem.

Ben, *v.* S. to be, 19, 905, 1006, &c. *Ben, pr. t. pl.* are, 1787, 2559. *Be, Ben, part. pa.* been, 1428, 2799. *Bes, Beth, imp.* and *fut.* be, shall be, 1261, 1744, 2007, 2246. *Lat be,* 1265, 1657, leave, relinquish, a common phrase in the Old Romances. *Lat abee,* Sc. V. Jam.

Benes, *n. pl.* S. beans, 769.

Beneysun, *n.* Fr. blessing, benediction, 1723. R. Br., Web., Chauc. C. T. 9239. Lynds. Gl.

Bere, *n.* S. bear, 573, 1838, 1840, 2448.

Bere, Beren, *v.* S. to bear, to carry, 581, 762, 805. *Ber,* 2557; *Bar, pa. t.* bore, 557, 815, 877. *Bere,* 974. *Beres, pr. t. pl.* bear, 2323.

Bermen, *n. pl.* S. bar-men, porters to a kitchen, 868, 876, 885. The only author in which this term has been found is Laȝamon, in the following passages:

Vs selve we habbet cokes,
  to quecchen to cuchene,
Vs sulue we habbet *bermen*,
  & birles inowe.—l. 3315.

Weoren in þeos kinges cuchene
  twa hundred cokes,
& ne mæi na man tellen
  for alle þa *bermannen.*—l. 8101.

Bern, *n.* S. child, 571. *Barn, bearne,* R. Br. *Bairn,* Sc.

Berwen, *v.* S. [*beorgan*] to defend, preserve, guard, 697, 1426; *burwe,* 2870. *Barw, pa. t.* 2022, 2679. The original word is found in Beowulf:

Scyld-weall gebearg
Líf and líce.
(The shield-wall defended
Life and body.)—l. 5134.

So in K. Horn, MS. Laud. 108.

At more ich wile the serue,
And fro sorwe the *berwe.*—f. 224*b,* c. 2.

Bes. *See* Ben.

Bes for Best, 354.

Best, Beste, *n.* Fr. beast, 279, 574, 944, 2691.

Bete, *v.* S. [*beátan*] to beat, fight, 1899, 2664, 2763. *Beten, pa. t. pl.* beat, struck, 1876. Chauc. C. T. 4206, to which Tyrwh. gives a Fr. derivation.

Betere, *adv. comp.* S. better, 1758.

Beye, *v.* S. to buy, 53, 1654. *Byen,* 1625.

Beyes, *pr. t.* for Abeyes, S. suffers, or atones for, 2460.
   His deth thou *bist* to night,
   Mi fo. *Sir Tristr.* p. 146.
   We shulden alle deye
   Thy fader deth to *beye.*
   *K. Horn,* 113.
   An of yow schall *bye* thys blunder.
   *Le bone Flor.* 1330.
   See Jam. in v. Aby. Web. Gl. and Lynds. Gl.; also Nares, v. Bye.
Bicomen, *pa. t. pl.* became, 2257; *part. pa.* become, 2264. *Bicomes, imp. pl.* become (ye), 2303.
Bidd, Bidde, *v.* S. offer, 484, 2530; order, bid, 529, 1733. *Ut bidde,* 2548, order out. *Biddes, pr. t.* bids, orders, 1232. *Bidde,* to ask, 910. R. Glouc., Lynds. Gl. *See* Bede.
Bidene, *adv.* forthwith, 730, 2841.
   "Rohand told anon
   His aventours *al bidene.*"
   *Sir Tr.* p. 45.
   From Du. *bij dien,* by that.
Bifalle, *v.* S. to happen, befall, 2981. Bifel, *pa. t.* 824. *Fel,* 1009; appertained, 2359.
Biforn, *prep.* S. (1) before, 1022, 1034, 1364, &c.; *bifor,* 1357; *biforen,* 1695; (2) in front of, 2406; *bifor,* 1812.
Bigan, *pa. t.* began, 1357. *Bigunnen, pl.* 1011, 1302. *Biginnen, pr. t. pl.* begin, 1779.
Bihalue, *v.* S. to divide into two parts, or companies, 1834. *Halue* occurs as a *noun* in Chauc. Troil. 4, 945.
Bihel for Beheld, 1645. *Bihelden, pa. t. pl.* beheld, 2148.
Bihetet, *pa. t.* S. promised, 677. *Bihight,* Sir Tr. p. 105. *Behet, Bihet,* R. Gl. *Be-hette,* R. Br. *Behete,* Web., Rits. M. R. *Behighte,* Chauc.
Bihoten, *part. pa.* promised, 564. *Behighte,* Chauc.

Bihoue, *n.* S. behoof, advantage, 1764. R. Gl., R. Br., Chauc.
Bikenneth, *pa. t.* S. betokens, 1268. *Bikenne,* R. Br.
Bileue, *imp.* tarry, remain, 1228. Bilefte, *pa. t.* remained, 2963. From v. S. *belifan,* to be left behind.
   Winde thai hadde as thai wolde,
   A lond *bilaft* he.
   *Sir Tristr.* p. 29. Cf. pp. 38, 60.
   He schal wiþ me *bileue,*
   Til hit beo nir eue.
   *K. Horn,* ed. Lumby, 363.
   Horn than, withouten lesing,
   *Bilaft* at hom for blode-leteing.
   *Horn Childe,* ap. Rits. M. R. V. 3, p. 298.
   Sojourn with us evermo,
   I rede thee, son, that it be so.
   Another year thou might over-fare,
   But thou *bileve,* I die with care.
   *Guy of Warw.* ap. Ellis, M. R. V. 2, p. 23.
   See also the Gl. to R. Gl., R. Br. and Web., to which add *Emare,* 496, and Gower, Conf. Am. This is sufficient authority for the reading adopted in the text, and it may hence be reasonably questioned, whether *bilened* in Lye, and *belenes* in *Sir Gawan and Sir Galoran,* i. 6, quoted by Jamieson in v. Belene, be not the fault of the scribe, or of the Editors.
Bimene, *v.* S. mean, 1259.
Binden, *v.* S. to bind, 1961. Used passively, 2820, as *Bynde,* 42. *Bounden, pa. t. pl.* 2442. *Bunden,* 2506. *Bounden, part. pa.* 545. *Bunden,* 1428.
Binne, *adv.* S. within, 584. *Byn,* Rits. M. R. *But and ben,* Doug., Virg., 123, 40; without and within. V. Jam., in v. Ben.
Birde. *See* Birþe.
Birþe (*should rather be* birþ), 3 *p. s. pres.* it behoves, 2101. *Hence* birde, 3 *p. s. pt. t.* behoved, 2761. A.S. *byrian, gebyrian,* to fit, suit, be to one's taste. *See Buren* in Stratmann.

Birþene, *n.* S. burden, 900, 902.

Bise, *n.* Fr. a north wind. *Bise traverse*, a north-west or north-east wind. *Cotgr.*

Après grant joie vient grant ire,
Et après Noel *vent bise.*
*Rom. de Renart*, 13648.

The term is still in common use.

Biseken, *v.* S. to beseech, 2994.

Biswike, *part. pa.* S. cheated, deceived, 1249.

Hu þu *biswikest*
Monine mon.
*La3am.* 1. 3412.

*Byswuke*, K. Horn, 296; Yw. and Gaw. 2335. *Bisuike*, R. Br. *Beswyke*, R. Cœur de L. 5918.

Bitaken, *v.* S. [*bitǽcan, tǽcan*] to commit, deliver, give in charge, 1226. *Bitechen*, 203, 384, 395. *Bi-teche, pr. sing.* 384; *imp. sing.* 395. La3am. 5316. *Bitake*, Sir Tr. p. 87. *Byteche*, K. Horn, 577. *Biteche*, Web. *Betake, Beteche,* Chauc., Barb., Wall. *Bitaucte, pa. t.* delivered, 206, 558. *Bitauhte*, 2212, 2317, 2957. *Bitawchte*, 1224. *Bitawte*, 1408. *Tauhte*, 2214. *Bitǽht, Bitachet,* La3am. *Bitaught,* Sir Tr. p. 85. *Bitoke*, K. Horn, 1103. *Betok*, Ly Beaus Desc. 82. *Betauht, bitauht, tauht, biteched*, R. Br. *Bitake*, R. Gl. *Betake*, Sir Guy. *Betaught*, Chauc. *Betaucht*, Doug., Lynds.

Bite, *v.* S. to taste, drink, 1731.

Horn toc hit hise yfere,
Ant seide, Quene, so dere,
No beer nullich *bite*,
Bote of coppe white.
*K. Horn* (Ritson), 1129.

Biþ for By the, 474. Cf. l. 2470.

Bituene, Bitwenen, Bitwene, *prep.* S. between, 748, 2668, 2967.

Blac, *adj.* S. black, 555, 1008. *Pl. Bluke*, 1909, 2181, &c.

Blakne, *v.* S. to blacken in the face, grow angry, 2165.

And Arthur sæt ful stille,
ænne stunde he wes *blac*,
and on heuwe swithe wak,
ane while he wes reod.
*La3am.* 1. 19887.

Tho Normans were sorie, of contenance gan *blaken*.
*R. Brunne*, p. 183.

Blawe, *v.* S. to blow, 587. *Blou, imp.* blow, 585.

Blede, *v.* S. to bleed, 2403.

Bleike, *pl. adj.* bleak, pale, wan, 470. A.S. *blác*, bleak, Su.-G. *blek*.

Blenkes, *n. pl.* blinks, winks of the eye, in derision, 307. R. Br. p. 270; Sc. V. Jam. Suppl. Derived from S. *blican*, Su.-G. *blǽnka*, Belg. *blencken*, to glance. *See* Gl. Lynds.

Blinne, *v. n.* S. to cease, 2367, 2374. Sir Tr. p. 26; Rits. M. R. Web., R. Gl., Chauc.; so in Sc. V. Jam. Gl. Lynds. *Blinne, pa. t. pl.* ceased, 2670. *Blinneth, pr. t.* ceases, 329.

Blissed, *part. pa.* S. blessed, 2873.

Bliþe, *adj.* S. happy, 632, 651.

Blome, *n.* S. bloom, flower, 63.

Bloute, *adj.* soft, 1910. Sw. *blöt*, soft, pulpy.

Bode, *n.* S. command, 2200, 2567. Sir Tr. p. 121, Web.

Bok, *n.* S. book, 1173, 1418, &c. *See* Messe-bok.

Bole, *n.* [Isl. *bolli*, W. *bwla*. Cf. A.S. *bulluca*] bull, 2438. *Boles, pl.* 2330.

Bon, Bone. *See* O-bone.

Bondemen, *n. pl.* S. husbandmen, 1016, 1308. R. Gl.

Bone, *n.* S. [*bén*] boon, request, 1659. Sir Tr. p. 31, and all the Gloss.

Bor, *n.* S. boar, 1867, 1989. *Bores, pl.* 2331.

Bord, *n.* S. (1) table, 1722. K. Horn, 259; Rits. M. R., Web.,

Chauc.; (2) a board, 2106. See the note on l. 2076.

Boren, *part. pa.* S. born, 1878.

Boru, *n.* S. borough, 773, 847, 1014, 1757, 2086, 2826. *Borwes, pl.* 1293, 1444, 1630. *Burwes,* 55, 2277. Sir Tr. pp. 12, 99. Chalmers is certainly mistaken when he says it does not signify *boroughs,* but *castles.* Introd. Gl. p. 200. In Laʒamon the word is always clearly distinguished from *castle,* as it is in many other writers. V. Spelm. in v. *Burgus.*

Bote, *adv.* S. but, only, 721. *See* But.

Bote, *n.* S. remedy, help, 1200. Laʒam., Sir Tr. p. 93; Web., Rits. M. R., Rob. Gl., R. Br., Minot, Chauc., Doug., Lynds. Gl.

Boþen, *adj. pl.* S. both, 173, 697, 958; *g. c.* of both, 2223.

Bounden, Bunden. *See* Binden.

Bour, Boure, Bowr, *n.* S. [*búr*] chamber, 239, 2072, 2076, &c. In Beowulf the apartment of the women is called *Bryd-bur;* l. 1846.

Ygarne beh to *bure*
& lætte bed him makien.
*Laʒam.* l. 19042.

Honder hire *boures* wowe, *K. Horn,* 982, MS., where Rits. Ed. reads *chambre wowe.* Cf. Sir Tr. p. 114; Rits. M. R., Web., R. Br., Doug., V. Jam. *See* note on l. 2076.

Bouthe, *pa. t.* S. bought, 875, 968. Cf. Sir Tr. p. 104.

Bouth, *part. pa.* bought, 883.

Boyes, *n. pl.* S. boys, men, 1899.

Brayd, *pa. t.* S. (1) started, 1282. Chauc., Gaw. and Gal. iii. 21; R. Hood, II. p. 83; (2) drew out, 1825, a word particularly applied to the action of drawing a sword from the scabbard.

Sone his sweord he ut *abræid.*
*Laʒam.* l. 26533.

Cf. Am. and Amil. 1163; Sir Ferumbras, ap. Ellis, M. R. V. 2, p.

387. Rauf Coilzear, ap. Laing, and Wall. i. 223.

Brede, *n.* S. bread, 98. *Bred,* 1879.

Breken, *v.* S. to break, 914. *Broken, pa. t. pl.* broke, 1238.

Brennen, Brenne, *v.* S. to burn, 916, 1162; Rits. M. R., Rob. Gl., R. Br., Chauc. *Brenden, pa. t. pl.* burnt, 594, 2125. *Brend, part. pa.* burnt, 2832, 2841, &c. Sir Tr. p. 93.

Brenne. *See* On brenne.

Brigge, *n.* S. bridge, 875. Sir Tr. p. 148. Still used in Sc. and N. E.

Brihte. *See* Brith.

Brim, *adj.* S. furious, raging, 2233; R. Br. p. 244; Chauc. Rom. Rose, 1836. *Breme,* Rits. M. R. It originally signified the sea itself, and was afterwards used for the raging of the sea, Beowulf, l. 56; Compl. of Scotland, p. 62. V. Jam.

Bringe, Bringen, *v.* S. to bring, 72, 185, &c.

Brini, Brinie, *n.* S. [Mœso-Goth. *brunjo*] cuirass, 1775, 2358, 2551. *Brinies, pl.* 2610. Sir Tr. p. 20. *Burne,* Laʒam. *Brenye,* K. Horn, 719, MS. *See* Merrick's Gl. to Ess. on Anc. Armor. The *Brini* then worn was of *mail,* as appears from l. 2740, *Of his brinie ringes mo.* Hence in Beowulf it is termed *Breostnet,* l. 3100; *Here-net,* 3110; *Hringedbyrne,* 2495. So in the French K. Horn, MS. Douce, *Mes vnc de sun halberc maele ne falsa.* *See* Rits. Gl. M. R.

Brisen, *v.* S. to bruise, beat, 1835. *See* To-Brised.

Brith, *adj.* S. bright, 589, 605, &c. *Brihte,* 2610. *Bryth,* 1252. *Brithter, comp.* brighter, 2141.

Brittene, *part. pa.* S. destroyed, 2700; R. Br. p. 244. *Pistill of Sussan,* ap. Laing. In Doug., Virg. pp. 76, 5; 296, 1, the verb has the sense of *to kill,* which it may also bear here. See *Bruten* in *Will. of Palerne*.

Brod, *adj*. S. broad, 1647.

Broucte, *pa. t. and pp.* brought, 767. *Brouht*, 1979. *Broute*, 2868. *Brouth*, 336, 64. *Browt*, 2412. *Browth*, 2052. *Brouct of liue*, 513, 2412, dead. *Brouthen, pl.* brought, 2791.

Brouke, 1 *p. pres. sing*. S. brook, enjoy, use, 311, 1743, 2545 (cf. Ch. *Non. Pr. Ta.* 480).
So *brouke* thou thi croune!
*K. Horn*, 1041.
Cf. Rits. Gl. M. R., Rich. C. de Lion, 4578; Chauc. C. T. 10182, 15306, R. Hood, V. I. 48, II. 112; Lynds. Gl. Percy, A. R. In Sc. *Bruike*. With these numerous instances before him, it is inconceivable how Jamieson, except from a mere love of his own system, should write: 'There is no evidence that the Engl. *brook* is used in this sense, signifying only to bear, to endure.'

Broys, *n*. S. broth, 924. *Brouwys*, R. Cœur de L. 3077; Sc. V. Jam. and Brockett's North country words, v. *Brewis*; also Nares. Sc. *brose*.

Brune, *adj. pl.* S. brown, 2181, 2249.

Bulder, *adj.* or *n.* 1790. In the north a *Boother* or *Boulder*, is a hard flinty stone, rounded like a bowl. Brockett's Gl. So also in Grose, *Boulder*, a large round stone. *Bowlders*, Marsh. Midl. Count. Gl. The word has a common origin with Isl. *balla$\eth$r*, Fr. *boulet*, Sc. *boule*, in Doug. V. Jam.

Bunden. *See* Binden.

Burgeys, *n*. S. burgess, 1328. *Burgeis*, 2466, *pl.* 2012. *Burgmen*, 2049. *Burhmen, Borhmen*, La3amon., V. Spelm. in v. *Burgarii*.

Burwe. *See* Berwen.

Burwes. *See* Boru.

But, Bute, *conj.* S. except, unless, 85, 690, 1149, 1159, 2022, 2031, 2727. *But on*, 535, 962, except. *Butand*, Sc. *But yf*, 2972, unless. [It should be noted that *but on* should properly be *one* word, being the A. S. *búton* or *bútan*, except. But it is written as two words in the MS.]

But, *n.* 1040. Probably the same as *Put*, q. v. The word *Bout* is derived from the same source.

But, *part. pa.* contended, struggled with each other (*or perhaps* struck, thrust, pushed), 1916. *Buttinge, part. pr.* striking against with force, 2322. From the Fr. *Bouter*, Belg. *Botten*, to impel, or drive forward. V. Jam. Suppl. in v. *Butte*, and *Butt* in Wedgwood.

Butte, *n.* a flounder or plaice, 759. Du. *bot. See* Halliwell.

Byen. *See* Beye.

Bynde. *See* Binden.

Bynderes, *n. pl.* S. binders, robbers who bind, 2050.

Caliz, *n*. S. chalice, 187, 2711.
Lunet than riche relikes toke,
The *chalis* and the mes boke.
*Yw. and Gaw.* 3907.

Callen, *v.* S. to call, 747, 2899.

Cam. *See* Komen.

Canst, *pr. t.* S. knowest, 846. *Cone*, 622, canst. *Kunne, pl.* 435. V. Gl. Chauc. in v. *Conne*. Jam. and Gl. Lynds. *See* Couthe.

Carl, *n.* S. churl, slave, villain, 1789. *Cherl*, 682, 684, 2533. *Cherles, q. c.* churl's, 1092. *Cherles, pl.* villains, bondsmen, 262, 620. Sir Tr. p. 39; V. Spelm. in v. *Ceorlus*, and Jam. and Gl. Lynds.

Casten. *See* Kesten.

Catel, *n.* Fr. chattels, goods, 225, 2023, 2515, 2906, 2939. Web. Gl., R. Br., P. Plowm., Chauc.
Nowe hath Beuis the treasure wone,
Through Arundell that wyll runne,

Wherefore with that and other *catel*,
He made the castle of Arundel.
*Syr Bevys*, O. iii.

Cauenard, *n.* Fr. [*cagnard caignard*] a term of reproach, originally derived from the Lat. *canis*, 2389. V. Roquef. Menage.

This crokede *caynard* sore he is adred.
Rits. A.S. p. 36.
Sire *olde kaynard*, is this thin aray?
Chauc. C. T. 5817.

Cayser, Caysere, *n.* Lat. emperor, 977, 1317, 1725. *Kaysere*, 353.

Cerges, *n. pl.* Fr. wax tapers, 594. *Serges*, 2125. Chauc. Rom. 6251; V. Le Grand. *Vie privée* s F.; V. 3, p. 175.

Chaffare, *n.* S. merchandise, 1657. R. Cœur de L. 2468, R. Gl., Sir Ferumbras, ap. Ellis, M. R. V. 2, p. 412, Chauc., R. Hood, I. 87. *Chaffery*, Sc. V. Lynds. Gl.

Cham for Came, 1873.

Chanbioun, *n.* Fr. champion, 1007. Sir Tr. p. 97. *Chaunpiouns*, *pl.* 1015, 1031, 1055; V. Spelm. in v. *Campio*. Cf. A.S. *cempa*.

Chapmen, *n. pl.* S. merchants, 51, 1639; R. Gl., R. Br., Chauc. In Sc. pedlars. V. Jam., and Gl. Lynds.

Charbucle, *n.* Fr. Lat. a carbuncle, 2145. *Charbocle*, Syr Bevys. *Charbokull*, Le bone Flor. 390. *Charboucle*, Chauc. C. T. 13800. *Charbukill*, Doug. Virg. 3, 10.

Cherl. *See* Carl.

Chesen, *v.* S. to choose, select, 2147. Sir Tr. p. 27; K. Horn, 666; Rits. M. R., Web., R. Br., Chauc., V. Jam. in v. *Cheis*.

Chinche, *adj.* Fr. niggardly, penurious, 1763, 2941.

Bothe he was scars, and *chinche*.
*The Sevyn Sages*, 1244.

So in Chauc. Rom. Rose, 5998, and Gower, *Conf. Am.* 109 b.

Chiste, *n.* S. Lat. chest, 222.

Kiste, 2018. *Kist*, Yorksh. and Sc.; V. Jam. and Lynds. Gl.

Citte, *pa. t.* S. cut, 942. *Kit*, Web. M. R. *Kyt*, Syr Eglam. B. iv. *Kette*, Syr Bevys, C. iii. So Chauc. C. T. 6304.

Claddes, *pa. t.* 2 *p.* S. claddest, 2907.

Clapte, *pa. t.* S. struck, 1814, 1821.

Clare, *n.* Fr. spiced wine, 1728. *See* Claret *in* Prompt. Parv.

Clef, *pa. t.* S. cleft, 2643, 2730.

Cleue. *n.* S. dwelling, 557, 596. A.S. *cleofa*.

Cleuen, *v.* S. to cleave, cut, 917.

Clothe, Clothen, *v.* S. to clothe, 1138, 1233. In l. 1233, Garnett suggests that *cloþen* may be a *nom. pl.* = clothes. If so, *dele* the comma after it.

Clutes, *n. pl.* S. clouts, shreds of cloth, 547. *Clottys*, Huntyng of the hare, 92. Cf. Chauc. C. T. 9827, and *Clut* in Bosworth.

Clyneden, *pa. t. pl.* S. cleaved, fastened, 1300.

Cok, *n.* Lat. cook, 967. *Kok*, 903, 921, 2898. *Cokes, Kokes, g. c.* cook's, 1123, 1146.

Comen, Comes, Cometh. *See* Komen.

Cone. *See* Canst.

Conestable, *n.* Fr. constable, 2286. *Conestables, pl.* 2366.

Conseyl, *n.* Fr. counsel, 2862.

Copes. *See* Kope.

Corporaus, *n.* Fr. Lat. the fine linen wherein the sacrament is put, 188; Cotgr. V. Du Cange, and Jam. in v. *Corperale*.

After the relics they send;
The *corporas*, and the mass-gear,
On the handom [halidom?] they gun swear,
With wordes free and hend.
*Gny of Warw.* ap. Ellis, M.R. V. 2, p. 77.

Corune, *n.* Lat. crown, 1319, 2944.

Coruning, *n.* Lat. coronation, 2948.

Cote, *n.* S. cot, cottage, 737, 1141.

Couel, *n.* coat, garment, 768, 858, 1144. *Cuuel,* 2904. *Kouel,* 964. The word is connected with A.S. *cufle, cugele,* a cowl.

Couere, *v.* Fr. to recover, 2040.
And prayde to Marie bryght,
Kevere hym of hys care.
*Ly Beaus Desc.* 1983.
Hyt wolde *covyr* me of my care.
*Erl of Tol.* 381.

Coupe, *v.* buy, buy dearly, get in exchange, 1800. Icel. *kaupa.*

Couth. *See* Quath.

Couþe, *pa. t.* of Conne, *v. aux.* S. knew, wa able, could, 93, 112, 194, 750, 772. *Kouþen, pl.* 369. More he *couthe* of veneri, Than *couthe* Manerious.
*Sir Tristr.* p. 24.
*See* Canst.

Crake, Crakede. *See* Kraken.

Cranede, *pa. t.* S. craved, asked, 633.

Crice, *n.* explained to mean *rima podicis* in Coleridge's Glossarial Index, 2450. Cf. A.S. *crecca.* Icel. *kryki,* a corner. In Barb. x. 602, *crykes* is used for *angles,* corners. *See* Krike.

Crist, *n.* Lat. Gr. Christ, 16, &c. *Cristes, g. c.* 153. *Kristes,* 2797.

Croiz, *n.* Fr. Lat. cross, 1263, 1268, 1358, &c. *Croice,* Sir Tr. p. 115.

Croud, *part. pa.* crowded, oppressed (?) 2338. K. Alisaund, 609. Cf. A.S. *crydan,* p. p. *gecróden.*

Croun, Croune, *n.* Fr. crown, head, 568, 902, 2657. *Crune,* 1814, 2734
Fykenildes *crowne*
He fel ther doune.
*K. Horn,* 1509.

Cf. K. of Tars, 631; Le bone Flor. 92, and Erle of Tol. 72.

Cruhsse. *See* To-cruhsse.

Crus, brisk, nimble, 1966. It is the Sw. *krus.* excitable, Sc. *crouse.* See *Crouse* in Atkinson's Cleveland Glossary.

Cunnriche, *n.* S. kingdom, 2318. *Kinneriche,* 976. *Kuneriche,* 2400. *Kunerike,* 2804. *Kunrik,* 2143. In the last instance it means *a nark of royalty, or monarchy.* Web. *Kyngriche, Kyaryche.*

Curt, *n.* Fr. court, 1685.

Curteys, Curteyse, *adj.* Fr. courteous, 2875, 2916.

Cuuel. *See* Couel.

Dam, *n.* 2468, here used in a reproachful sense, but apparently from the same root as the Fr. *Dam, Damp, Dan,* and *Don,* i. e. from *Dominus.*

Dame, *n.* Fr. Lat. mistress, lady, 558, 1717. V. Gl. Chauc.

Danshe, *n. pl.* Danish men, 2689, 2945, &c. *See* Denshe.

Datheit, *interj.* 296, 300, 926, 1125, 1887, 1914, 2047, 2447, 2511. *Datheyt,* 1799, 1995, 2604, 2757. An interjection or imprecation, derived from the Fr. *Deshait, dehait, dehet,* explained by Barbazan and Roquefort, *affliction, malheur;* [from the O. F. *hait,* pleasure]. It may be considered equivalent to Cursed! I'll betide! In the old Fabliaux it is used often in this sense:

Fils à putain, fet-il, lechiere,
Vo jouglerie m'est trop chiere,
*Dehait* qui vous i aporta,
Par mon chief il le comparra.
*De S. Pierre et du Jougleor,* 381.

The term was very early engrafted on the Saxon phraseology. Thus in the *Disputation of Ane Hule and a Niʒtingale,* l. 99.

*Dahet* habbe that ilke best,
That fuleth his owe nest!

GLOSSARIAL INDEX. 115

It occurs also frequently in the Old English Romances. *See* Sir Tristr. pp. 111, 191; Horn Childe, ap. Rits. V. 3, p. 290; Amis and Amil. 1569; Sevyn Sages, 2395; R. Brunne, where it is printed by Hearne *Dayet*. To this word, in all probability, we are indebted for the modern imprecation of *Dase you! Dise you! Dash you!* still preserved in many counties, and in Scotland. V. Jam. Suppl. v. *Dash you*.

Dawes, *n. pl.* S. days, 27, 2344, 2950. *Dayes*, 2353.

Ded, Dede, *n.* S. death, 149, 1(?), 332, 1687, 2719, &c.

Ded, *part. pa.* S. dead, 2007.

Dede, *n.* S. deed, action, 1356.

Dede, Deden, Dedes. *See* Do.

Deide. *See* Deye.

Del, *n.* S. deal, part, 218, 818, 1070, &c. Web., R. Gl., R. Br., Chauc. *Deil*, Sc. V. Jam.

Deled, *part. pa.* S. distributed, 1736. *See* To-deyle.

Demen, *v.* S. to judge, pass judgment, 2467. *Deme, Demen, pr. t. pl.* judge, 2476, 2812. *Demden, pa. t. pl.* judged, 2820, 2833. *Demd, part. pa.* judged, 2488, 2765, 2838.

Denshe, *adj.* Danish, 1403, 2575, 2693. *See* Danshe.

Deplike, *adj.* S. deeply, 1417. Synonymous with *Grundlike*, q. v.

Dere, *n.* S. dearth, scarcity, 824, 841. R. Gl. p. 416.

Dere, *adv.* S. dearly, 1637, 1638.

Dere, *v.* S. to harm, injure, 490, 574, 806, 2310. *Dereth, pr. t.* injures, 648. K. Horn, 148; R. Br. p. 107; K. of Tars, 192; Chauc. *Deir*, Sc. Doug. Virg. 413, 52; Lynds. Gl.

Dere, *adj.* S. dear, 1637, 2170, &c.

Deuel, *n.* S. devil, 446, 496, 1188. *Deueles, g. c.* devil's, 1409.

Deus. This is undoubtedly the vocative case of the Lat. *Deus*, used as an interjection, 1312, 1650, 1930, 2096, 2114. "Its use was the same in French as in English. Thus in King Horn :

Enuers Deu en sun quer a fait grant clamur,
Obi, *Deus!* fait il, ki es uerrai creatur,
Par ki deuise, &c.
*Harl. MS.* 527, f. 66 b. c. 2.

It was probably introduced into the English language by the Normans, and its pronunciation remained the same as in the French. And gradde 'as armes,' for *Douce Mahons!—K. Alisaunder*, 3674. It is curious to remark, that we have here the evident and simple etymology of the modern exclamation *Deuce!* for the derivation of which even the best and latest Lexicographers have sent us to the *Dusii* of St Augustine, the *Dues* of the Gothic nations, *Diis* of the Persians, *Teus* of the Armoricans, &c. Thomson very justly adds, that all these words, 'seem, like dæmon, to have been once used in a good sense,' and in fact are probably all corruptions of the same root. Cf. R. Brunne, p. 254, and Gl. in v. *Deus*. For the first suggestion of this derivation the Editor is indebted to Mr Will. Nicol."—M.

Deye, *v.* S. to die, 840. *Deide, pa. t. pl.* died, 402.

Dide, Diden, Dides. *See* Do.

Dike, *n.* S. ditch, 2435. *Dikes, pl.* 1923. N.E. and Sc., V. Jam. and Brockett.

Dine, *n.* S. din, noise, 1860, 1868.

Dinge, *v.* S. to strike, scourge, beat, 215, 2329. *Dong, pa. t.* struck, 1147. *Dungen, part. pa.* beaten, or scourged, 227. Sc. and N. E. *See* Jam. Gl., Lynds., and Ray.

Dint, *n.* S. blow, stroke, 1807, 1817, 1969, &c. *Dent*, Sir Tr. p. 92; Chauc. *Dynt*, R. Br. *Dintes*, *pl.* 1437, 1862, 2665. *Duntes*, K. Horn, 865. *Dentys*, Rits. M. R. *Dyntes*, R. Gl. *Dintes*, Minot, p. 23; V. Gl. Lynds.

Dunten, *pa. t. pl.* S. struck, beat, 2148.

Do, Don, *v.* S. The various uses of this verb in English and Scotch, in an auxiliary, active, and passive sense, have been pointed out by Tyrwhitt, Essay on Vers. of Chauc. Note (37), Chalmers, Gl. Lynds. and Jamieson. It signifies: to do, *facere*, 117, 528, 1191; to cause, *efficere*, 611; *do casten*, 519; *do hem fle*, 2600, to put or place (used with *in* or *on*), 535, 577, &c. *Dones on* = don es on = do them on, put them on (*see* Es), 970. *Dos*, *pr. t. 2 p.* dost, 2390. *Dos, pr. t. 3 p.* does, 1994, 2434, 2698. *Doth, Don, pr. t. pl.* do, 1838, 1840. *Doth, imp.* do, 'cause (ye), 2037. *Dos, imp. pl.* do ye, 2592. *Dede, Dide, pa. t.* caused, 658, 970, &c. *Dede, Dide, pa. t.* put, placed, 659, 709, 859. *Dedes, Dides, pa. t. 2 p.* didest, 2393, 2903. *Deden, Diden, pa. t. pl.* caused, 242; did, performed, 953, 1176, 2306. *Don, part. pa.* caused, 1169. *Don, part. pa.* done, 667. *Of line haue do*, 1805, have slain.

Dom, *n.* S. doom, judgment, 2473, 2487, 2813, &c. Sir Tr. p. 127.

Dore, *n.* S. door, 1788.

Dore-tre, *n.* S. bar of the door, 1806. *See* Tre.

Douhter, *n.* S. daughter, 120, 2712. *Douthe*, 1079. *Douther*, 2867, 2914. *Douhtres*, *pl.* 350, 2982. *Douthres*, 2979. *Doutres*, 717.

Doun. *See* Adoun.

Doutede, *pa. t.* Fr. feared, 708.

Douthe, *n.* Fr. fear, 1331, 1377.

Douthe, *pa. t.* of Dow, *v. imp.* S. [*dugan*, valere, prodesse] was worth, was sufficient, availed, 703, 833, 1184. It is formed in the same manner as *Mouthe*, Might. *See* Sir Tr. p. 77; Jam. and Gl. Lynds. in v. Dow.

Drad. *See* Dred.

Drawe, Drawen. *See* Drou.

Dred, *imp.* dread, fear (thou), 2168. *Dredden, Dredde, pa. t. pl.* dreaded, feared, 2289, 2568. *Drad, part. pa.* afraid, 1669. *See* Adrad.

Drede, *n.* S. dread, 1169; doubt, anxiety, care, 828, 1664. Chauc.

Dremede, *pa. t.* S. (used with *me*), dreamed, 1284, 1304.

Dreinchen, Drenchen, Drinchen, *n.* S. to drown, 553, 561, 583, 1416, 1424, &c. *Drenched, part. pa.* drowned, 520, 669, 1368, 1379. V. Gl. Web., R. Gl., Chauc.

Dreng, *n.* *See* note on l. 31.

Drepen, *v.* S. to kill, slay, 1783, 1865, &c. *Drepe*, would slay, 506. *Drop, pa. t.* killed, slew, 2229. Bosworth gives *drepan*, to slay. Cf. Sw. *dräpa*.

Dreping, *n.* slaughter, 2684. Cf. A.S. *drepe*.

Drinchen. *See* Dreinchen.

Drinken, *v.* S. to drink, 459, 800.

Drinkes, *n. pl.* S. drinks, liquors, 1738.

Drit, *n.* [Icel. *drítr*, Du. *dreet*] dirt, 682. A term expressing the highest contempt. K. Alisaund. 4718; Wickliffe. So, in an ancient metrical invective against Grooms and Pages, written about 1310,

Thah he ȝeue hem cattes *dryt* to huere compuuage,
ȝet hym shulde arewen of the arrerage.
MS. Harl. 2253, f. 125.

Cf. Jam. Suppl. in v. *Dryte*, and Gl. Lynds.

Driuende. *See* Drof.

Drou, *pa. t.* S. drew, 705, 719, &c. *Vt-drow, pa. t.* out-drew, 2632. *With-drow,* withdrew, 498; (*spelt* wit-drow), 502. *Drawe, Drawen, part. pa.* drawn, 1925, 2225, 2477, 2603, &c. *Ut-drawe, Ut-drawen,* out-drawn, 1802, 2631. *See* To-Drawe.

Drof, *pa. t.* S. drove, 725; hastened, 1793, 1872. *Driuende, part. pr.* driving, riding quickly, 2702.

Drurye,*n.* Fr. courtship, gallantry, 195. Web., Rits. M. R., P. Plowm., Chauc., Lynds.

Dubbe, *v.* Fr. S. to dub, create a knight, 2042. *Dubbede, pa. t.* dubbed, 2314. *Dubban to ridere,* Chron. Sax. An. 1085, [1086]. *To cnihte hine dubben,* Laʒam. l. 22497. "Hickes, Hearne, Gl. R. Gl., and Tyrwhitt, Gl. Chauc., all refer the word to the Saxon root, which primarily signified *to strike,* the same as the Isl. *at dubba.* Todd on the contrary, Gl. Illustr. Chauc., thinks this questionable, and refers to Barbazan's Gl. in v. *Adouber,* which is there derived from the Lat. *adaptare.* Du Cange and Dr Merrick give it also a Latin origin, from *Adoptare,* and by corruption *Adobare.*"—M. The etymology is discussed in Wedgwood, s. v. *Dub. See* Note on l. 2314.

Duelle, *v.* S. to dwell, give attention, 4.

A tale told Ysoude fre,
Thai *duelle :*
Tristrem that herd he.
*Sir Tristr.* p. 181.

Cf. Sir Otuel, l. 3, and Sevyn Sages, 1. *Dwellen,* to dwell, remain, 1185; to delay, 1351. *Dwellen, pr. t. pl.* dwell, tarry, 1058. *Dwelleden, pa. t. pl.* dwelt, tarried, 1189.

Dwelling, *n.* delay, 1352

Dun. *See* Adoun.

Dungen. *See* Dinge.

Dursten, *pa. t. pl.* S. durst, 1866.

Eie, *n.* S. eye, 2545. *Heie,* 1152. *Eyne, pl.* eyes, 680, 1273, 1364; *eyen,* 1340; *eyn,* 2171.

Eir, *n.* Fr. Lat. heir, 410, 2539. *Eyr,* 110, 289, &c. Jam. gives it a Northern etymology, in v. Ayr.

Ek, *conj.* S. [*eac*] eke, also, 1025, 1038, 1066, &c. *Ok* [Su.-G. *och,* Du. *ook*] 187, 200, 879, 1081, &c. V. Jam. in v. Ac.

Eld, *adj.* S. old, 546. *Helde,* 2472. *Heldeste, sup.* 1396.

Elde, *n.* S. age, 2713. *Helde,* 128, 174, 387, 1435.
Ælde hæfde heo na mare
Buten fihtene ʒere.
*Laʒam.* l. 25913.
R. Br. In Sc. *Eild.* It was subsequently restricted to the sense of *old age,* as in Chauc.

Elles, *adv.* S. else, 1192, 2590.

Em, S. uncle, 1326. Sir Tr. p. 53. Properly, says Sir W. Scott, an uncle by the father's side. It appears however to have been used indifferently either on the father's or mother's side. *See* Hearne's Gl. on R. Gl. and R. Br., Web., Erle of Tol. 988 ; Chauc. Troil. 2, 162, and Nares. Prov. Eng. *Eam.*

Er, *adv.* S. before, 684. *Her,* 541. *Are,* Sir Tr. p. 152. *Er,* K. Horn, 130. *See* Are, Or.

Er, *conj.* S. before, 317, 1261, 2680. *Her,* 229.

Erl, *n.* S. earl, 189, &c. *Erles, g. c.* 2898, earl's. *Herles,* 883. *Erldom,* earldom, 2909.

Ern, *n.* S. eagle, 572. Rits. M. R. Octovian, 196 ; R. Gl. p. 177; Will. of Palerne.

Erþe, *n.* S. earth, 740 ; ground, 2657.

Erþe, *v.* S. to dwell, 739. A.S. *eardian.*

Es, a plural pronoun signifying *them*, as in *don es on* = put them on, 970. See *Gen. and Exod.* ed. Morris, pref. p. xix.

Et, a singular pronoun, equivalent to *it*, used in *hauenet* = *hauen et*, 2005; *hauedet* = *haued et*, 714.

Ete, Eten, *v.* S. to eat, 791, 800, 911, &c. *Hete, Heten*, 146, 317, 457, 641. *Et, imp.* eat (thou), 925. *Et, Het, pa. t.* ate, 653, 656. *Etes, fut.* 2 *p.* thou shalt eat, 907. *Eteth, fut.* 3 *p.* shall eat, 672. *Eten, part. pa.* eaten, 657.

Eþen, *adv.* S. hence, 690. *Heþen*, 683, 845, 1085, 2727.

Eþer. See Ayþer.

Euere, Eure, *adv.* S. ever. 207, 424, 704, &c. *Heuere*, 17, 327, 830.

Euereich, *adj.* S. every, 137. *Euere il*, 218, 1334, 1644. *Euere ilc*, 1330. *Eueri*, 1070, 1176, 1383. *Eueril*, 1764, 2318, &c. *Euerilk*, 2258, 2432. *Euerilkon*, every one, 1062, 1996, 2197. See Il.

Euere-mar, *adv.* S. evermore, 1971.

Eyen, Eyn, Eyne. See Eie.

Eyr. See Eir.

Fader, *n.* S. Lat. father, 1224, 1403, 1416. Sir Tr. p. 35; K. Horn, 114. The cognate words may be found in Jam.

Faderles, *adj.* fatherless, 75.

Fadmede, *pa. t.* S. fathomed, embraced, 1295. From *fœthmian*, Utraque manu extensa complecti, Cod. Exon., ed. Thorpe, p. 334. It has the same meaning in Sc. V. Jam.

Falle, *v.* S. to fall, 39, &c. *Falles, imp. pl.* fall ye, 2302. *Fel, pa. t.* fell, appertained. 1815, 2359. *Fellen, pa. t. pl.* fell, 1303.

Fals, *adj.* S. false, 2511.

Falwes, *n. pl.* S. fallows, fields, 2509. Chauc. C. T. 6238, where Tyrwh. explains it *harrowed lands*.

Fare, *n.* S. journey, 1337, 2621. R. Gl. p. 211; R. Br., Minot, p. 2 (left unexplained by Rits.); Barb. iv. 627. *Schip-fare*, a voyage, Sir Tr. p. 53.

Faren, *v.* S. to go, 264. *Fare*, 1378, 1392, &c. *Fare, pr. t.* 2 *p.* farest, behavest, 2705. *Fares, pr. t.* 3 *p.* goes, flies, 2690. *Ferde, pa. t.* went, 447, 1678, &c.; behaved, 2411. *For* (went), 2382, 2943. *Foren, pa. t. pl.* went, 2380, 2618.

Faste, *adv.* S. attentively, earnestly, 2148.

Tristrem as a man
*Fast* he gan to light.
Sir *Tristr.* p. 167.

Bidde we ȝeorne Ihū Crist, and seint Albon wel *faste*,
That we moten to the Ioye come, that euere schal i-laste.
Vita S. Albani, MS. Laud. 108. f. 47 b.

Fastinde, *part. pr.* S. fasting, 865.

Fauth. See Fyht.

Fawen, *adj.* S. fain, glad, 2160. *Fawe*, K. of Tars, 1058; Octovian, 307; R. Gl. p. 150; Chauc. C. T. 5802.

Fe, *n.* S. fee, possessions, or money, 386, 563, 1225, &c. See Jam. and Lynds. Gl.

Feble, *adj.* Fr. feeble, poor, scanty, 323.

Feblelike, *adv.* feebly, scantily, 418. *Febli*, Sir Tr. p. 179, for *meanly*.

Feden, *v.* S. to feed, 906. *Feddes, pa. t.* 2 *p.* feddest, 2907.

Fel. See Bifalle, Falle.

Felawes, *n. pl.* S. fellows, companions, 1338.

Feld, *n.* S. field, 2634, 2685, 1291.

## GLOSSARIAL INDEX. 119

Felde, Felede. *pa. t.* S. felled, 67, 1859, 2694. *Felden* (? read *he ne fellen,* they did not fall), 2698. *Feld, part. pa.* felled, 1824. Sir F. Madden writes—"in l. 2698, I prefer reading *ne felden,* did not fell, governed by *that.* In l. 67, Garnett suggested *felede,* pursued, from Swed. *följade*."

Fele, *adj.* S. many, often, 778, 1277, 1737, &c. Sir Tr. p. 19.

Fele, *adv.* S very, 2442.

Fend, *n.* S. fiend, 506, 1411, 2229.

Fer, *adv.* S. far, 359, 1863, 22ʳ, &c. *Ferne,* far, 1864; *pl. ı j.* foreign, 2031.

þa kingges buh stronge, And of *ferrene* lond.
*Laȝam.* l. 5528.

Cf. Chauc. Prol. l. 14.

Ferd, *n.* S. army, 2384, 2548, &c. *Ferde,* 2535. Laȝam., R. Gl., R. Br., Web. *Ferdes, pl.* 2683.

Ferde. *See* Fare.

Fere, *n.* S. companion, wife, 1214. Sir Tr. p. 157. K. Horn, Web., R. Gl., R. Br., Minot, Chauc. *Feir,* Sc. V. Jam. and Gl. Lynds.

Ferlike, *n.* S. wonder, 1258. *Ferlik,* 1849. Sir Tr. p. 21. Originally in all probability an *adj.*

Ferþe, *adj.* S. fourth, 1810.

Feste, *n.* Fr. feast, 2344, &c.

Feste, *v.* Fr. to feast, 2938.

Festen, *v.* S. to fasten, 1785; (used passively) 82. *Fest, pa. t.* fastened, 144.

Fet. *See* Fot.

Fete, *v.* S. to fetch, bring, 642, 912, 937, &c. Used passively, 316, 2037. *Fetes, pr. t. s.* fetch, 2341. V. Pegge's Anecd. of Engl. Lang. p. 135.

Fetere, *v.* S. to fetter, chain, 2758. Used passively.

Feteres, *n. pl.* S. fetters, 82, 2759.

Fey, *n.* Fr. faith, 255, 1666. *Feyth,* 2853.

Fiht, *n.* S. fight, 2668, 2716.

Fikel, *adj.* S. fickle, inconstant, 1210, 2799.

File, *n.* vile, worthless person, 2499.

Men seth ofte a muche *file,*
They he serue boten a wile,
Bicomen swithe riche.
*Hending the hende,* MS. Digb. 86.

So in R. Br. p. 237.

David at that while was with Edward the kyng,
Ʒit auanced he that *file* vntille a faire thing.

It is used for *coward* by Minot, pp. 31, 36. Cf. Du. *vuil,* foul, malicious.

Finden, *v.* S. to find, 1083. *Finde,* 220. *Fynde,* 42. *Funden, pa. t. pl.* found, 602. *Funde, part. pa.* found, 2376. *Funden,* 1427.

Fir, *n.* S. fire, 585, 1162, &c. *Fyr,* 915.

Firrene, *adj.* S. made of fir, 2078. *Firron,* Doug. Virg. 47. 34.

Flaunes, *n. pl.* Fr. custards, or pancakes, 644. *See* Way's note in Prompt. Parv.

Fledden, *pa. t. pl.* S. fled, 2416.

Flemen, *v.* S. to drive away, banish, 1160. R. Gl., R. Br., Chauc., Rits. A.S. So in Sc. V. Jam.

Flete, *pres. subj.* S. float, swim, 522. Sir Tr. p. 27; K. Horn, 159; Chauc. *Fleit,* Sc. V. Jam.

Fleye, *v.* S. to fly, 1791, 1813, 1827, 2751. *Fley, pa. t.* flew, 1305.

Flo, *v.* S. to flay, 612, 2495. K. Horn, 92. *Flow, pa. t.* flayed, 2502. *Flowe, pa. t. pl.* 2433.

Flok, *n.* S. flock, troop, 24. *See* Trome.

Flote, *n.* S. boat, 738. A.S. *flóta,* a ship; Icel. *floti,* (1) a ship, (2) a fleet; cf. Laȝam. 4530.

Flour, *n.* Fr. flower, 2917.

Fnaste, *v.* S. to breathe, 548. Cf. A.S. *Fnæstiað*, the wind-pipe, *Fnæstan*, puffs of wind. *Fnast* = breath in *Owl and Nightingale*, l. 44.

Fo, *n.* S. foe, 1363, 2849; *pl.* foos, 67.

Fol, *n.* Fr. fool, 298. *Foles, pl.* 2100.

Folc, Folk, *n.* S. men collectively, people, 89, 438, &c.

Folwes, *imp.* S. follow ye, 1885, 2601.

Fonge, *v.* S. to take, receive, 763; 2 *p. pres. subj.* 856. In common use from Laȝam. to Chauc. and much later.

For, *prep.* S. *For to* is prefixed to the inf. of verbs in the same manner as the Fr. *pour*, or Sp. *por*. It is so used in all the old writers, and in the vulgar translation of the Scriptures, and is still preserved in the North of England. Cf. 17, &c. *For* = on account of, 1670. Sir Tr. p. 62.

For, Foren. *See* Faren.

Forbere, *v.* S. spare, abstain from, 352. Chauc. Rom. R. 4751. *Forbar, pa. t.* spared, abstained from, 764, 2623.

Forfaren, *v.* S. to perish, 1380. R. Br. *Forfard* (*p. p.*) Ly Beaus Desc. 1484. The inf. is also used in Web., P. Plowm., Chauc. In Sc. *Forfair*. V. Compl. of Scotl. p. 100, and Gl. Lynds.

Forgat, *pa. t.* S. forgot, 2636, &c. *Foryat*, 249.

For-henge, *v.* to kill by hanging, 2724. Cf. Du. *verhangen zich*, to hang one's self.

Forlorn, *part. pa.* S. utterly lost, 770, 1424. *Forloren*, 580. R. Br., Rits. M. R., Chauc. Used actively, Sir Tr. p. 35.

Forþi, *adv.* S. on this account, therefore, because, 1194, 1431,
2043, 2500, 2578. Sir Tr. p. 14, and in all the Gloss.

Forthwar, *adv.* S. forthward; i. e. as we go on, 731.

Forw, *n.* S. furrow, 1094.

Forward, *n.* S. promise, word, covenant, 486. *Forwarde*, 554. Laȝam. l. 4790. Sir Tr. p. 13. Rits. M. R., Web., R. Gl., R. Br., Minot, Chauc.

Fostred, *part. pa.* S. nourished, 1434, 2239.

Fot, *n.* S. *Euerilk fot*, 2432, every foot, or man. *Fet, pl.* 616, 1022, 1303, 2479. *Fote*, 1054, 1199.

Fouhten. *See* Fyht.

Fourtenith, *n.* S. fortnight, 2284.

Fremde, *adj.* (used as a *n.*) S. stranger, 2277.

Vor hine willeth sone uorgiete
Tho *fremde* and tho sibbe.
MS. Digb. 4.
Ther ne myhte libbe
The *fremede* ne the sibbe.
K. Horn, 67.
See also R. Gl. p. 346; Chron. of Eng. 92; P. Plowm., Chau., Jam. and Gl. Lynds.

Freme, *v.* S. to perform, 441.

Fri, *adj.* S. free, liberal, 1072. Chauc.

Frie, *v.* to blame, 1998. Icel. *fryja*, to blame. Cf. *frelrs*, blameless. *Allit. Poems*, ed. Morris, A. 431.

Fro, *prep.* S. from, 265, &c.

Frusshe. *See* To-frusshe.

Ful, *adv.* S. very, much, completely, 6, 82, &c. *Ful wo*, 2589, much sorrow.

Ful, Fule, *adj.* S. foul, 506, 555, 626, 965, &c. *Foule*, 1158.

Fulike, *adv.* S. foully, shamefully, 2749.

Fulde, *part. pa.* S. filled, complete, 355.

## GLOSSARIAL INDEX.   121

Funde, Funden. *See* Finde.

Fyht, *v.* S. to fight, 2361. *Fauth, pa. t.* fought, 1990. *Fouhten, pa. t. pl.* fought, 2661.

Fyn, *n.* Fr. Lat. ending, 22. R. Br., Minot, Chauc., &c.

Ga, *v.* S. to go. *See* Ouer-ga.

Gad, *n.* S. goad, 279. *Gaddes, pl.* 1016. In Gl. Ælfr. among the instruments of husbandry occur *Gad,* stimulus, and *Gadiron,* aculeus. So in *The Fermeror and his Docter,* printed by Laing:
Quhen Symkin standis quhisling with ane quhip and ane *gaid,*
Priking and ȝarkand ane auld ox hide.
V. Jam. in v. *Gade,* 4. and Nares.

Gadred, *part. pa.* S. gathered, 2577.

Gadeling, *n.* S. an idle vagabond, low man, 1121.

Þa wes æuer alc cheorl
Al swa bald alse an eorl,
& alle þa *gadelinges*
Alse heo weoren sunen kinges.
*Laȝam.* l. 12333.
Cf. K. Alisaund. 1733, 4063. *Gadlyng,* Rob. of Cicyle, MS. Harl. 1701. R. Gl. p. 277, 310. Chauc. Rom. Rose, 938. The word originally meant *Vir generosus. See* Beowulf, l. 5227.

Gaf. *See* Yeue.

Galwe-tre, *n.* S. the gallows, 43, 335, 695. Le Bone Fl. 1726. Erle of Tol. 657. *Galues, Galwes, Galewes,* 687, 1161, 2477, 2508. R. Br., Chauc. Cf. Ihre Gl. Suiog. in v. *galge,* ab Isl. *gayl,* ramus arboris.

Gamen, *n.* S. game, sport, 980, 1716, 2135, 2250, 2577; joy, 2935, 2963. *Gamyn,* Barb. iii. 465. V. Jam.

Gan, *pa. t.* S. began, 2443. V. Jam.

Gangen, *v.* S. to go, walk, 370, 845, &c. *Gange,* 796. *Gongen,*
855. *Gonge,* 1185, 1739, &c. *Gonge, pr. t.* 2 *p.* goest, 690, 843. *Gangande, part. pr.* on foot, walking, 2283. Wynt. V. Jam.

Garte, *pa. t.* S. made, 189, 1857, &c. *Gart,* 1001, 1082. *Gert,* Sir Tr. p. 147. V. Jam. and Gl. Lynds.

Gat, Gaten. *See* Geten.

Gate, *n.* S. (1) way, road, 846, 889. Sir Tr. p. 27; (2) manner, fashion (*see* þus-gate), 783, 2419, 2586.

Genge, *n.* S. family, company, 786, 1735; retinue, 2353, 2362, 2383.

Þe king of þan londe
Mid muchelere *genge.*
*Laȝam.* l. 6156.
Hence *Gang.* V. Todd's Johns.

Gent, *adj.* Fr. neat, pretty, 2139. Sir Tr. p. 87, R. Br., Chauc.

Gere. *See* Messe-gere.

Gest, *n.* Fr. tale, adventure, 2984. *See* Note in Warton's Hist. E. P., V. I. p. 69. Ed. 1840.

Gete, *v.* to guard, watch, keep, 2762, 2960. Icel. *gæta,* to guard. Cf. *Ormulum,* 2079. [Suggested by Garnett.]

Geten, *v.* S. to get, take, 792. *Gete,* 1393. *Gat, pa. t.* begot, got, 495, 730. *Gaten, Geten, pa. t. pl.* begot, 2893, 2934, 2978. *Getes, f. t.* 2 *p.* shalt get, 908.

Ghod *for* Good, 255.

Gisarm, *n.* Fr. a bill, 2553. *See* Gl. Rits. M. R., Speln. in v., Jam. Dict., and Merrick's Gl. in v. *Gesa, Gesum.* ["Distinguished from other weapons of the axe kind by a spike rising from the back. There were two kinds, viz. the *glaive-gisarme,* with a sabre-blade and spike; and the *bill-gisarme,* in shape of a hedging-bill with a spike." Godwin's Archæol. Handbook, p. 254.]

Giue. *See* Yeue.

Giue, *n.* S. gift, 2880. *Gyue,* 357. *Yeft,* 2336.

Giueled, piled up, 814. [The O.Fr. *gavelé* means piled up, heaped together. To *gavel* corn (*see* Halliwell) is to put it into heaps, and a *gavel* is a heap of corn. But this may very well be derived from *gable*, since a heap takes the shape of a peaked end of a house; and the O.Fr. term is probably originally Teutonic, and connected, as *gable* is, with Mœso-Goth. *gibla*, a pinnacle, with which compare German *giebel*, Du. *gevel*, and hence our word would be taken from a verb *givelen*, to pile up. The fish in Havelok's basket would be what the Dutch call *gevelvormig*, or formed like a gable, or like the peaked end of a *stack* of hay or corn, whence the author's expression—*giueled als a stac*, piled up in the shape of a stack. Other explanations are *flayed*, from Du. *villen*, to flay; or *filed*, ranged in rows upon a stick, where *stick* is represented by *stac*. But the latter supposition would require the reading *on* rather than *als*; not to mention the fact that if fish are carried *in a pannier* they would not resemble fish carried *on a stick*. Nor is it quite satisfactory to say that *giueled* is put for *gefilled*, filled; for this is not elucidated by the expression *als a stac*, any more than the explanation *flayed* is. *Gable* is Icel. *gafl*, Sw. *gafvel*, Dan. *gavl*, Du. *gevel*, Ger. *giebel*, *gipfel*, &c. Its forked shape seems to give rise to Ger. *gabel*, Sw. *gaffel*, a fork; respecting which set of words see *Gaff* in Wedgwood.]

Gladlike, *adv.* S. gladly, 805, 906, 1760.

Glede, *n.* S. a burning coal, 91, 869. Rits. M. R., Web., R. Br., Chauc. *See* Note on l. 91.

Gleiue, Gleyue, Fr. a spear, lance, 1770, 1844, 1981. *Gleiues, Gleyues, pl.* 267, 1748, 1864. Dr Merrick explains it, "A weapon composed of a long cutting blade at the end of a staff." See R. Gl. p. 203; Guy of Warw. R. iii.; Chauc. Court of Love, 544; Percy, A. R.

Glem, *n.* S. gleam, ray, 2122. *See* Stem.

Gleu, *n.* S. game, skill, 2332. Properly, says Sir W. Scott, the joyous science of the minstrels. Cf. Sir Tr. p. 24, 35, 150.

Gleymen, *n. pl.* S. gleemen, 2329. *Glewemen*, Sir Tr. p. 110.

Whar bin thi *glewmen* that schuld thi *glewe*,
With harp and fithel, and tabour bete.
Disp. betw. the bodi & saul, ap. Leyd. Compl. of Scotl.

Glotuns, *n. pl.* Fr. gluttons, wicked men, 2104.

Va, *Glutun*, envers tei nostre lei se defent.
K. Horn, 1633, MS. Douce.

Cf. K. Horn, 1124, ap. Rits., Yw. and Gaw. 3247; R. Cœur de L. 5953, and Chauc.

Gnede, *adj.* S. niggardly, frugal, 97. Nearly equivalent to *chinche*, l. 1763. Printed *guede* in Sir Tr. p. 169. [Cf. *Gnede* in Halliwell, and A.S. *gneadlícnes*, frugality.]

God, *n.* S. gain, wealth, goods, 797, 2034; *pl.* gode, 1221. R. Gl., R. Br., Chauc.

God, Gode, *adj.* S. good, excellent, 7, &c.

Goddot, Goddoth, *interj.* god wot! 606, 642, 796, 909, 1656, 2543; cf. 2527. It is formed probably in the same manner as *Goddil*, for God's will, in Yorksh. and Lanc. V. Craven dialect, and View of Lanc. dialect, 1770, 8vo. The word before us appears to have been limited to Lincolnshire or Lancashire, and does not appear in the Glossaries. Other instances are in the *Cursor Mundi*, MS. Cott. Vesp. F. iii. fol. 87*b*, and in MS. Cott. Galba E. ix. fol. 61. It also occurs in a translation of a French Fabliau, written in the reign of Edw. I.

## GLOSSARIAL INDEX. 123

*Goddot!* so I wille,
And loke that thou hire tille,
And strek out hire thes.
*La fablel & la cointise de dame Siriz*, MS. Digb. 86.
Grundtvig told me (adds Sir F. Madden) that it is "undoubtedly the same interjection spelled *Ioduth* in the old Danish rime-chronicle."

Gome, *n.* S. man, 7.

Gon, *v.* S. to go, walk, 113, 1045. *Goth, imp.* go ye, 1780. *Gon, part. pa.* gone, 2692.

Gonge, Gongen. *See* Gange.

Gore, 2497. *See* Grim.

Gos, *n.* S. goose, 1240. *Gees, pl.* 702.

Gouen. *See* Yeue.

Goulen, *pr. t. pl.* 2 *p.* S. howl, cry, 454. *Gouleden, pa. t. pl.* howled, cried, 164.
An *yollen* mote thu so heye,
That ut berste bo thin ey.
*Hule and Nihtingale,* l. 970.
Used also by Wickliffe. In Scotland and the North it is still preserved, but in the South *Yell* is used as an equivalent. *See* Jam. and Gl. Lynds.

Gram, *n.* S. grief, 2469.

Graten, *v.* S. [*grǽtan*] to weep, cry, cry out, 329. *Grede,* 96. *Grete, pres. pl.* 454, 2703. *Gret, pa. t.* cried out, wept, 615, 1129, 2159. *Gredde,* 2417. *Greten, pa. t. pl.* wept, 164, 415, 2796. *Grotinde, part. pr.* weeping, 1390. *Graten, part. pa.* wept, 241. *Igroten,* 285. *See* Jam. and Gl. Lynds.

Graue, *v.* S. to bury, 613. *Grauen, part. pa.* buried, 2528. Web., Sir Guy, Ii. iv., Chauc.

Greme, *v.* S. to irritate, grieve, 442. In R. Br. *Gram* is used as a verb, in the same sense.

Grene, *n.* desire, lust, 996. It is simply the Mœso-Goth. *gairuni,* lust; Icel. *girni,* desire. V. Jam. in v. Grene. Halliwell suggests *sport, play,* to which it is *opposed.*

Greting, *n.* S. weeping, 166.

Gres, *n.* S. grass, 2698.

Gret, *adj.* S. great, heavy, loud, 807, 1860. *Greth,* 1025 ; *pl.* grete, 1437, 1862. *Grettere, comp.* greater, 1893.

Grete. *See* Graten.

Greþede, 2003. Explained as *greeted, accosted,* by Sir F. Madden; but the use of þ (not *th*) renders this doubtful. May it not signify *treated, handled* (lit. *arrayed*), from the *vb.* greyþe ?

Grethet. *See* Greyþe.

Grette, *pa. t.* S. accosted, greeted, 452, 1811, 2625. *Gret, part. pa.* accosted, greeted, 2290.

Greu, *pa. t.* S. grew, prospered, 2333 ; *pl.* grewe, 2975.

Greue, *v.* S. to grieve, 2953.

Greyþe. *v.* S. [*gerǽdian*] to prepare, 1762. *Greyþede, pa. t.* prepared, 706. *Greyþed, part. pa.* prepared, made ready, 714. *Grethet,* 2615. Laȝam. l. 4414. Sir Tr. p. 33. Sc. *Graith.* V. Jam. and Gl. Lynds.

Greyue, *n.* S. [*geréfa*] greave, magistrate, 1771. *Greyues, g. c.* greave's, 1749. *Greyues, pl.* 266. V. Spelm. in v. *Grafio,* and Hickes, Diss. Epist. p. 21, n. p. 151.

Grim, *adj.* S. cruel, savage, fierce, 155, 680, 2398, 2655, 2761. R. Br., Rits. M. R. *See* Beowulf, l. 204.

Grim, *n.* [smut, dirt, 2497. The explanation is that Godard, on being flayed, did not bear his sentence as one of rank and blood would have done, but began to roar out as if he were mere *dirt* or *mud,* i. e. one of the dregs of the common herd. This curious expression is ascertained to have the meaning here assigned to it by observing (1) that *grim* and *gore* must be substantives, and (2) that they must be of like signification; but chiefly by comparing the line with others similar to it. Now the context, in the couplet following, repeats that "men might hear him roar, that *foul vile* wretch, a mile off;" and in l. 682, Godard calls Grim "*a foul dirt*, a thrall, and a churl." The author clearly uses *dirt* and *churl* as synonyms. The word *grim* is the Danish *grim*, soot, lampblack, smut, dirt, answering to the English *grime*; see *grime* in Atkinson's Glossary of the Cleveland dialect. *Gore* is the A.S. *gór*, wet mud, or clotted blood, in the latter of which senses it is still used. See "*Gore. Limus*" in Prompt. Parv., and Way's note.]

Grip, *n.* griffin, 572. Web. *Graip*, Sc., V. Jam. The plural *gripes* is in Laȝam. l. 28062, and K. Alisaund. 4880. Swed. *grip*.

Grip, *n.* S. [*græp*] ditch, trench, 2102. *Gripes, pl.* 1924. V. Jam. in v. *Grape;* and Skinner, v. *Groop*. Cf. Swed. *grop*.

Gripen, *pr. t. pl.* S. gripe, grasp, 1790. *Gripeth, imp.* gripe ye, 1882. *Grop, pa. t.* grasped, 1776, 1871, 1890, &c.

Grith, *n.* S. peace, 61, 511. *Grith-sergeans*, 267, legal officers to preserve the peace. These must not be confounded with the *Justitiarii Pacis* established in the beginning of Edw. III. reign, and called *Gardiani Pacis*. V. Spelm. in v. Cf. Icel. *grið*.

Grom, *n.* male child, youth, 790; young man, 2472. Belgic *grom* has the same sense of *boy*. Cf. Icel. *gromr*, homuncio. So in *Sir Degore*, A. iv.
He lyft up the shete anone
And loked upon the lytle *grome*.
It generally elsewhere signifies *lad, page*.

Gronge, *n.* Fr. grange, 764. [Halliwell says that, in *Lincolnshire*, a lone farm-house is still called a *grange*. In old English it is sometimes spelt *graunge*, which comes near the form here used. Cf. Fr. *grange;* Ital. *grangia* (Florio), a country-farm.]

Grop. See Gripen.

Grotes, *n. pl.* S. [*grot*] small pieces, grit, dust, 472, 1414.

Grotinde. See Graten.

Grund, *adj.* used as *adv.* 1027. See Grundlike.

Grunde, *n.* S. *dat. c.* ground, 1979, 2675.

Grunden, *part. pa.* S. ground, 2503. Yw. and Gaw. 676. *Grounden*, Chauc.

Grundlike, *adv.* heartily, 651, 2659; deeply, 2013, 2268, 2307, where it is equivalent to *Deplike*, q. v. The word is undoubtedly Saxon, but in the Lexicons we only find *Grundlinga*, funditus, from Ælf. Gl. It is used by Laȝamon, l. 9783.
Cnihtes heom gereden
*Grundliche* feire.

Gyue. See Giue.

Hal, all, 2370.

Halde, *v.* S. to hold, take part, 2308. *Holden*, to keep or observe, 29, 1171. *Haldes, pr. t.* 3 *p.* holds, 1382. *Hel, pa. t.* held, 109. *Helden, pa. t. pl.* held, 1201. *Halden, part. pa.* held, holden, 2806.

Hals, *n.* S. neck, 521, 670, 2510. Sir Tr. p. 109.

Halue, *n.* S. side, part; *bi bothe halue*, 2682. See Bi-halue.

Haluendel, *n.* S. the half part, 460. R. Gl. p. 5; R. Br.; K. Alisaund. 7116; Emare, 444; Chron. of Engl. 515; R. Hood, i. 68.

## GLOSSARIAL INDEX. 125

Handlen, v. S. to handle, 347. *Handel,* 586.

Hangen, v. S. to hang, 335, 695. *Hengen,* 43, &c. *Honge,* 2807. *Henged, part. pa.* hung, 1922, 2480. Cf. For-henge.

Harum *for* Harm, 1983, 2408.

Hasard, n. Fr. game at dice, 2326. *See* Note on l. 2320.

Hatede, *pa. t.* S. hated, 1188.

Hauen, v. S. to have, 78, &c. *Hawe,* 1188. *Haue,* 1298. *Haues, Hauest, pr. t.* 2 *p.* hast, 688, 848. *Haues, Haueth, pr. t.* 3 *p.* haveth, hath, has, 1266, 1285, 1952, 1980, &c. *Hauet,* hath, 564. *Hauen, pr. t. pl.* have, 1227. *Hauenet,* have it, 2005. *Hauede, pa t.* had, 649, 775, &c. *Hauedet,* 714, had it. *Haueden, pa. t. pl.* had, 238, &c. *Aueden,* 163. *Haue, Hauede, Haueden, subj.* would have, 1428, 1643, 1687, 2020, 2675.

Haui *for* Haue I, 2002.

He, *pron.* S. Is often understood, as in ll. 869, 1428, 1777, and hence might perhaps have been designedly omitted in ll. 135, 860, 1089, 2311, though the metre seems to require *he* in 135 and 1089. *He, pl.* they, 54, &c.

Heie, *n. See* Eie.

Heie, *adj.* S. tall, 987. *Hey,* 1071, 1083; high, 1289. *Heye se,* 719. *Heye curt,* 1685. *Heye and lowe,* 2431, 2471, &c.

Hel, Helden. *See* Halde.

Helde, Heldeste. *See* Eld.

Helen, v. S. [hǽlan] to heal, 1836. *Hele,* 2058. *Holed, part. pa.* healed, 2039.

Helm, n. S. helmet, 379, 624, 1653, &c. *Helmes, pl.* 2612.

Helpen, v. S. to help, 1712. *Helpes, imp. pl.* help ye, 2595. *Holpen, part. pa.* helped, 901.

Hem, *pron.* S. them, 367, &c.

Hend. *See* Hond.

Hende *for* Ende, 247.

Hende, n. S. a duck, 1241. A.S. *ened;* Lat. *anas (anat-is);* Du. *eend;* Icel. *önd.* "Ende mete, for dookelyngys, *Lenticula;"* and again, "Ende, dooke byrde, *Anas.*" Prompt. Parv.

Hende, *adj.* courteous, gentle, 1104, 1421, 1704, 2793, 2877, 2914; skilful, 2628. It certainly is the same word with *hendi, hendy. See* Tyrwh. on C. T. 3199; Gl. R. Glouc.; Amis and Amil. 1393; Ly Beaus Desc. 333; Morte Arthur, ap. Ellis, M. R. V. i. p. 359, &c.; Dan. and Sw. *händig,* dexterous.

Hende, *adv.* S. near, handy, 359, 2275. Web.

Hendeleik, n. courtesy, 2793. Cf. *Allit. Poems,* ed. Morris, B. 860.

Henged, Hengen. *See* Hangen.

Henne, *adv.* S. hence, 843, 1780, 1799. In the same manner is formed *Whenne,* K. Horn, 169, which Ritson thought a mistake for *whence.*

Henne, n. S. hen, 1240. *Hennes, pl.* 702.

Her. *See* Er.

Her, *adv.* S. here, 689, 1058, &c. *Her offe,* 2585, hereof.

Her, n. S. hair, 1924. *Hor,* 235.

Herboru, n. S. habitation, harbour, lodging, 742. *Herberowe,* Web.; *Herbegerie,* R. Br.; *Harbroughe,* Sq. of Lowe Degre, 179; *Herberwe,* Chauc.; *Herbry,* Wynt.; *Herberye,* Lynds. Gl. q. v. and Jam.

Herborwed, *pa. t.* S. lodged, 742. Laʒam., Chauc., V. Jam. in v. *Herbery.*

Here, *pron.* S. their, 52, 465, &c.

Here, n. S. army, 346, 379, 2153, 2942. R. Br., K. Alisaund., 2101.

Here, Heren, v. S. to hear, 4,

126                     GLOSSARIAL INDEX.

732, 1640, 2279, &c. *Y-here*, 11. *Herd, Herde*, pa. t. heard, 286, 465, &c. *Herden, pa. t. pl.* 150.

Herinne, *adv.* S. herein, 458.

Herkne, *imp. s.* S. hearken, 1285. *Herknet, imp. pl.* hearken ye, 1.

Herles. See Erl.

Hernes, *n.* Fr. armour, harness, 1917. R. Br., &c.

Hernes, *n. pl.* S. brains, 1808.

Hern-panne, *n.* S. skull, 1991. Yw. and Gaw. 660; R. Cœur de L., 5293. *Hardynpan,* Compl. of Scotl. p. 241; V. Gl.

Hert, *n.* S. hart, deer, 1872.

Herte, *n.* S. heart, 479, 2054, &c. *Herte blod*, 1819. Laȝam. l. 15846; Sir Tr. p. 98; Chauc.

Hertelike, *adv.* S. heartily, 1347, 2748.

Het, *part.* S. hight, named, 2348. *Hoten, part. pa.* called, named, 106, 284.

Het, Hete, Heten. See Ete.

Hetelike, *adv.* S. hotly, furiously, 2655.
And Guy bent his sword in hand,
And *hetelich* smot to Colbrand.
  *Guy of Warw.* ap. Ellis, M. R. V. 2, p. 82.
In Sir Tr. p. 172, *Hethelich* is explained *Haughtily* by the Editor, and by Jam. *reproachfully*. Cf. *Hetterly* in Gloss. to *Will. of Palerne*.

Hethede, *pa. t.* commanded, 551. A.S. *hetan*. The *th* is here pronounced like *t*, as elsewhere.

Heþen. See Eþen.

Heu, *n.* S. hue, colour, complexion, 2918. Very common. We may hence explain the "inexplicable phrase" complained of by Mr Ellis, Spec. E. E. P. V. I. p. 109. "On *heu* her hair is fair enough" —occasioned by Ritson having inadvertently copied it *hen*, from the MS.; see Anc. Songs, p. 25.

Heued, *n.* S. head, 624, 1653, 1701, 1759, &c. *Heuedes, pl.* 1907.

Heuere. See Euere.

Heui, *adj.* S. heavy, 808; laborious, 2456.

Hew, *pa. t.* S. cut, 2729. Sir Tr. p. 20.

Hext, *adj. sup.* S. highest, tallest, 1080. *Hast*, Laȝamon; *Hext*, K. Alisaund. 7961.; R. Gl.; Chauc.

Hey, Heye. See Heie.

Heye, *adv.* S. on high, 43, 335, 695, &c.

Heylike, *adv.* S. highly, honourably, 2319. *Heyelike*, 1329.

Heyman, *n.* S. nobleman, 1260. Sir Tr. p. 82. *Heymen, Heyemen, pl.* 231, 958.

Hi, Hic. See Ich.

Hider, *adv.* S. hither, 868, 885, 1431.

Hides, *n. pl.* S. hides, skins, 918.

Hijs, *pron.* S. his, 47, 468. *Hise*, 34, &c. *Hyse*, 355. [The final *e* is most used with *plural* nouns.]

Hile, *v.* S [*helan*] to cover, hide, 2082. *Hele*, Sir Tr. p. 19, Web., Rits. M. R., Chauc. *Hilles*, Yw. and Gaw. 741. V. Jam. in v. *Heild.*—Somersetsh.

Him, *pron.* S. them, 257, 1169.

Hine, *n. pl.* S. hinds, bondsmen, 620. Web. *Hinen,* R. Gl., V. Jam. in v.

Hinne. See þer-inne.

Hire, *pron.* S. her, 127, &c. *Hire semes,* it beseems her, 2916.

His *for* Is, 279, 1973, 2692.

Hise. See Hijs.

Hof *for* Of, 1976.

Hof, *pa. t.* S. heaved, 2750.

Hok, *n.* S. hook, 1102.

Hol, *adj.* whole, well, 2075.

Holi, *adj.* S. holy, 1361. [*Printed* hoh *in the former edition.*]

## GLOSSARIAL INDEX.     127

Hold, *adj.* S. firm, faithful, 2781, 2816.
   Ant suore othes *holde*,
   That huere non ne sholde
   Horn never bytreye.
           *K. Horn*, 1259.
   Cf. R. Glouc. p. 377, 383, 443; K. Alisaund. 2912; Chron. of Engl. 730.

Hold, Holde. *adj.* S. old, 30, 192, 417, 956, &c.; former, 2460.

Holden. *See* Halde.

Hole, *n.* S. socket of the eye, 1813.

Holed. *See* Helen.

Holpen. *See* Helpen.

Hond, *n.* S. hand, 2446. *Hon*, 1342. *Dat. c.* hend, 505, 2069; *pl.* hondes, 215, 636. *Hond-dede*, *n.* S. handiwork, 92.

Honge. *See* Hangen.

Hor. *See* Her, *n.*

Hore, *n.* mercy, 153. *See* Ore.

Horn, *n.* S. 779. [This probably refers to the *shape* of the simnel. Halliwell says, a Simnel is "generally made in a *three-cornered* form." Cracknels are still made with pointed and turned up ends, not unlike *horns.*]

Hors, *n.* S. horse, 2283. *Horse-knaue*, groom, 1019. So in a curious satirical poem, temp. Edw. II.
   Of rybaudz y ryme,
   Ant rede o my rolle,
   Of gedelynges, gromes,
   Of Colyn, & of Colle;
   Harlotes, *hors knaues*,
   Bi pate & by polle.
           MS. Harl. 2253, f. 124 b.
Used also by Gower, Conf. Am. *See* Todd's Illustr. p. 279.

Hosen, *n. pl.* S. hose, stockings, 860, 969. In Sir Tr. p. 94, trowsers seem to be indicated.

Hoslen, *v.* S. to administer or receive the sacrament, 212. *Hoslon*, 362. *Hosled*, *part. pa.* 364.

Hoscied, 2598. Le Bone Flor. 776. Chauc.

Hoten. *See* Het.

Houes, *pr. t.* S. behoves, 582. [*Read* bi-houes?]

Hul, *n.* S. hollow, i. e. vale, 2687 A.S. *hole.* Cf. l. 2439.

Hund, *n.* S. hound, 1994, 2435. *Hundes, pl.* 2331.

Hungred *for* Hunger, 2454.

Hungreth, *pr. t.* hunger, 455. *Hungrede, pa. t.* hungered, 654.

Hure, *pron.* S. our, 338, 842, 1231, &c.

Hus *for* Us, 1217, 1409.

Hus, *n.* S. house, 740. *Huse*, 2913. *Hws*, 1141. *Milne-hous*, mill-house, 1967.

Hyl, *n.* S. heap, 892. *Hil*, hill, 1287.

Hw, W, *adv.* S. how, 120, 288, 827, 960, 1646, &c. *Hwou*, 2411, 2946, 2987, &c.

Hwan, *adv.* S. when, 408, 474, &c. *See* Quan.

Hware, *adv.* S. where, 1881, 2240, 2579. *Hwar-of*, whereof, 2976. *Hwere*, 549, 1083.

Hwat, *pron.* S. what, 596, 635, 1137, 2547. *Wat*, 117, 541, &c. *Wat is yw*, 453. *Hwat* or *Wat is þe*, 1951, 2704.

Hwat. *See* Quath.

Hwel, *n.* S. whale, or grampus, 755. *Hwæl*, balena, vel cete, vel cetus. Ælf. Gl. *See* Qual.

Hweþer, *adv.* S. whether, 294, 2098.

Hwi, *adv.* S. why, 454. *See* Qui.

Hwil, *adv.* S. whilst, 301, 363, 538, 2137.

Hwile, *n.* S. time, 722, 1830.

Hwil-gat, *adv.* S. how, lit. which way, 836. *Howgates*, Skinner.

Hwit, *adj.* S. white, 1729.

Hwo, *pron.* S. who, 296, 300, 368, 2604, &c. *See* Wo.

Hwor, *adv.* S. whether, 1119. *Hwore-so*, wheresoever, 1349.

Hwou. *See* Hw.

Hws. *See* Hus.

Hyse. *See* Hijs.

Ich, *pron.* S. I, 167, &c. *Ihc*, 1377. *Ilic*, 305. *Hi*, 487. *I*, 686. *Y*, 15, &c.

Id *for* It, 2424.

I-gret, 163. *See* Grette.

I-groten. *See* Graten.

Il, *adj.* S. each, every, 818, 1740, 2112, 2483, 2514. *Ilc*, 1056, 1921. *Ilke*, 821, 1861, 2959, 2996; (=same), 1088, 1215, 2674, &c. *Ilker*, each (of them), 2352. *Ilkan*, each one, 1770, 2357. *Ilkon*, 1842, 2108. *See* Eueri.

Ille, *adv.* S. *Likede hire swithe ille*, 1165, it displeased her much. Sir Tr. p. 78. A common phrase. *Ille maked*, ill treated, 1952.

I-maked. *See* Maken.

Inne, *adv.* S. in, 762, 807. *See* þerinne.

Inow, *adv.* S. enough, 706, 911, 931, &c. *Ynow*, 563, 1795. *Ynou*, 904.

Intil, *prep.* S. into, 128, 251, &c. *See* Til.

Ioie, *n.* Fr. joy, 1209, 1237, 1278, &c. *Ioye*, 1315.

Ioyinge, *n.* gladness, 2087.

Ioupe, *n.* Fr. a doublet, 1767. Roquefort gives the form *Jupe*, but *Jupon* or *Gipoun* is more usual. See *Japon* in Halliwell, and *Gipe* in Roquefort.

Is *for* His, 735, 2254, 2479.

Iuele, *n.* S. evil, injury, 50, 1689. *Yuel*, 2221. *Yuele*, 994. *Iuel*, sickness, 114. *Yuel*, 144, 155.

þa þe he wes ald mon, þa com him *vfel* on.
*Laȝam.* 1. 19.82.

*Ful iuele o-bone*, very lean, 2505; cf. 2525.

Iuele, *adv.* S. evilly, 2755. *Me yuele like*, displease me, 132. Cf. Ille liken.

Kam. *See* Komen.

Kaske, *adj.* strong, vigorous, 1841. Sw. *karsk*.

Kaym, *n. p.* Cain, 2045. *See* note in loc.

Kayn, *n.* 31, 1327. Evidently a provincial pronunciation of *Thayn*, which in the MS. may elsewhere be read either *chayn* or *thayn*. By the same mutation of letters *make* has been converted into *mate*, *cake* into *cate*, *wayke* into *wayte*, *lake* into *late* (R. Hood, I. 106), &c., or *vice versa*. *See* Thayn.

Kaysere. *See* Cayser.

Keft, *part. pa.* purchased, 2005. *Sure keft* = sourly (bitterly) purchased it. *See* Sure *and* Coupe.

Keling, *n.* 757, cod of a large size, Jam. q. v. The *kelyng* appears in the first course of Archb. Nevil's Feast, 6 Edw. IV. *See* Warner's *Antiq. Cul.* Cotgrave explains *Merlus*, A Melwall or *Keeling*, a kind of small cod, whereof stockfish is made.

Keme. *See* Komen.

Kempe, *n.* S. knight, champion, 1036. V. Jam. in v.

Kene, *adj.* S. keen, bold, eager, 1832, 2115. A term of very extensive use in old Engl. and Sc. poetry, and the usual epithet of a knight.

Kesten, *v.* S. to cast in prison, or to overthrow, 81, 1785 (used passively). *Casten*, cast, throw, 2101. *Keste, pa. t.* cast, 2449. *Keste, part. pa.* cast, placed, 2611; [or it may be the infin. mood.]

Keuel, *n.* S. a gag, 547. See *Kevel* in Hall., *Kewl* in Jam. A.S. *cæfli*, a halter, headstall.

Kid, *part. pa.* S. made known, discovered, 1060. Sir Tr. p. 150; R. Br.; Yw. and Gaw. 530; Minot, p. 4; Chauc. From *cýþan*, notum facere.

Kin, Kyn, *n.* S. kindred, 393, 414, 2045.

Kines, *n.* S. *gen. c.* kind, 861, 1140, 2691. *None kines* = of no kind; *neuere kines* = of never a kind.

Kinneriche. *See* Cunnriche.

Kippe, *v.* S. [*cépan*] to take up hastily, 894. *Kipt, Kipte, pa.* snatched up, 1050, 2407, 2638.

   Horn in is armes hire *kepte.*
               *K. Horn*, 1208.

*Kypte* heore longe knyues, and slowe faste to gronde.
            *Rob. Glouc.* p. 125.

*Kept up*, snatcht up, Gl. R. Br. Jamieson derives the word from Su.-G. *kippa*, to take anything violently. V. in v. *Kip.* Ihre quotes the Icel. *kipti up* = snatched up.

Kirke, *n.* S. church, 1132, 1355. *Kirkes, pl.* 2583. V. Gl. Lynds. and Jam.

Kiste. *See* Chiste.

Kiste, *pa. t. s.* kissed, 1279. *Kisten, pa. t. pl.* S. kissed, 2162.

Kiwing, *n.* 1736. [Respecting this word I can only record my conviction that it is not safe to quote it, as the MS. is indistinct. I read the word as *kilþing*, which I believe to be merely miswritten for *ilk þing* (which the scribe also spells *il þing*), and I suppose the sense of the line to be—" when they had there distributed *everything*."]

Knaue, *n.* S. lad, 308, 409, 450, &c. Attendant, servant, 458. *Cokes knaue*, scullion, 1123.

   Heore cokes & heore *cnaues*
   Alle heo duden of lif dæʒen.
            *Laʒam.* l. 13717.

V. Jam. in v. Gl. Lynds. and Gl. Todd's Illustr. Chauc.

Knawe, *v.* S. to know, 2785. *Knawe, pr. t. pl.* know, 2207. *Kneu, pa. t.* knew, 2468. *Knawed, part. pa.* known, 2057.

Knicth, Knith, *n.* S. knight, 77, 343, &c. *Knictes, pl.* 239. *Knithes*, 1068. *Knihtes*, 2706.

Kok, *n.* a cook, 873, 180, 891, 903, 921, 2898. *See* Cok.

Komen, *v.* S. to come, 1001. *Comes, Cometh, imp. pl.* come ye, 1798, 1885, 2247. *Kam, pa. t.* came, 766, 863. *Kom*, 1309. *Cam*, 2622. *Komen, pa. t. pl.* came, 1012, 1202. *Comen*, 2790. *Keme*, 1208. *Comen, part. pa.* come, 1714.

Kope, *n.* Lat. cope, 429. *Copes, pl.* 1957.

Koren, *n.* S. corn, 1879.

Kouel. *See* Couel.

Kouþen. *See* Couþe.

Kradel-barnes, *n. pl.* S. children in the cradle, 1912.

Kraken, *v.* S. to crack, break, 914. *Krake*, 1857. *Crake*, 1908. *Crakede, pa. t.* cracked, broke, 568. *Kraked, part. pa.* 1238.

Krike, *n.* S. creek, 708.

Kunne. *See* Canst.

Kuneriche, Kunerike, Kunrik. *See* Cunnriche.

Kyne-merk, *n.* S. mark or sign of royalty, 604. In the same manner are compounded *cine-helm, cine-stol,* &c.

   & Cador þe kene
   scal beren þas *kinges marke ;*
   hæbben haʒe þene drake,
   biforen þissere duʒeðe.
            *Laʒam.* l. 19098.

   Thyll ther was of her body
   A fayr chyld borne, and a godele,
   Hadde a dowbyll *kynges marke.*
            *Emare*, 502.

Lac, *n.* S. fault, reproach, 191, 2219. Yw. and Gaw. 264, 1133. *Lak*, R. Br., Rom. of Merlin, ap. Ellis, M. R. V. I. p. 252. Sir Orpheo, 421. *Lakke*, P. Plowm. Chauc. So in Sc. V. Jam. and Gl. Lynds. v. *Lak*, *Lack*.

Ladde, *n.* S. lad, 1786. *Ladden*, *pl.* 1038. *Laddes*, 1015, &c. A term subsequently applied to persons of low condition. "When *laddes* weddeth leuedis—" Prophecy of Tho. of Essedoune, MS. Harl. 2253, f. 127.

Large, *adj.* Fr. Lat. liberal, bountiful, 97, 2941. R. Gl. Yw. and Gaw. 865. Sir Orpheo, 27. Sevyn Sages, 1251. Chauc.

Late, *v.* S. [*lǽtan*] *pres. subj.* let, suffer, 486. *Late*, *pr. t.* let, permit, 1741. *Late*, *imp.* let, suffer, 17, 1376, 2422. *Leth*, *pa. t.* let, suffered, 2651 ; caused, 252. *Late*, *part. pa.* or *inf.* put, 2611.

Laten, *v.* S. [*lǽtan*] to leave, 328. *Late be*, *imp.* leave, relinquish, 1265 ; *inf.* 1657. *Let*, *pa. t.* left, 2062. *Laten*, *part. pa.* left, abated, 240, 1925.

Lath, *n.* S. injury, 76. *Lathe*, 2718, 2976.

Lauhwinde, *part. pr.* S. laughing, 946.

Laute, *pa. t.* S. [*lǽccan*, *lǽhte*] received, took, 744. *Lauthe*, 1673. *Lauth*, *part. pa.* received, taken, 1988. *I-lahte*, Laʒam. l. 29260.
    Horn in herte laʒte
    Al þat he him taʒte.
    *K. Horn* (ed. Lumby), 243.
*Laught*, Yw. and Gaw. 2025. *Laught*, K. Alisaund. 685, 1109. *Lauht*, R. Br. (*See* Hearne's blundering Gl. in voc.) Rits. A.S. p. 46. *Laucht*, Wall. ix. 1964.

Laumprei, *n.* S. lamprey, 771. *Laumprees*, *pl.* 897.

Lawe, Lowe, *adj.* S. low, 2431, 2471, 2767, &c.

Lax, *n.* S. [*lœx*] salmon, 754, 1727. *Laxes*, *pl.* 896. V. Spelm. and Somn. in v. Jamieson says, it was "formerly the only name by which this fish was known." Cf. Dan. Sw. Icel. *lax*.

Layke, *v.* S. [*lácan*] to play, 1011. *Leyke*, *Leyken*, 469, 950, 997. *Leykeden*, *pa. t. pl.* played, 954. In the same sense the verb is found in P. Plowman, and Sevyn Sages, 1212. So in Sc. and N.E. V. Jam. v. *Laik*, Ray, Brockett, and Crav. Dial. v. *Lake*.

Leche, *n.* S. physician, 1836, 2057.

Led, a caldron, kettle, 924. Chauc. Prol. 202.

Lede, Leden, *v.* S. to lead, 245, &c.; *utlede*, 89. Cf. 346, 379. *Ledes*, *pr. t.* 3 *p.* uses, carries, 2573. *Ledde*, *pa. t.* led, 1686. *Ledden*, *pa. t. pl.* led, 2451.

Lef, *adj.* S. agreeable, willing, *lef and loth*, 261, 440, 2273, 2313, 2379, 2775. A very usual phrase. *See* Beowulf, l. 1026. Chauc. C. T. 1839. R. Hood, I. 41. *Leue*, 431, 909. Sir Tr. p. 187. K. Horn, 949, &c. *Leuere*, *comp.* more agreeable, rather, 1193, 1423, 1671, &c. *Lef*, used as *adv.* willingly, in the phrase "Ye! lef, ye!" = yes, willingly, yes, 2606; cf. l. 1888.

Leidest. *See* Leyn.

Leite, *adj.* S. light, 2441.

Leme, *n.* S. limb, 2555. *Lime*, 1409. *Limes*, *pl.* 86.

Leman, *n.* S. mistress, lover, 1191. *Lemman*, 1283, 1312, 1322. Used by all the old writers, and applied equally to either sex.

Lende, *v.* S. to land, 733. Sir Tr. p. 13. R. Br. *See* Jam. in v. *Leind*.

Lene, *v.* S. [*leanian*] to lend, grant, 2072.
    I sal *lene* the her mi ring.
    *Yw. and Gaw.* 737

Lenge, *n.* the fish called *ling*, 832. [*Asellus longus*, or *Islandicus*, Ray.] It was a common dish formerly. Thus we have *Lynge in jelly*, in Archb. Nevil's Feast, 6 Edw. IV., and *Lyng in foyle*, in Warham's Feast, 1504. *See* Pegge's *Form of Cury*, p. 177, 184, and MS. Sloane, 1986.

Lenge, *v.* S. to prolong, 1734, 2363. P. Plowm.

Leoun, *n.* Lat. lion, 573. *Leun*, 1867.

Lepe, *v.* S. escape from (?) 2009. *Loupe*, to leap, 1801. *Lep*, *pa t.* leapt, 891, 1777, 1942. *Lopen*, *a. t. pl.* 1896, 2616.

Lere, Leren, *v.* S. to learn, 797, 823; to teach, 2592. *Y-lere*, 12.

Lese, *v.* S. *imp. s.* 3 *p.* loose, 333. Sir Tr. p. 110.

Leth. *See* Late.

Lette, *v.* S. [*lǽtan, lettan*] to hinder, retard, 1164, 2253, 2819; to stop, cease, 2445, 2627. *Let*, *pa. t.* stopped, stayed, 2447, 2500. *Leten*, *pa. t. pl.* stopped, delayed, 2379.

Leue, *n.* S. leave, 1387, 1626, 2952, &c.

Leue, *adj. See* Lef.

Leue, *v.* S. [*lýfan*] *imp. s.* grant, 334, 406, 2807. K. Horn, 465, MS.; R. Gl., Erle of Tol. 365. Guy of Warw. ap. Ellis, M. R. V. 2, p. 77, where it is misprinted *lene*. It is very frequently used in the old Engl. Metrical Lives of the Saints, MS. Laud, 108. [The true distinction between *leue* and *lene* is, that the former is the A.S. *lýfan*, G. *erlauben* = grant in the sense of *allow, permit*, and is invariably intransitive; whilst *lene* is the A.S. *lǽnan*, G. *leihen* = grant in the sense of *give*. The confusion between the senses of *grant* has led to confusion between *lene* and *leue*, and in at least five passages of Chaucer (C. T. 7226, 13613; Tro. ii. 1212, iii. 56, v. 1749, ed. Tyrwhitt) many editions wrongly have *lene*. In the last three instances Tyrwhitt rightly prints *leve*, but unnecessarily corrects himself in his Glossary. I regret to add that I have thrice made a similar mistake. In Piers Plowman, A. v. 263, and in Pierce the Ploughman's Crede, ll. 366 and 573, for *lene* read *leue*. Halliwell's remark, that "the [former] editor of Havelok absurdly prints *leue*" is founded upon the same misconception, and he is wrong in his censure. *See* the use of *lefe* in the Ormulum, ed. White.]

Leued, *pa. t.* S. left, 225.

Leuedi, *n.* S. lady, 171, &c. *Leuedyes, pl.* 239. V. Hickes, Diss. Ep. p. 52, n.

Leuere. *See* Lef.

Leues, *pr. t.* 3 *p.* S. believes, 1781, 2105. From *lefan*.

Leuin, *n.* S. lightning, 2690. R. Br. p. 174. Yw. and Gaw. Chauc. C. T. 5858. Doug. Virg. 200, 53.

Lewe, *adj.* S. warm, 498, 2921.

A opened wes his breoste,
þa blod com forð *luke*.
*Laʒam.* l. 27556.

Leyd, Leyde. *See* Leyn.

Leye, *n.* S. lie, falsehood, 2117.

Leye, *v.* S. to lie, speak false, 2010.

Leyke, Leyken. *See* Layke.

Leyk, *n.* S. game, 1021, 2326. So in Beowulf, l. 2084, *sweorda-gelác*, and Sir Tr. p. 118, *love-laike*. In the pl. *laykes*, Minot, p. 10. In Lanc. a player is still called a *laker*.

Leyn, *v.* S. to lay, 718. *Leyde, pa. t.* laid, 50, 994, &c.; stopped, 229. *Leidest, pa. t.* 2 *p.* laidest, 636. *Leyden, pa. t. pl.* laid, 1907. *Leyd, part. pa.* laid, 1689, 1722, 2839.

Lich, *adj.* like, 2155.

Lict, Lith, *n.* S. light, 534, 576, 588, &c.

Lift, *adj.* S. left (*lævus*), 2130.

Ligge, Liggen, *v.* S. to lie down, 802, 876, 882, 1374. *See* Lyen.

Lime, Limes. *See* Leme.

Lite, *adj.* S. little, 276, 1730. *Litel*, 1858, &c. *Litle*, 2014.

Lith. *See* Lict.

Lith, *imp.* S. light (thou), 585.

Lith, *adv.* S. lightly, 1942.

Lith, *n.* S. alleviation, comfort, peace, 1338. *Lyþe*, 147. It also occurs as a sb. in Laȝam. l. 5213. As an adj. it occurs in Laȝam. l. 7242. Sir Tr. p. 43, 82. R. Cœur de L. 2480, and Emare, 348, from the v. *liðian*, alleviare. Cf. Icel. *lið*, sometimes used to mean *help*. See *Leathe* in Atkinson's Cleveland Glossary.

Lith, *n.* S. 2515: This word is explained by Ritson *plains*, by Hearne *tenements*, and by Jamieson a *ridge* or *ascent*. Its real signification seems unknown, but may be conjectured from the following passages.

No asked he lond no *lithe*.
        Sir Tristr. p. 101.
Ther wille not be went, ne lete ther lond ne *lith*.
        R. Brunne, p. 194.
where it answers to the Fr. Ne volent lesser tere ne *tenement*.

Who schall us now geve londes or *lythe*.    Le Bone Flor. 841.

Here I gif Schir Galeron, quod Gaynour, withouten ony gile,
Al the londis and the *lithis* fro laver to layre.
        Sir Gaw. and Sir Gal. ii. 27.
[*See* Glossary to *William of Palerne*, s. v. *Lud*.]

Lithes, *n. pl.* S. the extreme points of the toes, or articulations, 2163. *Fingres lith*, extremum digiti, Luc. 16, 24.

Liþes, *imp. pl.* S. listen, 1400, 2204. *Lyþes*, 2576. The verb in the Sax. is *hlystan*, but in Su.-G. *lyda*, and Isl. *hlyda*, which approaches nearer to the form in the poem. So also in K. Horn, 2, *wilen lithe*, MS.; R. Br. p. 93; R. Hood, I. p. 2; Minot, p. 1. Still used in Sc. and N.E. V. Jam. and Brockett.

Littene, *part. pa.* [or *inf. ?*] 2701. " *Qu.* cut in pieces, from the same root as to *lith*, divide the joints. V. Jam. Suppl."—M. [Or it may mean disgraced, wounded, defeated. Cf. Su.-Goth. *lyta*, to wound; Icel. *lyta*, to disgrace; Sw. *lyte*, a defect, *litt*, deformed; Dan. *lyde*, a blemish.]

Liue, *n.* S. *dat. c.* life, 232; *brouth of liue*, dead, 513, 2129. K. Horn, 188. *Of liue do*, kill, 1805. *Liues, gen. c. as adv.* alive, 509, 1003, 1307, 1919, 2854. *See* Ouliue.

Liuen, *v.* S. to live, 355. *Liuede*, *Liueden, pa. t. pl.* lived, 1299, 2044.

Lof, *n.* S. loaf, 653.

Loke, Loken, *v.* S. to look after, take care of, to behold, 376, 2136. *Lokes, pr. t.* 2 *p.* lookest, 2726. *Loke, imp.* look, 1680, 1712. *Lokes, imp. pl.* look ye, 2240, 2292, 2300, 2579, 2812. *Lokede, pa. t.* looked, 679, 1041.

Loken, Lokene, *part. pa.* S. fastened, locked, closed, 429, 1957. So in the Const. Othonis, Tit. *de habitu Clericorum;* " In mensura decenti habeant vestes, et *cappis clausis* utuntur in sacris ordinibus constituti." V. Spelm. in v. *Cappa clausa*. So also in the *Ancren Riwle*, fol. 17—" gif he haues a wid hod and a *lokin* cape, &c."

Lond, Londe, *n.* S. land, 64, 721, &c. *Lon*, 340.

Long, *adj.* S. tall, 987, 1063. So K. Horn, 100.

Longes, *pr. t.* 3 *p.* S. belongs, 396. R. Br., Chauc., &c.

Lopen. *See* Lepe.

Loth, *adj.* S. loath, unwilling, 261, 440, &c. *See* Lef.

Louede, *pa. t.* S. loved, 71. *Loueden, pa. t. pl.* 955.

Louerd, *n.* S. lord, master, 96, 483, &c. *Lowerd*, 621.

Louerdinges, *n. pl.* S. lordings, masters, 515, 1401. *See* Note in Warton's Hist. Engl. Poet. V. I. p. 19. Ed. 1840.

Loupe. *See* Lepe.

Low, *pa. t.* S. laughed, 903. Horn, 1502. *Lowen, pa. t. pl.* 1056.

Lowe, *n.* S. [*hlœw*] hill, 1291, 1699. Rits. M. R., Web., &c. V. Jam. and Brockett's Gl. v. *Lawe*.

Luue, *n.* S. love, 195. [*Luuedrurye* seems here to be a compound word, meaning *love-courtship. Lufedrowrie* also = love-token, *Lyndesay's Sq. Meidrum*, 1003. *See* Drurye.]

Lyen, *v.* S. to lie (in bed), 2134. *Leyen, pt. pl.* lay, 475.

Lyþe. *See* Lith.

Maght, Mait. *See* Mowe.

Make, *n.* S. mate, companion, wife, 1150. K. Horn, 1427. K. Alisaund. 3314. Le Bone Flor. 881. Chauc. Sc. *Maik.* V. Jam.

Maken, *v.* S. to make, 29, &c. *Make*, 676. *Makeden, pa. t. pl.* made, 554. *I-maked, part. pa.* made, 5.

Male, *n.* Fr. a budget, bag, wallet, 48. Laȝamon, l. 3543. Web., Chauc., R. Hood.

Malisun, *n.* Fr. malediction, curse, 426. Sir Tr. p. 179.

Manred, Manrede, *n.* S. homage, fealty, 484, 2172, 2180, 2248, 2265, 2312, 2774, 2816, 2847, 2850. Leg. of S. Gregori, ap. Leyd. Compl. of Scotl. *See* Jam. for further examples.

Marz, *n.* Lat. March, 2559.

Maugre, Fr. in spite of, 1128, 1789. *See* Tyrwh. Gl. to Chauc. and Jam. in v.

Maydnes, *n. pl.* S. maidens, 467, 2222.

Mayster, *n.* Fr. master, 1135; chief, 2028, 2385.

Mayt, Mayth. *See* Mowe.

Mede, *n.* S. reward, 102, 685, 1635, 2402.

Mele, *n.* S. oat-meal, 780.

Mele, *v.* Fr. to contend in battle, 2059. Gaw. and Gol. ii. 18. *Mellay*, Wynt. viii. 15, 19. V. Jam.

Meme, 2201, *probably miswritten for* neme; *see* Nime.

Men (used with a sing. vb. like the Fr. *on*), men, people, 390, 647, 2610.

Mene, *v.* S. to mean, signify, 2114. *Menes, pr. t.* 3 *p.* means, 597.

Menie, *n.* Fr. family, 827. *Meynie*, 834. This word is to be found from the time of Laȝamon to Shakespeare. Jamieson attempts to derive it from the North. V. in v. *Menzie*. *See maisnie* in Roquefort.

Mere, *n.* S. mare, 2449, 2478, 2504.

Messe, *n.* Fr. Lat. the service of the mass, 243, 1176. *Messe-bok*, mass-book, 186, 391, 2710. *Messegere*, all the apparel, &c., pertaining to the service of the mass, 188, 389, 1078, 2217.

Mest, *adj. sup.* S. greatest, 233. *Moste*, 1287; tallest, 983.

Mester, *n.* Fr. trade, 823. K. Horn (ed. Lumby), 229.

Met, *pp.* S. dreamt, 1285.

Mete, *n.* S. meat, 459, &c. *Metes, pl.* 1733.

Meynie. *See* Menie.

Michel, *adj.* S. much, 510, 660. *Mik*, 2342. *Mike*, 960 (cf. Horn Childe, ap. Rits. V. 3, 292), 1744, 1761, 2336. *Mikel*, 122, 478, &c.

Micte, Micten, Micthe, Mithe, Mithest, Mithen. *See* Mowe.

Micth, *n.* S. might, power, 35.

Middelerd, *n.* S. the earth, world, 2244. *Middelærd*, Laȝam., Rits., Web., R. Gl., Minot, &c. So in Sc. V. Jam.

Mik, Mike, Mikel. *See* Michel.

Milce, *n.* S. [*mildse*] mercy, 1361. A! me do þine *milce*, Laȝam. l. 4681; R. Gl. It is usually coupled with *ore*.

Milne-hous. *See* Hus.

Mirke, *adj.* S. dark, 404. R. Br., Lynds.; *merke*, Chauc. Still used in Sc. and N.E. V. Jam.

Misdede, *pa. t.* S. did amiss, 337; injured, 992, 1371. *Misdo*, *part. pa.* misdone, offended, 2798.

Misferde, *pa. t.* S. behaved, or proceeded ill, 1869. *See* Faren.

Misgos, *pr. t.* 2 *p.* S. goest or behavest amiss, 2707.

Misseyd, *part. pa.* S. spoken to reproachfully, 1688.

Mithe, Mythe, *v.* S. [*miðan*] to conceal, hide, dissemble, 652, 948, 1278. Sche might no lenger *mithe*. Horn Childe, ap. Rits. M. R. V. 3, p. 310.

Mixed, *adj.* vile, base, 2533. From S. *myx*, fimus. Cf. *Mix* in *William of Palerne*.

Mo, *adj. comp.* S. more, 1742, 1846.

Mod, *n.* S. mood, humour, 1703.

Moder, *n.* S. mother, 974, 1388, &c.

Mone. *n.* S. moon, 373, 403.

Mone, *n.* S. mind, say, opinion, 816. Cf. A.S. *myne, monian, mo-*

nung; Icel. *munr*. Hence, to *mone*, to *relate*, R. Cœur de L. 4636, and to *animadvert*, in Barbour. It appears to express the Fr. phrase *par le mien escient*, K. Horn, 467, MS. Douce. In nearly the same sense *mone* may be found in K. Alisaund. 1281, R. Gl. pp. 281, 293. Cf. ll. 1711, 1972.

Mone, *v. pl.* [Isl. *mun*] must, 840. *Maun*, Sc. *Mun*, Yorksh. Cumb. V. Jam.

Morwen, *n.* S. morning, 811, 1131, 2669, &c. *To-morwen*, 530, 810. *Amorwe*, Sir Tr., K. Horn.

Moste. *See* Mest.

Mote, *v.* S. may, 19, 406, 1743, 2545. *Moten*, *pl.* 18.

Moun. *See* Mowe.

Mowe, *v.* S. *pres. sing.* may, be able, 175, 394, 675. *Mowen*, *pl.* 11. *Moun*, 460, 2587. *Mait*, *pr. t.* 2 *p.* mayest, 689. *Mayt*, 845, 852, 1219. *Mayth*, 641. *Maght*, *pa. t.* 2 *p. s.* mightest, 1348. *Mithe, Mithest*, 855, 1218. *Micte, Micthe, Mithe, pa. t.* 3 *p.* might, 42, 233, 1030, 1080. *Mouchte, Moucte, Moucthe, Mouthe, Mowcte*, 145, 356, 376, &c. *Micte, Micten, Mithen, pl.* 232, 516, 1929, 2017. *Mouhte, Mouthe. Mouthen*, 1183, 2019, 2039, 2328, 2330, &c. V. Pegge's Anecd. of Engl. Lang. p. iii.

Na, *adv.* S. no, 2363, 2530.

Nam. *See* Nime.

Nayles, *n. pl.* S. nails, 2163.

Ne, *adv.* S. nor, 44, &c.

Nede, *n.* S. need, necessity, 9, &c. *Nedes*, *pl.* 1692.

Neme. *See* Nime.

Ner, *adv.* S. near, 990, 1949.

Nese, *n.* S. nose, 2450.

Nesh, *adj.* S. [*nesc*] soft, tender, 2743. *Neys*, 217. Web., Rits. M. R., Rob. Br., Chauc. Still used in N.W. part of England.

Neth, *n*. S. net, 752, 808, 1026; *pl. netes*, 783.

Neth, *n*. S. neat, cattle, 700, 1222. *Netes, g. c.* neat's, 781.

Neþeles, *conj*. S. nevertheless, 1108, 1658.

Neue, *n*. S. fist, 2405. *Neues, pl.* 1917. V. Jam.

Neure, *adv*. S. not, never, 80, 672; *neuere a polk*, ne'er a pool, 2685. *Neuere kines*, of no kind, 2691.

Ney, *adv*. nigh, near to, nearly, 464, 640, 2619.

Neys. *See* Nesh.

Neyþer, Neþe, *pron*. S. neither, not either, 458, 764, 2970, &c. *Noþer*, 2623. *Noyþer*, 2697.

Newhen, *v*. S. [*nehwan*] to approach, 1866. In the more recent form to *neigh* it is used in several of the old Romances, Chauc., and Minot.

Nicht, Nicth, *n*. S. night, 533, 575. *Niht*, 2669. *Nith*, 404, 1247, 1754. *Nithes, g. c.* of night, 2100. *Nihtes, nithes, pl.* 2353; *nihtes*, 2999.

Nime, *v*. S. *pr. s*. take, *or* go, 1931. *Nim, imp*. take, 1336. *Nam, pa. t*. took, 900; went, 2930. *Neme, pl*. went, 1207; cf. l. 2201. *Nomen*, took, 2790. *Nomen, Numen, part. pa*. taken, 2265, 2581. *Nimes, imp. pl*. go ye, 2594; *nime*, go we, 2600. In the first sense this verb is common in all the Glossaries, but in the latter sense *To go* it occurs nowhere but in the Gl. to Rob. Brunne, who, from being a Lincolnshire man, approaches nearer to the language of the present poem than any other writer. [In N. E. to *nim* is to walk with quick, short steps.]

Nis, *for* Ne is, is not, 462, 1998, 2244.

Nither-tale, *n*. S. night-time, 2025. *See* Chaucer, Prol. l. 97.

Noblelike, *adv*. S. nobly, 2640.

Nok, *n*. [Belg. *nock*] nook, corner, 820; *nouth a ferthinges nok*, not the value of a farthing. The same phr. is in the *Manuel des Pechés* of Rob. of Brunne, MS. Harl. 1701, fol. 39.

Nomen. *See* Nime.

Non, *adj*. S. no, 518, 685, 1019; no one, 931, 974.

Note, *n*. S. a nut, 419. *Nouthe*, 1332.

Noþer. *See* Neyþer.

Nou, *adv*. S. now, 328, 1362, &c. *Nu*, 2421, 2460, 2650, &c.

Nout, Nouth, Nouht, *n*. or *adv*. S. not, naught, nothing, not at all, 249, 505, 566, 648, 1733, 2051, 2822. *Nowt, Nowth*, 770, 2168, 2737.

Nouthe. *See* Note.

Noyþer. *See* Neyþer.

Nu. *See* Nou.

Numen. *See* Nime.

Nytte, *v*. S. make use of, require for use, 941. A.S. *nyttian, neotan*, G. *nützen*, Du. *nutten*.

O. *See* On.

Of, *prep*. S. off, 130, 216, 603, 857, 1850, 2444, 2626, 2676, 2751, &c. *Of londe*, out of the land, 2599. Sir Tr.

Offe, *prep*. S. of, 435. *Of*, 436.

Offrende, Dan. Fr. offering, 1386

Ofte, *adv*. S. often, 226, &c.

Ok. *See* Ek.

On, *adj*. S. one, 425, 1800, 2028, 2263, &c.

On, *in* But on. *See* But.

On, *prep*. S. in, on. *On liue*, 281, 363, 694, 793, &c. *O liue*, 2865. *On two*, 471, 1823, 2730, in two; *a two*, 1413, 2643. *O londe*, 763, on, *or* in land. *On knes*, 1211,

1302, 2710, on knees; *o knes*, 2252, 2796. *On brenne*, 1239, in flame, on fire. *O nith*, 1251, in the night. *On nithes*, 2048. *O worde*, 1349, in the world (*see* Werd). *O mani wise*, 1713, in many a manner. *On gamen*, 1716, in sport. *On lesse hwile*, 1830, in less time. *O bok*, 2307, 2311, on the book. *Wel o bon*, 2355, 2525, 2571, strong of body. *Inele o bone*, 2505, lean. *On hunting*, 2382. *O stede*, 2549, on steed. *Up-o the dogges*, 2596, on the dogs. From these examples, added to those which occur in every Glossary, it is evident the Sax. prep. *On* was subsequently corrupted to *O* and *A*. *See* Tyrwh. and Jam. *A nycht* in Barb. xix. 657, explained by the latter *one night*, is according to the above rule *In the night*, as confirmed by l. 1251. Sir Tr. pp. 47, 114. R. Glouc.

One, *adj.* S. alone, singly, 815, 936, 1153, 1710, 1742, 1973, 2433.
There hue wonede al *one*.
K. *Horn*, 80.
*See* Tyrwh. Gl., Chauc. v. *On*.

Ones, *adv.* S. once, 1295.

Onfrest, *v.* delay, 1337. From Su.-G. *fresta*, to delay, A.S. *firstan*, from Su.-Goth. *frest* or *frist*, A.S. *fyrst*, a space of time. Cf. Dan. and Sw. *first*, a truce. *Frest*, delay, Barb. vii. 447.

Onlepi. *See* Anilepi.

Onne, *prep.* S. on, 347, 1940.

Onon, *adv.* S. anon, speedily, 136, 447, 1964, 2790.

Ontil, *prep.* S. unto, for, 761.

Or, *adv.* S. previously, before, 728, 1043, 1356, 1688, &c. *Or outh longe*, 1789, before any long time.

Ore, *n.* S. favour, grace, mercy, 153, 211, 2443, 2797. Ich hadde of hire milse an *ore*. Hule and Nihtingale, l. 1081. Sir Tr. p. 24. K. Horn (ed. Lumby), 1509. *See*

Tyrwhitt's Note on Chauc. C. T. 3724, and Ritson's Note, Metr. Rom. V. iii. p. 263. A.S. *ár*.

Ore, *n.* S. oar, 718, 1871, &c. *Ores, pl.* 711.

Osed *for* Hosed, 971.

Oth, *n.* S. oath, 2009, 2272, &c. *Oþes, pl.* 2013, 2231, &c.

Oþe *for* Oþer, 861, 1986, 2970.

Oþer, *conj.* S. either, or, 94, 674, 787, &c. *See* Ayther.

Oþer, *adj.* S. [*alter*] the other of two, second, 879. *þe oþer day*, 1755, the following day.
Day hit is igon & *oþer*,
Wiþute sail & roþer.
K. *Horn*, ed. Lumby, 187.
So also R. Br. p. 169, and Wynt.

Oþer, *adj.* S. [*alius*] other, 2490. *Oþre, pl.* others, 1784, 2413, 2416.

Ouer-fare, *v.* S. to pass over, cease, 2063. *See* Fare.

Ouer-go, *v.* S. to be disregarded, 2220.

Ouer-gange, *v.* S. to get the superiority over, 2587.

Ouer-þwert, *adv.* S. across, 2822. *Ouerthuert*, R. Br. p. 241. *Overtwert*, Ly Beaus Desc. 1017. *Overthwarte*, Syr Eglamore, B. iii. Chauc. C. T. 1993.

Oune, *adj.* S. own, 375, 2428.

Oure, *n.* bank, shore, 321. G. *ufer*. A.S. *ófer*. Cf. "to þan castle of Deoure on þere sæ *oure*." *Laȝamon*, l. 31117.

Outh, *n.* S. [*awiht*] any space of time, aught, 1189; cf. l. 1789; anything, 703. [*Outh douthe* = was worth anything, was of any value.]

Palefrey, *n.* Fr. saddle-horse, 2060. *See* Gl. on Chauc. in v. Pegge's Anec. Engl. Lang. p. 289.

Pappes, *n. pl.* Lat. breasts, 2132.

**Parred,** *part. pa.* confined, fastened in, barred in, 2439. We have met with this word only in one instance, where Ritson leaves it unexplained.
Yn al this [tyme] was sir Ywayn
Ful straitly *parred* with mekil payn.
*Yw. and Gaw.* 3227.
[It is undoubtedly equivalent to O.E. *sperre,* or *spere.* Halliwell, s. v. *Parred,* quotes "ȝe are *parred* in . . . ȝe are so *spered* in." So, too, the Ital. *sbarra* is the Fr. *barre.* Cf. A.S. *sparran,* O.N. *sperra,* Sc. *spar.* Hence the derivation of *park,* O.E. *parrock,* an enclosure.]

**Pastees,** *n. pl.* Fr. pasties, patés, 644.
Ther beth bowris and halles,
Al of *pasteiis* beth the walles.
*Land of Cokaygne,* MS. Harl. 913, f. 5.

**Pateyn,** *n.* Lat. the Plate used in the service of the Mass, 187.

**Paþe,** *n.* S. path, road, 2381, 2390. *Paþes, pl.* 268.

**Patriark,** *n.* Lat. patriarch, 428.

**Payed,** *part. pa.* Fr. satisfied, content, 184. Rits. M. R., Web., R. Gl., R. Br. *Apaied,* Chauc.

**Pelle,** *v.* drive forth (*intr.*), hurry forth, 810. Deriv. uncertain, unless it be connected with Lat. *pello,* Eng. *impel.* Cf. Eng. *pelt.*

**Peni,** *n.* S. penny, 705, 2147. *Penies, pl.* 776, 1172.

**Per,** *n.* Fr. peer, equal, 989, 2241, 2792.

**Pike,** *v.* to pitch (used passively), 707. Teut. *pecken,* Lat. *picare.* The verb in Saxon is not extant, but only the n. *pic.*

**Pine,** *n.* S. pain, grief, 405, 540, 1374. Sir Tr. p. 12. V. Jam.

**Pine,** *v.* S. to grieve, 1958.

**Plat.** *See* Plette.

**Plattinde,** *part. pr.* tramping along, moving noisily *or* hurriedly, 2282. From the beating noise of the feet, like Sc. *platch* (q. v. in Jam.). *See* Plette.

**Plawe,** *v.* S. to play, 950. *Pleye,* 951.

**Playces,** *n. pl.* plaice, 896.

**Pleinte,** *n.* Fr. complaint, 134. *Pleynte,* 2961.

**Plette,** *v.* S. [*plœttian*] to strike, 2444. *Plat, pa. t.* struck, 2755. *Plette,* 2626; *pl. plette,* hurried, moved noisily, 2613. [Cf. *Plattinde,* and note the double use of Sc. *skelp,* to beat, to hurry, and O.E. *strike,* to beat, to move along.]

**Plith,** *n.* S. [*pliht*] harm, 1370, 2002. Laȝam. l. 3897.

**Poke,** *n.* S. a bag, 555, 769. *Pokes, pl.* 780.

**Poles,** *n. pl.* S. pools, ponds of water, 2101.

**Polk,** *n.* S. pool, puddle, 2685. *Pow,* Sir Tr. p. 171. *Pulk,* Somersetsh.

**Pouere, Poure,** *adj.* Fr. poor, 58, 101, 2457, &c.

**Pourelike,** *adv.* poorly, 323.

**Prangled,** *part. pa.* compressed, 639. Cf. Du. *prangen,* to pinch; Dan. *prange Seil,* to crowd sail.

**Preie,** *pr. t.* S. pray, 1440. *Prey, imp.* pray (thou), 1343. *Preide, pa. t.* prayed, 209.

**Prest,** *n.* S. priest, 429, 1829. *Prestes, pl.* 2583.

**Priken,** *v.* S. to spur a horse, ride briskly, 2639.

**Prud,** *adj.* S. proud, 302.

**Pulten,** *pa. t. pl.* so reads the MS. l. 1023, instead of *putten.* Both have the same signification. So in the Romance of *Rob. of Cecyle,* Harl. MS. 1701, f. 94, c. 1, *pulte* occurs for *put,* placed, and *pylt* in R. Cœur de L. 4085; pelte, Sir Tr. p. 95. In the *imp. Pult* for *put, place*, is used in *Hending the Hende*, MS. Digb. 86. In the signification of *drove forward*, which is nearer to the sense we require, we find *pylte* in K. Horn, 1433, and R. Glouc. Hence the Engl. word *pelt*. *See* Putten. Cf. *Pult* in Gl. to *Will. of Palerne*.

Pund, *n. pl.* S. pounds, 1633.

Put, *n.* cast, throw, 1055. But, 1040.

Putten, *v.* to cast, throw, propel forward, 1033, 1044. *Puten*, 1051. *Putte, pa. t.* cast, 1052. *Putten, pa. t. pl.* cast, threw, 1023, 1031, 1844. From the Fr. *bouter*, Teut. *buitten*, or Belg. *botten*, to drive or propel forward, or, as others suggest, from the Br. *potiaw*, which has the same meaning, or Isl. *potta*. From the same root are derived both *Put* and *But*. Thus to *butt* in Sc. is to drive at a stone in curling, and to *put* in Yorksh. is to push with the horns. In the passage before us it is applied to a particular game, formerly in great repute. *See* Note on l. 1022. Cf. Ramsay's Poems, ii. 106. The word is still retained in the North, and Sc. V. Jam. and Brockett. See *But* and *Pulten*.

Putting, Puttinge, *n.* casting, 1042, 1057, 2324.

Pyment, *n.* B. L. spiced wine, 1728. *See* Note on l. 1726.

Qual, *n.* S. [*hwæl*] whale or grampus, 753. *See* Hwel.

Quan, Quanne, *adv.* S. when, 134, 204, 240, &c. *See* Hwan.

Quath, *pa. t.* S. quoth, 606, 642, &c. *Hwat*, 1650, 1878. *Wat*, 595. *Qvod*, 1888. *Quodh*, 1801. *Qvot*, 1954, 2808. *Couth*, 2606.

Queme, *adj.* S. agreeable, 130, 393. Web., Rits. M. R., Rob. Br., R. Glouc., Gower, Chauc.

Quen, *n.* S. queen, 2760, 2783, &c. *Quenes, pl.* 2982.

Qui. *See* Hwi.

Quic, Quik, *adj.* S. alive, 612, 613, 1405, 2210, 2476, &c., *quik and ded*. This is the usual language of the Inquisitiones post mortem, which commence at the early part of Henry III. reign. For the usage of the term, *see* Gl. to Sir Tr. p. 98. Yw. and Gaw. 668. Chron. of Engl. 762, &c. The word is preserved in the vulgar version of the Scriptures, and Creed. *Quike*, quick, alert, 1348. *Al quic wede*, 2641. Cf. l. 2387.

Quiste, *n.* S. [*cwide*] bequest, will, 219, 365. *Quede*, K. Alisaund. 8020.

Quod, Quodh, Quot. *See* Quath.

Radde. *See* Rede.

Ran. *See* Renne.

Rang, *adj.* S. [*ranc*] perverse, rebellious, 2561.

Rath, *n.* S. counsel; hence, an adviser, 75. *Dat. c. rathe*, in the phrase *to rathe*, 2542; for the meaning of which, *see* Red.

Rape, *adv.* S. speedily, readily, quickly, 358, &c. (In l. 1335, I prefer considering it as a verb.)

Rathe, *v.* S. [*ræedan*] to advise, 1335. A provincial pronunciation of *Rede*. In l. 2517, it is still broader, "Yif ye it wilen and ek *rothe*." In the same manner *Rod* is spelt, and was undoubtedly pronounced *Rothe*, Ly Beaus Desc. 425, and *Abode* is spelt *Abothe*, ib. 1118. Cf. ll. 693, 1681, 2585, of the present poem, in all which instances the *d* in *rede* has the sound of *th*.

Recke, *pr. t. subj.* S. may reck, may care, 2047, 2511. Sir Tr. p. 124, &c.

Red, *n.* S. advice, counsel, 180, 518, 826, 1194, 2871, &c. *To rede*, lit. for a counsel, i.e. advisable, 118, 693; spelt *to rathe*, 2542.

Rede, v. S. to direct, advise, 104, 148, 361, 687, &c. *Radde, pa. t.* advised, 1353. V. Jam. in v. and Hearne's Gl. to R. Glouc.

Reft, Refte, Reftes. *See* Reue.

Regne, *pr. t. pl.* Fr. Lat. reign, assume the superiority, 2586. *Reng, Ring,* Sc. V. Jam. in v.

Renne, v. S. to run, 1161, 1904. *Ran on blode, pa. t.* 432. So in Sir Tr. p. 176, *His heued ran on blod;* and in MS. Harl. 2253, f. 128,
Lutel wot hit any mon hou loue hym haueth y-bounden,
That for vs o the rode *ron,* ant bohte vs with is wounde.

Reue, *n.* S. magistrate, 1627. *See* Greyue.

Reue, Reuen, v. S. *[reafian]* to take away, bereave, rob, 480, 2590, 2991. *Refte, pa. t.* took away, bereaved, 2223, 2485. *Reftes, pa. t.* 2 p. tookest away, 2394. *Reft, part. pa.* taken away, bereaved, 1367, 1672, 2483; spoiled, 2004. Still used in the North.

Reures, *n. pl.* S. robbers, bereavers, 2104.
Alle bacbiteres wendet to helle,
Robberes & *reueres* & the monquelle.
*A lutel sermun,* MS. Cal. A. ix. f. 246, b.
V. Jam. in v. *Reyffar.*

Reunesse, Rewnesse, *n.* S. compassion, 502, 2227.

Rewe, v. S. to have pity, to compassionate, 497, 967. *Rewede, pa. t. (impersonal)* 503.

Richelike, *adv.* S. richly, 421.

Ricth, Ricthe. *See* Rith, Rithe.

Ricthwise, *adj.* S. *[rihtwis]* righteous, just, 37. Rits., Web. M. R., Rob. Br., Minot, Lynds., R. Hood. [MS. *has* rirth wise.]

Riden, v. S. to ride, 10, &c.

Rig, *n.* S. back, 1775. So in Laȝam. l. 6718. Burne he warp on *rigge.*

Rike, *n.* S. kingdom, 290. *Heuene riche,* 133, 407. *See* Cunnriche.

Rim, Rym, *n.* S. Fr. rhyme, poem, 21, 2995, 2998. So Chauc. *Rime of Sire Thopas.* [The modern false spelling *rhyme* is due to confusion of Eng. *rime* with the Gk. *rhythm.*]

Ringen, v. S. to ring, 242, 1106. *Ringes, pr. t. sing.* ring, 390. *Rungen, part. pa.* rung, 1132.

Ringes, *n. pl.* S. rings of mail, 2740. *See* Brini.

Rippe, *n.* fish-basket, 893. Hence a *Rippar,* B. Lat. *riparius,* is a person who brings fish from the coast to sell in the interior. V. Spelm. in v. Nares prefers the etymology of *ripa,* but without reason. *Rip* is still provincial for an osier basket. *See* Jam. and Moore. So also in a curious Latin and English Vocabulary, written out by Sire John Mendames, Parson of Bromenstrope [Broomsthorp, Co. Norf.] in the middle of the 15th cent., and now preserved in the valuable MSS. library of T. W. Coke, Esq. *Cophinus* is explained *A beryng lepe,* or *ryppe,* terms still retained in the county. Jam. gives Icel. *hrip,* a basket.

Rith, Ricth, *n.* S. right, justice, inheritance, 36, 395, 1099, 1383, 2717.

Rith, *adj.* S. right *(dexter),* 604, 1812, 2140, 2545, 2725.

Rithe, Ricthe, *adj.* S. right *(rectus),* 772, 846, 1201, 2235, 2473.

Rith, Rithe, *adv.* S. rightly, 420, 1701, 2611, &c.; exactly, just, 872, 2494, 2506.

Ritte, v. to rip, make an incision, 2495.
The breche adoun he threst,
He *ritt,* and gan to right.
*Sir Tristr.* p. 33.
[Cf. Sw. *rista,* Dan. *riste,* to slash, cut; G. *ritzen.* Perhaps connected also with Du. *rijten,* G. *reissen,* to tear.]

Robben, v. S. to rob, 1958.

Rode, n. S. the rood, cross, 103, 431, 1357, &c. V. Todd's Gl. Illustr. Chauc.

Rof, n. S. roof, 2082.

Rome, v. S. to roam, travel about, 64.

Rore, v. S. to roar, 2496, &c. Rorede, pa. t. roared, 2438.

Roser, n. Fr. rose-bush, 2919. Chauc., Pers. Tale, *De luxuria.*

Rothe. *See* Rathe.

Rowte, v. S. [*hrutan*] to roar, 1911. R. Cœur de L. 4304. V. Gl. Lynds. and Jam. in v. Cf. Icel. *hrjota,* Sw. *ryte.* The word is still retained in the provinces. V. Brockett and Wilbr.

Runci, n. B. Lat. a horse of burden, 2569. V. Du Cange and Spelm. The word is common both in Fr. and Engl. writers. Cf. Span. *Rozin-ante.*

Rungen. *See* Ringen.

Rym. *See* Rim.

Sal *for* Shall, 628.

Same *for* Shame, 1941. V. Jam.

Samen, adv. S. together, 467, 979, 1717, &c. Web., Rits. M. R., Rob. Br. So also in Sc. V. Jam.

Samened, *part. pa.* S. assembled, united, 2890. Web., R. Br. p. 2.

Sare, adv. S. sore, sorrowfully, 401.

Sat, *pa. t.* S. opposed, 2567. *See* Atsitte. In Sc. is *Sit, Sist,* to stop, from Lat. *sistere.* V. Jam.

Sautres, n. pl. Fr. Lat. Psalters, Hymns for the Office of the Dead, 244.

Sawe, *written for* sa we, i. e. say we, 338.

Sawe, Sawen, Say. *See* Se.

Sayse, v. B. Lat. to seise, give seisin or livery of land, 251, 2518.

Seysed, *pa. t.* seised, 2931, *part. pa.* 2513. Horn Childe, ap. Rits. M. R. V. 3, p. 309.

Scabbed, Skabbed, *adj.* S. Lat. scabby, scurvy, 2449, 2505.

Scaþe, n. S. harm, injury, 1352. *Scaþes, pl.* 269. R. Br., V. Gl. *Skaith,* Sc. V. Jam.

Sche, Scho, Sho, *pron.* S. she, 112, 126, 649, 1721, &c.

Schifte *for* Shrift, absolution, 1829.

Schoten, Shoten, *pa. t. pl.* S. shot, cast, 1838, 1864. *Scuten,* 2431.

Schulle, n. a plaice, 759. Sw. *skolla,* a plaice. *See* Coleridge's Glossarial Index.

Se (*the* S. *art.*) the, but perhaps a mistake of the scribe, l. 534, as it is not elsewhere used.

Se, n. S. sea, 535, &c.; *gen.* seis, 321.

Se, Sen, v. S. to see, 1021, 1273, &c. *Sest, pr. t.* 2 p. seest, 534. *Sen, pr. t. pl.* see, 168, 1217. *Sawe, Sowe, pa. t.* saw, 1182, 1323. *Say,* 881. *Sawen, Sowen, pa. t. pl.* 957, 1055, 2255. *Sene, part. pa.* 656.

Seckes, n. pl. S. sacks, 2019.

Segges, n. pl. Fr. [*seches*] 896. In Cotgr. the *Seche* is explained the Sound, or Cuttle fish. The *Seches de Coutance* were held in the highest estimation. V. Le Grand. *See* also Jam. v. *Sye.*

Sei, v. *See* Seyen.

Seis. *See* Se.

Seken, v. S. to seek, 1629. The reading is confirmed by an old poem in MS. Digb. 86.
Sire, we ben knizttes fer i-fare,
For to *sechen* wide-ware.
*La vie seint Eustace, qui out noun Placidas.*

Selcouth, n. S. wonder, strange thing, 124, 1059. *Selcuth,* 2119. It was in all probability originally

## GLOSSARIAL INDEX.

an *adj.* as *Selkuth.* Strange, wonderful, 1284.

Sele, *n.* S. seal, 755.

Seli, *adj.* S. simple, harmless, 477, 499. R. Gl., Chauc.

Selthe, *n.* S. success, 1338. A.S. *sélð.* [Cf. *selehðe* in *Laʒam.* l. 25136, and see *selehðe* in Stratmann's Dictionary of Old English. The line seems to be a proverb, and the meaning is—" Rest and success are companions." Goldborough tells him to avoid delay, since rest may accompany success, but cannot precede it.]

Sembling, *n.* Fr. assembling, 1018. It may also be compared with the Su.-G. *samlung,* conventus.

Semes, *pr. t.* in the phrase, *hire semes* = it beseems her, it becomes her, 2916. *Semede, pa. t.* was suitable, was fit, 976. See *Seem* in Wedgwood.

Sen, Sene. *See* Se.

Sendes, *pr. t.* sendeth, sends, 2392. *Sende, pa. t.* sent, 136, &c.

Serf-borw, *n.* S. surety, pledge, 1667. In MS. Soc. Antiq. No. 60, known by the name of *The Black Book of Peterborough,* is an instrument in which many names both of Saxon and Danish origin appear as the *Borhhanda,* or Sureties, otherwise called *Festermen.* See Jam. and the Glossaries, for further examples.

Serganz, *n. pl.* Fr. attendants, officers, 2088, 2091, 2116. *Sergaunz,* 1929, 2361, 2371. *Seriaunz,* 2066. V. Spelm. in v. *Servientes,* and Hickes, Thes. T. i. p. 148.

Serges. *See* Cerges.

Serk, *n.* S. shirt, 603. Emare, 501. R. Br.

Seruen, *v.* S. to serve, 1230.

Seruede, *pa. t.* S. deserved, 1914. Web. M. R. So in Sc. V. Jam.

Sest. *See* Se.

Sette, *v.* S. to set, descend, 2671.

Sette, *pa. t.* S. set, placed, 2405; appointed, 2571. *Setten, pa. t. pl.* set, 1211. *Sette, part. pa.* set, placed, 2612.

Seyen, *v.* S. to say, 2886. *Seyst, pr. t.* 2 *p.* sayest, 2008. *Seyde, pa. t.* 3 *p.* said, 117, &c. *Seyden, pa. t. pl.* said, 376, 1213. *Seyden,* have said, 456. *Sey, part. pa.* said, 2993.

Seysed. *See* Sayse.

Seyst. *See* Seyen.

Seyt, *pr. t. s.* put for *sey it,* i. e. say it; or else put for *seyth,* i. e. say, 647. So in Sir Tr. p. 117,
For mani men *seyt* ay whare.

Shaltou, shalt thou, 1800. *Shaltow,* 1322. *Shaltu,* 2180, 2186, 2882, 2901.

Shamelike, *adv.* S. shamefully, disgracefully, 2825. *Schamliche,* Sir Tr. p. 93

Shankes, *n. pl.* S. legs, 1903. *Sconke,* Laʒam. l. 15215. *See* Rits. A.S. p. 16, and Diss. p. xxxi. *Schank* Sc. V. Jam.

Shar, *pa. t.* S. share, cut, 1413. So in Am. and Amil. 2298, Her throtes he *schar atvo.*

Shauwe, Shawe, *v.* S. to shew, 2206, 2784. *Sheu,* 1401.

Shel, Sheld, *n.* S. shield, 489, 624, 1653, &c.

Shende, *v.* S. to ruin, destroy, 1422. Bevis of H. ap. Ellis, M. R. V. 2, p. 99. Chauc. *Shent, pa. t.* shamed, disgraced, 2749; *part. pa.* shend, 2845. The more common sense of this verb is the latter. V. Jam.

Shere. Clearly miswritten for *she were,* 1250.

Sheu. *See* Shauwe.

Shides, *n. pl.* S. It here expresses pieces of wood cleft at the end, 917. In Doug. Virg. *Schide* signifies a billet of wood, 223, 10;

or a chip, splinter, 207, 8. So in *Rauf Coilzear*, st. 39, Schaftes of schene wode they scheueride in *schides*. So also in P. Pl. The word is preserved in Lanc. This custom of skinning eels by inserting the head in a cleft stick, is still practised, we are informed, in the fish markets.

Shir, *adj.* S. bright, 588, 916, 1253, &c.

Shireue, *n.* S. sheriff, 2286. *Schireues, pl.* 266.

Sho, *pron. See* Sche.

Sho, *v.* S. to shoe, 1138.

Shof, *pa. t.* S. shoved, pushed, 871, 892.

Shol, 1 *p. s.* (if I) shall, 1782. *Sal*, I shall, 628. *Shole, pl.* shall, 562, 645, 1788. *Sholen*, 621, 1127, 1230, &c. *Shulen*, 731, 747, &c. *Shoren* (so in MS.), 1640. *Sule*, shall ye, will ye, 2419. *Shude*, I should, 1079. *Sholdest*, shouldst, 2712. *Sholden, pl.* 1020, 1195. *Shulden*, 941.

Sholdre, *n.* S. shoulder, 2738. *Shuldre*, 604, 1262. *Shudre-blade*, 2644. *Sholdres, pl.* shoulders, 1647, 1818. *Shuldren*, 982.

Shon, *n. pl.* S. shoes, 860, 969.

Shop, *qu.* Shok, shook, struck, destroyed, 1101. But Sewel gives Du. *schoppen*, to strike. Cf. Eng. *chop*.

Shotshipe, *n.* S. [*scot*, symbolum, *scipe*, societas] An assembly of persons who pay pecuniary contribution or reckoning, 2099.

> For al Sikelines quiden
> *Sotscipe* heo heolden,
> And swa longe swa beoð æuere,
> Ne scal hit stonde næuere.
> *Laʒam.* l. 23177.

Cf. *sotschipes, pl.* in Leg. of St. Kath. MS. Cott. Tit. D 18, fol. 144 *b. See* Nares, *v. Shot-clog*.

Shrede. *n.* S. a fragment, piece cut off, 99. [As it was given off the "board," to "feed the poor," it must mean a piece of bread or meat. Correct "*shrede =* clothing" in Coleridge's Glossarial Index.]

Shres, *n.* S. shears, 857.

Shride, *v.* S. to clothe (himself), 963. *Shrid, part. pa.* clothed, 978.

Shriue, Shriuen, *v.* S. to confess, make confession, 362, 2598. *Shriue, Shriuen, part. pa.* 364, 2489.

Shrud, *n.* S. clothing, 303.

Shude, Shul, Shulen. *See* Shol.

Shuldre, Shuldren. *See* Sholdre.

Shuldreden, *pa. t. pl.* S. shouldered, 1056.

Sibbe, *adj.* S. related, allied, 2277. Sir Tr. p. 44. *See* Fremde.

Siden, *n. pl.* S. sides, 371.

Sike, *v.* S. to sigh, 291.

Siking, *n.* S. sighing, 234.

Sikerlike, *adv.* S. surely, 422, 625, 2301, 2707, 2871. *Sikerly*, Sir Tr. p. 35, &c.

Sikernesse, *n.* S. surety, security, 2856. R. Glouc., R. Br., Chauc.

Simenels, *n. pl.* Fr. 779, a finer sort of bread, "q. a *simila* h. e. puriori farinæ parte." Spelm. Assis. pan. 51 Hen. III. *Symnellus* vero de quadrante ponderabit 2 sol. minus quam Wastellum. It elsewhere appears to be a sort of cake, or cracknel. So in the *Crieries de Paris*, v. 163, Chaudes tartes et *siminiaus*. V. Nares in v.

Sinne, *n.* S. fault, 1976. *Ne for loue ne for sinne*, 2375. *Wolde he nouth for sinne lette*, 2627. Traces of this phrase may be elsewhere found:

> Neyther for *love* nor yet for *awe*
> Lyuinge man none than they saw.
>     *Sir Degore*, c. iv.

> Maboun and Lybeauus
> Faste togedere hewes,
> And stente *for no synne*.
>     *Ly Beaus Desc.* 1957.

Sire, Syre, n. Fr. The term in ll. 310, 1229, is used not only to express respect, but command. A parallel passage is in R. Cœur de L. 2247. It simply means *Sir*, ll. 909, 2009.

Site, v. S. to sit, 2809. *Sittes, pr. t. 2 p.* sittest, 1316. *Sitten, pr. t. pl.* sit, 2098. *Site on knes,* i. e. kneel, 2708.

Siþe, Siþen, adv. S. then, afterwards, after, 399, 472, 1414, 1814, 1988, &c.

Siþe, n. S. time, 1052. *Siþe, Siþes, pl.* 213, 778, 1737, 2189. *Syþe, Syþes,* 2162, 2843. Sir Tr. p. 55, &c.

Sket, adv. quickly, soon, 1926, 1960, 2303, 2493, 2513, 2574, 2736, 2839. Sir Tr. pp. 36, 40, &c.; Ly Beaus Desc. 484; K. Alisaund. 3047; R. Cœur de L. 806; Rom. of Merlin, ap. Ellis, M. R. V. i. p. 228. [Icel. *skjótt,* quickly, from *skjótr,* quick, swift. The adj. is still preserved in the surname Skeat *or* Skeet.]

Skirming, n. Fr. skirmishing, 2323. Web. M. R. *See* Note on l. 2320.

Slawe, Slawen. *See* Slo.

Slenge, v. S. to sling, cast out, 2435. *Slenget, part. pa.* slung, 1923.

Slepes, *pr. t. 2 p.* sleepest, 1283.

Sleie, Sley, adj. skilful, expert, 1084, 2116. Sir Tr. pp. 23, 28; Horn Childe, ap. Rits. M. R. V. 3, p. 296; Emare, 67; R. Glouc. p. 350; Barb. xix 179; Doug. 137, 12. Jamieson derives it from Su.-G. *slug,* Isl. *slægr.* Cf. Sw. *slug.*

Slike, adv. or perhaps adj. smoothly, *or* smooth, 1157. "*Slyke,* or smothe. *Lenis.*" Prompt. Parv.

Slo, n. S. sloe, berry, 849, 2051.

Slo, v. S. to slay, 512, 1364, 1412, &c. *Slou,* 2543. *Slos, pr. t. 2 p.* slayest, 2706. *Slos, imp. pl.* strike ye, 2596. *Slou, Slow, pa. t.* slew, 501; struck, 2633. *Slowe, Slowen, pa. t. pl.* slew, 2414, 2427, 2432; struck, fought, 2683. *Slawe, Slawen, part. pa.* slain, 1803, 1928, 2000, &c. In l. 2747 (as in 2596, 2633, 2683) it has only the sense of *struck,* wounded, agreeably to the signification of the original word, *sleán, sleáhan,* Cædere, ferire.

Smerte, *adj. pl.* S. painful, 2055.

Smerte, v. S. to smart, 2647.

Smot, *pa. t.* S. smote, 2654.

So, a large tub, 933. See *So* in Halliwell. Dan. *saa,* a pail.

So, conj. S. as, 279, 349, *et pass.*

Softe, adj. S. of a mild disposition, 991.

Softe, adv. S. gently, 2618.

Somdel, adj. S. somewhat, in some measure, 240. *Sumdel,* 450, 497, 1054, 2306, 2950. Web., R. Gl., Chauc.

Sond, n. S. sand, 708, 735.

Sone, n. S. son, 660, 839. *Sones, pl.* 2980.

Sone, adv. S. soon, 78, &c. ; so soon as, 1354.

Sor, n. S. sorrow, 234. *Sorwe,* 1374; pain, sore, 1988.

Sor, adj. S. sore, detestable, 2229. [Perhaps it should be *sori.*]

Sorful, adj. S. sorrowful, 151, 2541.

Sori, adj. S. sorrowful, 151, 477.

Soth, Sothe, n. S. truth, 36, 647, 2008, &c.

Soþlike, adv. S. truly, 276.

Soupe, v. Fr. to sup, 1766.

Southe, *pa. t.* S. sought, 1085.

Sowe, Sowen. *See* Se.

Sowel, n. victuals, 767, 1143, 2905. Properly, anything eaten with bread as a relish. See *Suol* in Halliwell. Dan. *suul.*

Span-newe, *adj.* quite new, 968. This is the earliest instance on record of the use of this word. For its disputed etymology see Jam., Nares, Todd's Johns., and Thoms. Etymons; but especially Wedgwood's Etym. Dict. *Span* = chip; *Span-new*, chip-new. A.S. *spón*. It occurs in Chauc. Troil. iii. 1671.

Sparkede, *pa. t.* S. sparkled, 2144.

Spede, *v.* S. to speed, prosper, 1634.

Speke, *n.* S. speech, 946.

Speke, Speken, *v.* S. to speak, 326, 369, 548, 1070, &c. *Spak, pa. t.* spoke, 2389, 2968. *Speken, part. pa.* spoken, 2369.

Spelle, *n.* S. story, relation, 338. K. Horn, 951.

Spelle, *v.* S. to relate, tell forth, 15, 2530.

Spen *for* Spent, 1819.

Sperd, Sperde, *part. pa.* S. barred, bolted, 414, 448. Still common in the North. V. Brockett.

Spille, *v.* S. to perish, 2422. Of *limes spille*, 86, suffer the loss of limbs. K. Horn, 202. Web., Chauc.

Spired, *part. pa.* S. speered, inquired, 2620. V. Jam. in v.

Spore, *n.* S. spur, 2569.

Sprauleden, *pa. t. pl.* S. sprawled, 475.

Sprong, *pa. t.* S. sprung, 959. See the Note. *Sprongen,* 869. *Sprungen, part. pa.* risen, 1131.

Sprote, *n.* S. sprout, 1142. A.S. *sprote*, a sprig, sprout.

Spuse, Spusen, *v.* S. to espouse, marry, 1123, 1170, 2875. *Spusede, pa. t. pl.* espoused, 2887. *Spused, part. pa.* 1175, 2928. *Spuset,* 1266.

Spusing, *n.* S. espousals, marriage, 1164, 1177, 2886.

Stac, *n.* S. 814. [This I believe to mean simply a stack, or heap, like the Dan. *stak*, Sw. *stack*. I add Sir F. Madden's note in the edition of 1828.] A stack, or, more properly, *stick* of fish, a term applied to eels when strung on a row, 'sic dicta, quod trajecta vimine (quod *stic* dicimus) connectebantur.' *Spelm.* A *stica* consisted of 25 eels, and 10 *Sticæ* made a *Binde.* Glanv. lib. 2, c. 9.

Stalworþi, Stalworþe, Stalwrthe, *adj.* S. strong, valiant, courageous, 24, 904, 1027, &c. *Stalworþeste, sup.* 25.

Stan-ded, *adj.* S. dead as a stone, completely dead, 1815. *Stille als a ston,* 928. Cf. K. of Tars, 549; Erle of Tol. 754; Launfal, 357. See Gl. to *Partenay.*

Star, *n.* Icel. a species of sedge, 939. Icel. *stör;* Sw. *starr;* Dan. *stær.* See the Note.

Stareden, *pt. t. pl.* 1037. Probably miswritten for Stradden, contended. Cf. Su.-Goth. and Sw. *strida,* to contend.

Starinde, *part. pr.* staring, 508.

Stark, *adj.* S. stiff, stout, strong, 341, 380, 608, &c. V. Jam. in v.

Stede, *n.* S. steed, horse, 10, &c.

Stede, *n.* S. place, 142, 744. *Stedes, pl.* 1846.

Stem, *n.* S. a ray of light, beam, 591. It is equivalent to *Glem,* l. 2122.

Therewith he blinded them so close,
A *stime* they could not see.
R. *Hood,* I. 112.

Cf. Brockett's Gl. in v. *Stime.*

Sternes, *n. pl.* stars, 1809. *Ageyn* þe *sternes* = exposed to the sky, or to the open air.

Stert, *n.* S. leap, 1873. Chaucer has *at a stert* for immediately, C. T. 1707.

Stert, *n.* S. [*steort,* cauda] tail, 2823. *Start* is still retained in the North.

Steuene, *n.* S. voice, 1275.

## GLOSSARIAL INDEX. 145

Sti, *n.* S. road, way, 2618. Sir Tr. p. 192; Yw. and Gaw. 599; Emare, 196; Sevyn Sages, 712; R. Br. Chaucer uses *stile* in the same sense, C. T. 12628, and Minot, p. 5, in both which passages the respective Editors have made the same mistake in explaining it. [Cf. G. *steg*, a pass.]

Stille, *adj.* S. quiet, 955, 2309.

Stille, *adv.* S. in a low voice, secretly, 2997. Sir Tr. p. 55; K. Horn, 315.

Stirt, Stirte, *pa. t.* S. started, leaped, 398, 566, 873, 1049, ′ ⁀. *Stirte, Stirten*, *pa. t. pl.* star .l, hurried, 599, 1964, 2609. Derived by Skinner from S. *astirian*, movere, by Jam. from Teut. *steerten*, volare. *See* Astirte. Cf. G. *stürzen;* and see *Start* in Wedgwood.

Stith, *n.* S. anvil, 1877. Chauc. Still provincial. V. Moore, and Brockett.

Stiward, *n.* S. steward, 666.

Stonden, *v.* S. to stand, 689. *Stondes, pr. t.* 3 *p.* standeth, stands, 2240, 2983. *Stod, pa. t.* stood, 591, 679. *Stoden, pa. t. pl.* 1037.

Stor, *adj.* S. hardy, stout, 2383. Laȝam. l. 9126; Yw. and Gaw. 1297; Chron. of Engl. 464; Sq. of Lowe D. 658; Ly Beaus Desc. 1766. *Steir, Sture*, Sc. ap. Jam. Cf. Sw. *stor.*

Stra, *n.* S. straw, 315, 466. A.S. *streow, streaw.* Cf. Strie.

Strenes, *pr. t.* 3 *p.* S. begets, 2983. From *streónan*, gignere. Cf. K. Alisaund. 7057.

Strie, *n.* a straw, 998. *See* Stra.

Strout, *n.* dispute, contention, 1039. Cf. A.S. *strúdan*, and *Strother* in Atkinson's Cleveland Glossary.

Stroute, *v.* S. to make a disturbance, 1779. Bosworth explains A.S. *strúdan, strútian*, as having originally the sense to bustle about.

Stunde, *n.* S. short space of time, 2614. V. Gl. to R. Glouc. *See* Vmbestonde.

Sturgiun, Sturgun, *n.* sturgeon, 753, 1727. Cf. Sw. *stör*, Dan. *stör.*

Suere, Suereth. *See* Sweren.

Suete, *adj.* S. sweet, 1338. Cf. l. 2927.

Sueyn, Sweyn, *n.* S. swain, villain, 343, 1328, &c. *Swegnes, pl.* 371, 2195. It is generally used in opposition to *knight.*

Svich, *adj.* S. such, 60.

Suilk, *adj.* such (things), 644. *See* Swilk.

Sule. *See* Shol.

Sumdel. *See* Somdel.

Sunne-bem, *n.* S. sun-beam, 592, 2123.

Swerd, *n.* S. sword, 1759, &c. *Swerdes, pl.* 1769, 2659.

Sweren, *v.* S. to swear, 494. *Suereth, pr. t. s.* swear, 647. *Swor, pa. t.* swore, 398, 2367. *Suere, pr. subj.* 2 *p. s.* 388.

Swike, *n.* S. deceiver, traitor, 423, 551, 626, 1158, 2401, 2451, &c. *Swikes, pl.* 2834, 2990. Laȝam. l. 12942; R. Gl. p. 105.

Swikel, *adj.* S. deceitful, 1108.

For alle þine witien
Beoð swiðe *swikele.*
Laȝam. l. 15848.

Hoe beth of *swikele* kunne
Ther mide the witherwinne.
*The sawe of Seint Bede*, MS. Digb. 86.

He was *suikel*, fals, ant fel.
*Chron. of Engl.* 791.

Swilen, *v.* S. [*swilian*, Ps. vi. 6] to wash, 919. It occurs also in Rob. of Brunne's *Handling Sinne*, l. 5828. Still provincial.

Swilk, *adj.* S. such, 1118, 1625, 2123, 2684, 2783. *Suilk*, 644.

10

Swinge, *v.* S. to beat, chastise (used *passively*), 214. *Swngen, part. pa.* beaten, 226. Laȝam. l. 21070. So in *Syr Bevys,* C. ii. All at ones on him they *swonge.* In the North the verb retains the same meaning; v. Brockett.

Swink, *n.* S. labour, 770, 801, 2456.

Swinken, *v.* S. to labour, 798. *Swank, pa. t.* laboured, 788.

Swire, *n.* S. neck, 311. Formerly in universal use, and still preserved in the provinces.

Swiþe, Swyþe, *adv.* S. very, exceedingly, 110, 217, 341. Quickly, 140, 682, 690; *ful swithe,* 2436, appears a pleonasm. *Swithe forth and rathe,* quickly forth, and soon, 2594.

Swot, *n.* S. sweat, perspiration, 2662. The word has the same meaning in Cædmon, f. 24, ed. Thorpe, p. 31, l. 8, which seems to contradict Mr Price's assertion to the contrary, in Warton's Hist. Engl. Poetr. p. lxxi., ed. 1840.

Swngen. *See* Swinge.

Syre. *See* Sire.

Syþe, Syþes. *See* Siþe.

Syþe, *n.* S. scythe, 2553, 2699.

Tabour, *n.* Fr. tabor, 2329.

Tale, *n.* S. number, 2026.

Taleuaces, *n. pl.* Fr. large shields, 2323. *See* the Note on l. 2320.

Tarst (*so in* MS.), 2688; almost certainly an error for *faste,* which appears in the next line. Also, the movements of Godard are compared to the course of lightning.

Tauhte, *pt. s.* committed, 2214, probably an error for *bitauhte. See* Bitaken.

Tel, *n.* S. deceit, reproach, 191, 2219. A.S. *tálu.*

Telle, *v.* S. to count, number,

2615. *Told, part. pa.* numbered, esteemed, 1036.

Tene, *n.* S. grief, affliction, 729.

Tere, *v.* S. to tar (used passively), 707.

Teth, *n. pl.* S. teeth, 2406.

Teyte, *adj.* S. 1841, 2331. [Explained "lively" by Coleridge, Stratmann, and Morris, as if from Icel. *teitr,* hilaris. This I believe to be completely wrong. The word occurs in Allit. Poems, ed. Morris, B. 871, with reference to *tight* lasses, and in l. 1841 of Havelok we have a reference to *tight* lads. In l. 2331 it may also mean *flawless,* staunch. "*Theet, adj.* water-tight. O.N. þiettr or þéttr, densus, solidus. O. Sw. *thæter,* Sw. Dial. *tjett* or *tjætt,* Dan. *tætt,* Germ. *dicht.* Ihre gives .... *ett tätt fat,* a flawless vessel. '*Thyht,* hool fro brekynge, not brokyn. *Integer, solidus.* Prompt. Parv.'" Atkinson's Glossary of the Cleveland dialect.]

þa, *written for* þat, 175.

þan, þanne, *adv.* S. then, 51, 1044, &c.; when, 226, 248, *et sæpius;* than if (*quàm*), 944, 1867.

þar, *adv.* where (?) 130. *See* the Note; and cf. þer.

þare, *adv.* S. there, 2481, 2739. Cf. þer, þore.

þarne, *v.* to lose, be deprived of, 2492, 2835. þarnes, *pr. t.* wants, is deprived of, 1913. þarned þe ded, 1687; [clearly miswritten for þoled þe ded, suffered death. The scribe was thinking of þarned þe lif; cf. l. 2492.] The verb only exists in the Sax. in the pt. t. þærnode, Chron. Sax. p. 222, ed. Gibs., which is derived by Lye from the Cimbr. *At thuerna,* or *thorna,* diminui, privari. V. Hickes Thes. I. p. 152. [I. e. it is from the root of the Sw. *tarfva,* Icel. *thurfa,* Goth. *thaurban,* with the *f* dropped, and with the addition of the *passive* or *neuter* infinitive-ending denoted by -*ne*, like -*na* in Sw., -*nan* in Mœso-Gothic. See þ*arrnenn* in Gl. to Ormulum.]

þas, *read* Was, 1129. [As þ at the beginning of a word is never put for *t*, it is not = Sc. *tas*, takes, as some have suggested.]

þaue, *v.* S. [þ*afian*] to grant, 296; bear, sustain, 2696. Ormulum, 5457.

Thayn, *n.* S. nobleman, 2184. *Thein*, 2466. *Thaynes, pl.* 2260. *Theynes*, 2194. *See* Kayn.

þe, *n.* S. thigh, 1950. þ*he*, 1( 4. þ*es, pl.* 1903. þ*hes*, 2289.

þe, *adv.* S. (*written for* þer), there, 142, 476, 863, 933. þ*e with*, therewith, 639. *See* þer.

þe, *conj.* S. though, 1682. þ*ei*, 1966. þ*ey*, 807, 992, 1165, 2501. *See* þou.

þede, *n.* S. country, dwelling, 105; place, 2890. Web., Le Bone Flor. 246. R. Br. p. 18. V. Jam.

þef, *n.* S. thief, 2434. þ*eues, pl.* 1780.

þei, *pron.* S. they, 1020, 1195, &c.

þei, þey, *conj.* though. *See* þe.

þenke, *pr. subj.* S. think, 2394. þ*enkeste, pr. t.* 2 *p.* thinkest thou, 578.

þenne, *adv.* S. thence, 1185. [Perhaps in l. 777, we should put the comma after þ*enne;* "when he came thence," &c.]

þer, *adv.* S. where, 318, 448, &c.; there, *passim;* the place whence, 1740. þ*erinne*, therein, 535, &c. þ*erhinne*, 322. þ*erof*, þ*eroffe*, thereof, 372, 466, 1068, &c. þ*erþoru*, by that means, 1098. þ*ertil*, þ*erto*, thereto, 396, 1041, 1045. þ*erwit*, þ*erwith*, therewith, 1031, 1046. *See* þe, þore.

þere, *pron.* S. their, 1350.

þerl *for* þe erl, the earl, 178.

þertekene, 2878. [Coleridge's Glossarial Index has "Thertekene = mark thereto. A.S. *tácnian.*" But this is a very awkward phrase, and I should prefer to suppose þ*er-tekene* = by the token, i. e. in token. Tekene answers to the Sw. *tecken*, a token; and þ*er* is found as a prefix in *P. Plowman* in the phr. þ*er-while* = þ*e while*, i. e. in the time that. The only difficulty is that þ*er* is properly *feminine* (A.S. þ*ære*), whilst *tecken* in Sw. and *tácen* in A.S. are neuter. *In tokne* ( = in token) occurs in Shoreham's poems, ed. Wright, 131.]

þet, *conj.* S. that (*quòd*), 330.

þet, *pron.* S. that, 879.

þeþe, þeþen, *adv.* S. thence, 2498, 2629.

þeu, þewe, *n.* S. in a servile condition or station, 262, 2205. R. Gl.

þewes, *n. pl.* S. manners, 282. Laȝam., Rits. M. R., Web., P. Plowm., Chauc., Gl. Lynds., Percy, A. R.

þi. *See* Forþi.

þi *for* þy, thy, 2725.

þider, *adv.* S. thither, 850, 1012, 1021, &c.

þigge, *v.* S. [þ*icgan*] to beg, 1373. This word is chiefly preserved in the Sc. writers. Wall. ii. 259; Doug. Virg. 182, 37; Evergreen, ii. 199; Bannatyne Poems, p. 120, V. Jam. in v., who derives it from Su.-G. *tigga*, Alem. *thigen*, petere. [See *tigga* in Ihre. "Thyggynge or beggynge, *Mendicacio.*" Prompt. Parv.]

þis *for* þise, these, 1145.

þisternesse, *n.* S. darkness, 2191.

Dalden from þan fihte
Al bi þ*ustere* nihte.

Laȝam. l. 7567; cf. *Gen. and Ex.*, 58.

Thit, *pp.* 2990. [The rime shews that the *i* is long; and, whether the *th* is sounded like *t*, or (which is more likely) the word should have been written *tiht* or *tith*, we may be tolerably confident that it is equivalent to the O.E. *tight* or *tiȝt*, a pp. signifying *intended, purposed, designed*, which is the exact sense here required. Stratmann gives five instances of it, of which one is—"To brewe the Crystene mennys banys Hy hadden *tyght ;* " Octovian, 1476.]

þo, *pron.* S. those, 1918, 2044.

þo, *pron.* thou. *See* þu.

þo, *adv.* S. then, 930 ; when, 1047. *Thow*, 1669.

þore, *adv.* S. there, 741, 922, 1014, &c. Þortil, thereto, 1443. Þorwit, therewith, 100. *See* Þe, þer.

þoru, *adv.* S. through, 627, 774, 848, &c. Þoruth, 1065, 2786. Þorw, 264, 367, 2646. Þuruth, 52.

þoruthlike, *adv.* S. throughly, 680.

þou, *conj.* S. though, 124, 299, &c. Þo, 1020. *See* Þe.

þoucte, *pa. t.* S. thought, 504, 507, &c. Þouthte, 1073. Þowthe, 1869. Þouthe, 1166. Þat god thoucte, 256, that seemed good. Cf. Sir Tr. pp. 30, 36. And so in MS. Vernon, Bodl.
Riche metes was forth brouht
To all men *that gode thouht.*
*Disp. betw. a Crystene mon and a Jew*, f. 301.
[Or, if we read " þat god *him* þoucte," this would mean "that seemed good *to him ;* " cf. l. 197.]

þouth, *n.* S. thought, 122, 1190.

þral, *n.* S. slave, villain, 527, 684, 1097, 1158, 2564, 2589. In an opprobious sense, 1408. Sir Tr. p. 175.

þrawe, *n.* S. space of time, moment, 276, 1215. Web., Rits. M. R., Rob. Br., Doug. Virg. Þrow, Chauc., Gower, &c.

þredde, þridde, *adj.* S. third, 867, 2633.

þrette, *pa. t.* S. threatened, 1163.

þrie, 730. [In the former edition it is glossed "trouble, affliction ; apparently the same as *Tray* or *Treye ;* " cf. A.S. *tréga*. But this renders the construction difficult, nor is it clear that *treye* and þrie can be identified. Without doubt, the usual meaning of þrie is *thrice*, which is easily construed, only it remains to be shewn why *thrice* should be introduced ; unless perhaps it signifies *in a threefold degree.*]

þrinne, *num.* S. three, 716, 761, 1977, 2091.

þrist, þristen, *v.* S. to thrust, 1152, 2019, 2725. Þrist, *part. pa.* thrust, 638.

þu, *pron.* S. thou, 527, &c. Þou, 527, &c. Þo, 388. Þw (*read* þat þw *instead of* þw that ?), 1316. *Tow*, 1322. *Tu*, 2903. It is often joined to the verb which precedes, as *Shaltow, Wiltu*, &c. The *gen.* is þin, 1128 ; the *acc.* is þe, 529.

þurte, *pt. t. s.* need, might, 10. [It answers to the A.S. þurfan, *pt. t. ic* þorfte, Icel. þurfa, *pt. t.* þurfti, Mœso-Goth. þaurban, *pt. t.* þaurfta. *See* Ormulum, l. 16164, and Sir F. Maddeu's note to þort in Gl. to *Will. of Palerne.*]

þuruth. *See* þoru.

þus *for* þis, 785, 2586. (*In comp.* þus-gate.)

Tid, *n.* S. time, hour, 2100.

Til, *prep.* S. to, 141, 762, 864, &c. *See* Intil, þertil.

Til, *v.* S. to tell, 1348.

Tilled, *part. pa.* S. obtained, acquired (lit. drawn, taken), 438. V. Gl. R. Br. in v. *tille*, and see quotation under *Goddot*.

Tinte, *pa. t.* S. lost, 2023. Sir Tr. p. 104. V. Jam.

Tirneden, *pa. t. pl.* S. turned, 603.

Tiþandes, *n. pl.* Icel. tidings, 2279.

To-, in composition with verbs, is usually augmentative, or has the force of the Lat. *dis-*. *To-brised, part. pa.* very much bruised, 1950. (*See* Brisen.) *To-cruhsse, inf.* crush in pieces, 1992. *To-deyle, inf.* divide, 2099. (*See* Deled.) *To-drawen, part. pa.* dragged or pulled to death, 2001. (*See* Dreu.) *To-frusshe, inf.* break in pieces, 1993. *To-hewen, part. pa.* hewn in pieces, 2001. *To-riuen, part. pa.* torn *or* riven in pieces, 195". *To-ref, pa. t.* burst open, 17' *To-shiuere, inf.* shiver in pieces, 1993. *To-shinered, part. pa.* shivered to pieces, 2667. *To-tere, inf.* tear in pieces, 1839. *To-torn, part. pa.* torn in pieces, 1948, 2021. *To-tusede, part. pa.* entirely rumpled or tumbled, 1948. In one case only we find it to be merely the prep. *to* in composition; viz. in *To-yede, pa. t.* went to, 765. (*See* Yede.) [*See* note on this prefix in Gloss. to *William of Palerne.*]

To, *adv.* S. too, 303, 689, 691, &c.

To, *n.* S. toe, 1743, 1847, &c. *Tos, pl.* 898, 2163.

To, *num.* S. two, 2664.

To, *prep.* follows its case in ll. 197, 325, 526.

To-frusshe, *v.* Fr. [*froisser*] to dash or break in pieces, 1993.

The Sarczynes layde on with mace, And al *to-frussched* hym in the place.
    *R. Cœur de L.* 5032. Cf. 5084.

He suld sone be *to-fruschyt* all.
    *Barb.* x. 597. So also Doug. Virg. 51, 53. V. Jam. in v. *Frusch.*

Togidere, Togydere, *adv.* S. together, 1128, 1181, 2683, 2891.

Tok, *pa. t.* S. took, 354, 467, 537. *Toke, pa. t.* 2 p. 1216. *Token, pa. t. pl.* 1194. *Token under fote,* 1199.

Told. *See* Telle.

Totede, *pa. t.* peeped, looked, 2106. This verb is thrice found in P. Ploughman's Crede, ll. 142, 168, 339. Although it would appear a rare word from its not appearing in Hearne, Ritson, or Weber, yet in later times it occurs often, and is instanced by Jamieson from Patten's Account of Somerset's Expedicion, p. 53, and by Nares from Hall, Latimer, Spenser, and Fairfax. It also occurs four times in the *Lacren Riwle,* ed. Morton, 1853. In Sc. it is pronounced *Tete,* which is derived by Jam. from the same stock as Su.-G. *titt-a,* explained by Ihre, " Per transennam veluti videre, ut solent curiosi, ant post tegmina latentes." V. the authorities quoted, Todd's Johns. and Wilbr. Gl. [Cf. Sw. *titta;* Dan. *titte,* to peep; Dan. *tittelege,* to play at bopeep.]

To-tusede, *part. pa.* entirely rumpled or tumbled, 1948. See Nares, in v. *Tose,* and *Toust, Toozle,* in Jam., Brockett, &c. Cf. G. *zausen.*

Toun, *n.* S. town, 1750, &c. *Tun,* 764, 1001, &c. *Tunes, pl.* 1444, 2277.

Tour, *n.* Fr. tower. 2073.

Tre, *n.* S. a bar or staff of wood, 1022, 1821, 1843, 1882, &c. *Doretre,* 1806, 1968, bar of the door.

Trewe, *adj.* S. true, 1756.

Tristen, *v.* to trust, 253.

Tro. *See* Trowe.

Trome, *n.* S. [*truma*] a troop, company, 8.

Heo makeden heore sceld-*trome*
    *Laʒam.* l. 9454.

Bisydes stondeth a feondes *trume,*
And waileth hwenne the saules cume.
    *Les Unze peyne,* &c. MS. Coll. Jes. 29.

The same mode of expression used above occurs lower down, l. 24.

"A stalworþi man in a *flok*," which is also found in Laʒamon,
Cador ther wes æc,
þe kene wes on *flocke*.—1. 23824.
And in *Sir Guy*, H. iii.
Then came a knight that hight Sadock,
A doughty man in every *flock*.

Trone, *n.* Lat. throne, 1316.

Trowe, *n.* S. to believe, trust, 1656. *Tro*, 2862. *Trowede, pa. t.* believed, 382. Sir Tr. p. 41.

Trusse, *v.* Fr. [*trousser*] to pack up, to truss, 2017. R. Gl. Hence to *make ready*, K. Alisaund. 7006. Minot, p. 50, which Ritson was unable to explain.

Tuenti, *num.* S. twenty, 259.

Tumberel, *n.* a porpoise, 757. In Spelm. *Timberellus* is explained, a small whale, on the authority of Skene, Vocab. Jur. Scot. L. Forest, *Si quis cetum.* In Cotgr. also we find " *Tumbe*, the great Sea-Dragon, or Quadriver ; also the Gurnard, called so at Roan." [But the Sw. *tumlare*, a porpoise, *lit.* a tumbler, suggests that the name may be given from its *tumbling* or *rolling*. The Dan. *tumler*, however, is a dolphin.]

Tun. *See* Toun.

Turues, *n. pl.* S. turf, peat, 939. Chauc. C. T. 10109. V. Spelm. in v. and Jennings' Somersetsh. Gl.

Twel *for* Twelve, 2455.

Ueneysun, *n.* Fr. venison, 1726.

Vmbestonde, *adv.* S. for a while, formerly, 2297.

& heo seileden forth,
þæt inne sæ heo comen,
pa *vmbe stunde*
ne sæge heo noht of londe.
*Laʒam.* l. 11967.
It is equivalent to *umbe-while* or *vmwhile*, Sc. *umquhile*. *See* Stunde.

Umbistode, *pa. t.* S. stood around, 1875. *See* Bistode, Stonden.

Vn-bi-yeden, *pa. t. pl.* S. surrounded, 1842. *See* Yede.

Vnblithe, *adj.* S. unhappy, 141. Sir Tr. p. 171.

Unbounden, *pa. t. pl.* S. unbound, 601.

Underfong, *pa. t.* S. understood, 115. This sense of the verb is not found elsewhere. It is in the present poem synonymous with *Understod* (as Lat. *accipere, percipere*).

Understonde, *v.* S. to receive, 2814. *Understod, pa. t.* received, 1760. *Understonde, pr. subj.* receive, 1159. So in K. Horn, 245, ed. Rits.

Horn child thou *vnderstond*,
Tech him of harpe and song.

where the MS. Laud 108 reads *vnderfonge*. See Lumby's ed. l. 339.

Unker, *pron. g. c. dual.* S. of you two, 1882.

Vnkeueleden, *pa. t. pl.* S. ungagged, 601. *See* Keuel.

Unkyndelike, *adv.* S. unsuitably, 1250.

Vnornelike, *adj.* S. basely, or degradingly, 1941. The only word in the Sax. remaining to which it can be referred, is *unornlic*, tritus, Jos. 9. 5. The following instances also approach the same stock :

Ne speke y nout with Horne,
Nis he nout so *vnorne*.
*K. Horn*, 337.

Mi stefne is bold & noʒt *vnorne*,
Ho is ilich one grete horne,
& þin is ilich one pipe.
*Hule and Niʒtingale*, l. 317.

[Thre shews that Icel. and Su.-Goth. *orna* mean to acquire vital heat, to grow warm. Hence *unorne* means unfervent, spiritless, feeble, old. Thus, in the *Hule and Niʒtingale* it means *feeble, weak* ; in Jos. 9. 5, it is used of *old, worn-out* shoes. In the Ormulum, *unn-orne* occurs frequently, in the sense of *poor, mean, feeble;* see ll. 827, 3668; also *unnornelig,* meaning *meanly, humbly, obscurely,* in ll. 3750, 4858, 7525, 8251.]

Unride, *adj.* S. [*ungereod, ungerydu*] It is here used in various significations, most of which, however, correspond to the senses given by Somner. Large, cumbersome (of a garment), 964; unwieldy (of the bar of a door), 1795; deep, wide (of a wound), 1981, 2673; numerous, extensive (of the nobility), 2947. *Unrideste, sup.* deepest, widest, 1985. In the second sense we find it in Sir Tristr. p. ? 7,
    Dartes wel *unride*
    Beliagog set gan.
And in *Guy of Warwick,* ap. Ellis, M. R. V. 2, p. 79.
    A targe he had ywrought full well,
    Other metal was ther none but steel,
    A mickle and *unrede.*
In the fourth sense we have these examples:
    Opon Inglond for to were
    With stout ost and *unride.*
        *Horn Childe,* ap. Rits. M. R.
            V. 3, p. 283.
    Schir Rannald raugh to the renk
    ane rout wes *unryde.*
        *Sir Gaw. and Gol.* ii. 25.
    The soudan gederet an ost *unryde.*
        *K. of Tars,* 142.
Cf. also *Sir Guy,* Ee. IV. in Garrick's Collect. 'Ameraunt drue out a swerde *unryde.*' In the sense of huge, or unwieldy, we may also understand it in Sir Tr. p. 148, 164; Guy of Warw. ap. Ell. M. R. V. 2, p. 78; Horn Childe, ap. Rits. V. 3, p. 295. In R. Brunne, p. 174, it expresses loud, tremendous. Sir W. Scott and Hearne are both at fault in their Glossaries, and even Jamieson has done but little to set them right, beyond giving the true derivation, and then, under the cognate word *Unrude,* Doug. Virg. 167, 35, &c., errs from pure love of theory.

Vnrith, *n.* S. injustice, 1369.

Unwrast, Unwraste, *adj.* S. [*unwræste*] feeble, worthless, 2821; rotten, 547. This word occurs in the Saxon Chron. 168, 4 (ed. Thorpe, p. 321), applied to a rotten ship, and this appears to have been the original meaning. The sense in which it was subsequently used may be learnt by comparing Laȝam. ll. 13943, 29609; R. Gl. p. 586; Chron. of Engl. 662, 921; Ly Beaus Desc. 2118 (not explained by Rits.); K. Alisaund. 878; R. Cœur de L. 872, and Sevyn Sages, 1917. It is not found in Jam. Cf. A.S. *wræst,* firm.

Uoyz, *n.* Lat. voice, 1264.

Vre, *pron.* S. our, 13, 596, &c.

Vt, *prep.* S. out, 89, 155, &c.
    Uth, 346, 1178.

Ut-bidde. *See* Bidd.

Ut-drawe, Ut-drawen, Vt-drow, Ut-drowen. *See* Drou.

Uten, *prep.* S. out, exhausted, 842; without, foreign, as in *Utenladdes,* 2153, 2580, foreigners.

Ut-lede. *See* Lede.

Utrage, *n.* S. outrage, 2837.

W. *See* Hw.

Wa, *n.* S. woe, wail, 465.

Wade, *v.* S. Lat. to pass, go, 2645.
    *Wede,* 2387, 2641. Vid. Nares.

Wagge, *v.* S. to wield, brandish, 89.

Waiten, Wayte, Wayten, *v.* Fr. to watch, 512, 1754, 2070. Chauc. Cf. O.Fr. *gaiter.*

Waken, *v.* S. to watch, 630. *Waked, part. pa.* watched, kept awake, 2999. *See* R. Br., Sq. of L. D. 852. Chauc.

Wakne, *v.* S. to wake, awaken, 2164.

Wan, *adv.* S. when, 1962.

War, *adj.* S. aware, wary, 788, 2139.

Warie, *v.* S. to curse,433. *Waried, part. pa.* cursed, 434. Emare, 667. *Wery,* Minot, p. 7. *Warrie,* Chauc. *See* Gl. Lynds.

Warp, *pa. t.* S. threw, cast, 1061.
  Al swa feor swa a mon
  Mihte *werpen* ænne stan.
      *La3am.* l. 17428.
  So in Se. Doug. Virg. 432, and Barb. iii. 642. V. Jam.

Washen, *v.* S. to wash, 1233.

Waste *for* Was þe, 87.

Wastel, *n.* Fr. cake, or loaf made of finer flour, 878. *Westels, pl.* 779. *See* Todd's Illustr. of Chauc., who derives the name from *wasteil,* the vessel or basket in which the bread was carried. V. Du Cange, Spelm. Jam. In Pegge's Form of Cury, p. 72, 159, we meet with *Wastels yfarced.*

Wat, *pron.* *See* Hwat.

Wat, *v.* *See* Quath.

Wat, *pp.* known, 1674. *See* Wot.

Wawe, *n.* S. wall, 474, 2470. The phrase *bith wawe,* 474, is also found in Rits. A.S. p. 46, which is left unexplained by the Editor, and is badly guessed at by Ellis. By the aid of Moor's Suffolk Gl. we are enabled to ascertain the meaning of an expression which is not yet obsolete. "By the walls." Dead and not buried. "A' lie bi' the walls"—said, I believe, only of a human subject. [This remark only applies to l. 474. In ll. 1963, 2470, the phrase refers to the benches placed round the walls in the great hall, whereon men slept at night, and sat in council by day.] *Wawe,* 1963, 2078. Still so pronounced in Lanc., &c.

Waxen. *See* Wex.

Wayke, *adj. pl.* S. weak, 1012.

Wayte, Wayten. *See* Waiten.

We, 115, 287, 392, 772. Apparently an error of the scribe for *wei,* but its frequent repetition may cause it to be doubted, whether the *l* may not have been purposely dropped.

Wede, *v.* *See* Wade.

Wede, *n.* S. clothing, garments, 94, 323, 861. In very general use formerly, and still preserved in the phrase, a widow's *weeds.*

Weddeth *for* Wedded, 1127.

Weie, *n.* S. way, road, 772, 942.

Weilawa, Weilawei, *interj.* S. woe! alas! 462, 570. *See* Gl. Sir Tr., Rits. M. R., and Chauc. [A.S. *wá la wá,* woe, lo! woe; now corrupted into *wellaway.*]

Wel, *adv.* S. full, *passim.* *Wel sixti,* 1747; *wel o-bon.* *See* On. *Wel with me,* 2878. *Wol,* 185.

Wel, *n.* S. weal, wealth, prosperity (*for wel ne for wo*), 2777.

Welde, *v.* S. to wield, govern (a kingdom), 129, 175; (a weapon), 1436; (possessions), 2034. *Weldes, pr. t. 2 p.* wieldest, governest, 1359.

Wende, *v.* S. to go, 1346, 1705, 2629. *Wenden, pr. t. pl. subj.* 1344. *Wende, pr. t. pl. 2 p.* go, 1440. *Wend, part. pa.* turned, 2138.

Wene, *v.* S. *pres. sing.* ween, think, 655, 840, 1260, &c. *Wenes, pr. t. 2 p.* thinkest, 598. *Wenestu,* 1787,thinkest thou. *Wend, Wende, pa. t.* thought, 374, 524, 1091, 1803, &c. *Wenden, pa. t. pl.* 1197, 2547.

Wepen, *pr. t.* or *pa. t. pl.* S. weep, wept, 401.

Wepne, *n.* S. weapon, 89, 490, 1436, &c.

Wer *for* Were, 1097.

Werd, *n.* S. world, 1290, 2241, 2335, 2792, 2968. *O worde,* in the world, 1349. Cf. *Ward* = world, in *Laucelot of the Laik*, and *Gen. and Exod.* ed. Morris, ll. 280, 591.

Were, *v.* S. [*werian*] to defend, 2152, 2298. Sir Tr. p. 156; Yw. and Gaw. 2578; Horn Childe, ap. Rits. M. R., V. 3, p. 289; K. of Tars, 189; Chauc. C. T. 2552, V. Note, p. 182. *Werie*, K. Horn, ed. Lumby, 785, Web., Minot, Gl. Lynds.

Were, should be, 2782. *Weren*, 3 *p. pl.* were, 156, &c.

Weren, 784. Sir F. Madden says—Garnett conjectured *weirs* or dams, from Isl. *ver.* [If *weren* be really a plural noun, I should prefer to translate it by *pools;* cf. A.S. *wær*, Icel. *ver*, Su.-Go. *wär*. Ihre says—" *Wär*, locus, ubi congregari amant pisces, ut solent inter brevia et vada. Isl. *ver, fiskaver.* A.S. id. unde *ver-hurde* apud Bens. custos septi piscatorii, Angl. *wier, wear,* &c." See *wer* in Stratmann. In this case the line means —" in the sea-pools he often set them," and the note on the line (q. v.) is wrong.]

Werewed, *part. pa.* S. worried, killed, 1915. [We should probably insert a mark of interrogation, thus —" Hwat dide he? þore weren he werewed," i. e. " What did they effect?" There were they slain." Spelt *wirwed*, 1921. Cf. Du. *woorgen*, and see Jam. s. v. *Wery*, and *Worry* in Atkinson's Gl. of Cleveland dialect.]

Werne, *v.* S. to refuse, deny, 1345. *Werne, pr. t.* 3 *p. s. subj.* refuses, forbids, 926. Sir Tr. p. 88; K. Horn, 1420, &c.

Wesseyl, *n.* S. wassail, 1246.

Wesseylen, *pr. t. pl.* wassail, 2098. *Wosseyled, part. pa.* 1737. *See* Rits. A.S. Diss. p. xxxiii. n. Hearne's Gl. to R. Glouc. in v. *Queme* and *Wasseyl*, Selden's Notes on Drayton's Polyolb. p. 150, and Nares.

Wex, *pa. t.* S. waxed, grew, 281. *Waxen, part. pa.* grown, 302, 791.

Wicke, Wike, Wikke, *adj.* S. wicked, vile, 66, 319, 425, 665, 688, &c. *Swithe wicke*, 965, very mean. *Swiþe wikke cloþes*, 2458, very mean clothing. *Wicke wede*, 2825, mean clothing.

Wicth, With, *n.* S. [*wiht*] whit, bit, small part, 97, 1763, 2500. Laȝam. l. 15031; Sevyn Sages, 293. 'The loue of hire ne lesteth no *wyht* longe,' MS. Harl. 2253, f. 128.

Wicth, With, *adj.* courageous, stout, active, 344, 1008, 1064, 1651, 1692, &c. *Wicteste, sup.* 9. An epithet used universally by the ancient poets, and to be found in every Gloss. merely differing in orthography, as spelt *Waite, Wate, Wight, Wich*, &c. [Sir F. Madden suggests a derivation from A.S. *hwæt* (Icel. *hvátr*), acute, brave. Wedgwood suggests Sw. *vig*, nimble. Cf. Su.-Goth. *wig*, Icel. *vigr*, fit for *war* (A.S. *wig*).]

Wider, *adv.* S. whither, where, 1139.

Widuen, Wydues, *n. pl.* S. widows, 33, 79.

Wif, *n.* S. wife, 2860; woman, 1713. *Wiues, pl.* 2855.

Wike, Wikke. *See* Wicke.

Wil, *adv.* S. while, 6.

Wil, *adj.* lost in error, uncertain how to proceed, 863; at a loss, without experience, 1042. Wynt. vi. 13, 115. V. Jam. who derives it from Su.-G. *vild*, Isl. *villr*. It is radically the same with *wild*.

Wile, will, 352, 485, &c. *Wilte*, 528, 1135, wilt thou; *Wiltu*, 681, 905. *Wilen, pl.* 732, 920, 1345, 2817, &c.

Wille, *n.* S. will, 528.

Winman, *n.* S. woman, 1139, 1168, &c. *Wman*, 281. *Wymman*, 1156.

## GLOSSARIAL INDEX.

Win, *n.* S. wine, 1729. *Wyn*, 2341.

Winan, *v.* S. to get to, arrive at, 174. V. Gl. to *Will. of Palerne.*

Winne, *n.* S. joy, gain, 660, 2965. *Muchere winne*, Laȝam. 1. 10233. Horn Childe, ap. Rits. M. R., V. 3, p. 294.

Wirchen, *v.* S. to work, cause, 510.

Wirwed. *See* Werewed.

Wis, *adj.* S. wise, prudent, 180, 1421, 1635; skilled, 282.

Wislike, *adv.* S. wisely, 274.

Wisse, *v.* S. to direct, ordain, advise, 104, 361. Sir Tr. p. 29; K. Horn, Chron. of Engl. 499; Chauc., Gl. Lynds.

Wissing, *n.* S. advice, *or* conduct, 2902.

Wiste, *pa. t.* S. knew, 115, 358, 541, &c. *Wisten, pa. t. pl.* 1184, 1187, 1200, &c.

Wit, *prep.* S. with, 52, 505, 701, 905, 1090, 2517, &c.; by, 2489. *Wituten*, 179, 247, 2860, without. *Withuten*, 425, except. *With than*, provided that, 532. *With that*, 1220.

Wite, *v.* S. [*witan*, decernere] *pres. subj. or imp.* decree, ordain, 19, 1316.

Wite, *v.* S. *pres. subj. or imp.* preserve, guard, defend, 405, 559. R. Gl. p. 98, 102. So in the *Carmen inter Corpus & Animam*, MS. Digb. 86.

The king that al this world shop thoru his holi miȝtte,
He *wite* houre soule from then heuele wiȝtte.

And in the French Romance of Kyng Horn, MS. Harl. 527, f. 72, b. c. 2.

Ben iurez *Wite God*, kant auerez beu tant,
Kant le vin uus eschaufe, si seez si iurant.

Wite, Witen, *v.* S. [*witan*, cognoscere] to know, 367, 625, 2201, 2786; to recollect, 2708. *Wite, pr. t. pl.* 2 *p.* know, 2808; *imp.* 3 *p. wite*, know, 517. *Wite*, 3 *p. s. subj.* (if) he know, 694. *Witen, pr. t. pl.* 2 *p.* know, 2208. *See* Wot.

With, *conj. See* Wit.

With, *n. See* Wicth.

With, *adj. See* Wicth.

With, *adj.* S. white, 48, 1144.

With-sitten, *v.* S. to oppose, 1683. R. Br., Web.

Wlf, *n.* S. wolf, 573.

Wluine, *n.* S. she-wolf, 573. Dan. *ulfinde*, a she-wolf.

Wman. *See* Wimman.

Wnden, *part. pa.* S. wound, 546.

Wo, *pron.* S. who, whoso, 76, 79, &c. *See* Hwo.

Wo, *n.* S. woe, sorrow, 510, &c.

Wod, *adj.* S. mad, 508, 1777, 1848, &c. *Wode, pl.* 1896, 2361.

Wok, *pa. t.* S. awoke, 2093.

Wol. *See* Wel.

Wole, will, 1150. *Wolde*, would, 354, 367, &c. *Wode*, 951, 2310. *Wolden, pl.* 456, 514, 1057.

Wombes, *n. pl.* S. bellies, 1911.

Wom so, *pron.* S. whomso, 197.

Won, Wone, great number, plenty, in phr. *ful god won*, in great quantity (*in* 1791 *it seems to mean* with great force), 1024, 1791, 1837, 1907, 2325, 2617, 2729. R. Gl., Horn Childe, ap. Rits. M. R., V. 3, p. 308, 314; R. Cœur de L. 3747; K. Alisaund. 1468; K. of Tars, 635; Minot, p. 14; Chauc. *Wane*, Yw. and Gaw. 1429; *Wayn*, Wall. viii. 947. Cf. Gl. to *Will. of Palerne.*

Wone, *n.* S. (probably the same as *ween*, Sir Tr. p. 59, 78), opinion, conjecture, 1711, 1972. Cf. l. 816, and the Glossaries, in v. *Wene.*

Wone, *v.* S. to dwell, 247, 406. *Woneth, pr. t.* 3 *p.* dwelleth, 105.

Wone, *part. pa.* wont, 2151, 2297. K. Horn, 36; R. Gl. Chron. of Engl. 632; Web., Chauc. [A.S. *wune*, a custom.]

Wonges, *n. pl.* S. fields, plains, 397, 1444. Cf. l. 1360. Spelman thinks arable land is meant by the term, rather than pasture.

Wore, 2 *and* 3 *p. s.* were, 504, 684, &c. *Wore, Woren, pl.* 237, 448, &c. It is not merely a licentious spelling, as conjectured by Sir W. Scott.

Worþe, *v.* S. *imp.* may he be, 1102, 2873. *Wrth,* 434. *Wurþe,* 2221. Laȝam. l. 28333. Sir Tr. p. 49, and all the Gloss., including Lynds.

Wosseyled. *See* Wesseylen.

Wot, Woth, *pr. t.* 1 *p.* S. know, 119, 213, 653, 1345, &c. *Wost, pr. t.* 2 *p.* knowest, 527, 582, 1384, &c. *Woth, pr. t.* 3 *p.* knows, 2527. *Wot, pl.* 1 *p.* know, 2803. *Wat, part. pa.* known, 1674.

Wowe. *See* Wawe.

Wrathe, *n.* S. wrath, anger, 2719, 2977. *See* Wroth

Wreieres, *n. pl.* S. betrayers, spoilers, 39.

The *wraiers* that weren in halle, Schamly were thai schende.
    *Sir Tristr.* p. 190.

Wreken, *v.* S. to avenge, revenge, 327, 1901. *Wreke, imp.* revenge (thou), 1363. *Wreken (miswritten for* wreke), 3 *p. imp.* 544. *Wreke, pr. pl. subj.* 1884. *Wreke, Wreken, part. pa.* revenged, 2368, 2849, 2993. Sir Tr. p. 190, &c.

Wringen, *v.* S. to wring, 1233.

Writ, *n.* S. writing, 2486. *Writes, pl.* writs, letters, 136, 2275. *See* note to l. 136.

Wrobberes, *n. pl.* S. robbers, 39.

Wros, *n. pl.* corners, 68. So in the *Leg. of S. Margrete,* quoted by Dr Leyden:

Sche seiȝe a wel fouler thing
Sitten in a *wro;*

which Jamieson aptly derives from the Su.-G. *wraa,* angulus. Cf. Dan. *vraa,* a nook, corner.

Wroth, *adj.* S. wrath, angry, 1117. *Wroþe,* 2973. *See* Wrathe.

Wrouht, *pa. t.* S. wrought, 2810. *Wrouth,* 1352. *Wrowht,* 2453.

Wrth. *See* Worthe.

Wunde, *n.* S. wound, 1980, 2673, &c. *Wounde,* 1978. *Wundes, pl.* 1845, 1898, 1986. *Woundes,* 1977, &c.

Wurþe. *See* Worþe.

Y, *pron.* I. *See* Ich.

Ya, *adv.* S. yea, yes, 1888, 2009, 2607. *Ye,* 2606. *See* Rits. note to Yw. and Gaw. l. 43. In l. 2009, we should probably have found *yis* in a more southern work. See the note to *ȝis* in Gl. to *Will. of Palerne.* The distinction between *no* (l. 1800) and *nay* (l. 1136) is rightly made.

Yaf. *See* Yeue.

Yare, *adj.* S. ready, 1391, 2788, 2954. Sir Tr. p. 28; Rits. M. R., Web., Chauc., Gl. Lynds.

Yaren, *v.* S. to make ready, 1350. This word in all the Gloss. has the form of *Yarken.*

Yede, *pa. t.* S. went, 6, 774, 821, &c. *Yeden, pa. t. pl.* 889, 952.

Yeft. *See* Giue.

Yelde, *v.* S. to yield, 2712; *imp.* 3 *p.* requite, 803. Very common formerly in this sense. *Yeld, imp.* yield (thou), 2717.

Yeme, *v.* S. to take charge of, govern, 131, 172, 182, 324, &c. *Yemede, pa. t.* governed, 975, 2276. Sir Tr. p. 115, Rits. M. R., Web., R. Gl., Chauc.

Yen. *See* Agen.

Yerne, *adv.* S. eagerly, anxiously, 153, 211, 880, 925. Web., Rits. M. R., Chauc.

Yerne, *v.* S. to desire earnestly, 299. Laʒam. l. 4427. K. Horn, 1419; R. Br., Chauc., Gl. Lynds.

Yete, *adv.* S. yet, 495, 973, 996, 1043.

Yeue, *v.* S. to give, 298, &c. *Yeueth, pr. t.* 3 *p.* giveth, 459. *Yif, imp.* give (thou), 674; 3 *p. yeue,* 22; *pl. yeuep,* 911. *Yaf, pa. t.* gave, *or* gave heed, 315, 419, &c. *Gaf,* 218, 418, 1311, &c. *Gouen, pa. t. pl.* 164 (in phr. *gouen hem ille,* gave themselves up to grief); Sir Tr. p. 129. *Giue, part. pa.*

2488; *gouen,* 220. *Youenet = Youen it,* given it, 1643. For *yaf* in l. 1174, see note on the line.

Y-here. *See* Here, *v.*

Yif, *prep.* S. if, 126, 377, 1974, &c. *Yf,* 1189.

Yif. *See* Yeue.

Y-lere. *See* Lere.

Ynow. *See* Inow.

Youenet. *See* Yeue.

Ys. *See* note to l. 1174.

Yuel, Yuele. *See* Iucle.

Yunge, *adj.* S. young, 368, &c.

Yure, *pron.* S. your, 171.

# INDEX OF NAMES TO "HAUELOK."

[In this Index, the references under words in large capitals are in general to the *pages* of the book; otherwise, the references are to the *lines* of the poem.]

ATHELWOLD (*spelt* Aþelwald, l. 1077), is king of England, and governs wisely, pp. 2, 3; feels he is dying, p. 4; bequeaths his daughter to the care of Godrich, pp. 6, 7; dies, p. 8. (Mentioned again in ll. 2709, 2803.)

Auelok, *another spelling of* Hauelok, 1395, 1793.

BERNARD BRUN (i. e. Bernard Brown; so called in ll. 1751, 1945), provides a supper for Havelok, p. 48; his house attacked by thieves, p. 49; fights against them, p. 52; tells Ubbe how well Havelok fought, p. 54.

BERTRAM (*named in* l. 2898), is cook to the Earl of Cornwall, and employs Havelok, pp. 27, 28; is made Earl of Cornwall, and marries Levive, Grim's daughter, p. 83.

BIRKABEYN (*spelt* Bircabein, l. 494; *gen.* Birkabeynes, 2150, 2209, 2296), is king of Denmark, p. 11; commends his three children to Godard, p. 12; dies, p. 13; his son Havelok's resemblance to him, p. 60.

Cestre (Chester), 2607, 2859, 2896.

Cornwayle (Cornwall), 178, 2908; Cornwalie, 884.

Crist, 16, &c.;—krist, 22; *gen.* kristes, 2797.

Dauy, seint, 2863.

Denemark (Denmark), 340, 381, 386, &c.

Denshe, *sing. adj.* Danish, 1403; *pl.* 2575, 2693, 2938. Danshe, 2689.

Douere (Dover), 139, 265. Doure, 320.

Engelond (England), 59, 202, 250, &c.;—Engellond, 1093;—Engelonde, 208;—Englond, 1270;—Engeland, 108, 610;—Hengelond, 999; *gen.* Engelondes, 63.

Englishe, *pl. adj.* (*followed by* men), 2766, 2795;—Englis (*used absolutely*), 254;—Henglishe, 2945.

Giffin [*Qu.* Griffin] Galle, 2029.

GODARD (*gen.* Godardes, l. 2415), is made regent of Denmark, pp. 12, 13; shuts up Birkabeyn's children in a castle, p. 13; kills Swanborow and Helfled, p. 15; spares Havelok, p. 16; but afterwards hires Grim to drown Havelok, p. 17; is attacked by Havelok, p. 67; is taken prisoner, p. 68; condemned, flayed, drawn, and hung, pp. 70, 71.

## INDEX OF NAMES.

GODRICH (*spelt* Godrigh, l. 178), is Earl of Cornwall, p. 6; is made regent of England, pp. 7, 8, 9; shuts Goldborough up in Dover castle, p. 10; makes Goldborough marry Havelok, p. 33; raises an army against Havelok, p. 72; excites his men, p. 73; marches to Grimsby, p. 74; fights with Ubbe, p. 75; fights with Havelok, pp. 77, 78; is taken prisoner, p. 78; taken to Lincoln, and burnt alive, pp. 80, 81.

GOLDEBORU (*or* Goldeborw, l. 2985), is daughter of King Athelwold, p. 4; is committed to the care of Godrich, pp. 8, 9; shut up in Dover castle, p. 11; is sent for to Lincoln, p. 33; is married to Havelok, p. 36; hears an angel's voice, p. 39; encourages Havelok to go to Denmark, p. 41; rejoices at Godrich's death, p. 81; is queen of England, p. 85. *See* Havelok.

GRIM, a fisher, is hired by Godard to drown Havelok, p. 17; discovers Havelok to be the right heir to the crown, p. 19; takes Havelok over to England, p. 20; founds Grimsby, p. 23; sends Havelok to Lincoln, p. 26; dies, p. 37. [In l. 2333, there seems to be an allusion to a spectacle, in which the history of Grim is represented.]

Grimes, *gen. c. of* Grim, 1343, 1392, 2867.

Grimesbi, 745, 2540, 2579, 2617, 2619;—Grimesby, 1202.

Gunnild (daughter of Grim, marries Earl Reyner of Chester), 2866, 2896.

Gunter (an English earl), 2606.

HAUELOK, son of king Birkabeyn of Denmark, p. 13; spared by Godard, p. 16; but given over by him to Grim to be drowned, p. 17; spared and fed by Grim, p. 20; goes to England, p. 22; sells fish, p. 25; works as a porter, p. 27; puts the stone, p. 31; marries Goldborough, p. 35; returns to Grimsby, p. 36; his dream, p. 39; returns to Denmark, p. 43; trades there, p. 44; is noticed by Ubbe, p. 45; defends Bernard's house against thieves, pp. 48—53; is known to be heir of Denmark by a miraculous light, p. 60; is dubbed knight by Ubbe, p. 65; is king of Denmark, p. 66; defeats Godard, p. 68; invades England, p. 72; defeats Godrich, p. 77; rewards Bertram and others, p. 82; lives to be a hundred years old, p. 83; is crowned king of England at London, p. 84; is king for sixty years, p. 85. [The story is called "þe gest of Hauelok and of Goldeborw," l. 2985.]

Helfled (Havelok's sister), 411.

Hengelonde (England), 999.

Henglishe (*pl.* English), 2945.

Humber (the river), 733.

Huwe Rauen (one of Grim's sons), 1398, 1868, 2349, 2636, 2677; *spelt* Hwe, 1878.

Iohan, seint; the patron saint to whom Havelok commits his Danes, 2957; bi seint Iohan! 1112, 2563. *Spelt* Ion, 177.

Iudas, 319, 425, 1133.

Lazarun (= Lazarum, *acc. of* Lazarus), 331. Cf. "Lord"— said Guy—"that reared *Lazaroun*," &c. Guy of Warwick, in Ellis, Met. Rom. (ed. Halliwell), p. 227.

Leue (Grim's wife), 558, 576, 595, 642.

Leuiue (Grim's daughter, married to Bertram), 2914.

Lincolne, 773, 847, 862, 980, 1105, 2558, 2572, 2824.

Lindeseye (N. part of Lincolnshire), 734.

Lundone (London), 2943.

INDEX OF NAMES. 159

Marz (March), 2559.

Reyner (earl of Chester), 2607.

Roberd þe rede (Grim's eldest son), 1397, 1686, 1888, &c.;— Robert, 2405, 2411, &c.; *gen.* Roberdes, 1691.

Rokesborw (explained by Prof. Morley to mean Rokeby, but it is surely Roxburgh), 265;—Rokesburw, 139. Roxburgh is spelt *Rokesburgh* in Walsingham, ed. Riley, i. 340, &c.

Sathanas (Satan), 1100, 1134, &c.

Swanborow (Havelok's sister), 411.

UBBE, a great Danish lord, p. 44; entertains Havelok, p. 45; takes him to his castle, p. 57; does homage to Havelok, p. 63; dubs him knight, p. 65; his combat with Godrich, p. 75; is sorely wounded, p. 76.

Willam Wendut (one of Grim's sons), 1690, 1881, 1892, 2348, 2632;—Wiliam Wenduth, 1398.

Winchestre, 158, 318.

Yerk (York), 1178.
Ynde, India, 1085.

The manufacturer's authorised representative in the EU for product safety is Oxford University Press España S.A. of El Parque Empresarial San Fernando de Henares, Avenida de Castilla, 2 - 28830 Madrid (www.oup.es/en or product.safety@oup.com). OUP España S.A. also acts as importer into Spain of products made by the manufacturer.
Printed and bound by CPI Group (UK) Ltd, Croydon, CR0 4YY

04/12/2025

02011944-0001